Advance Praise for
Black Indian

"Shonda Buchanan is a mesmerizing writer, one to watch."
—Janet Fitch, bestselling author of *White Oleander*,
The Revolution of Marina M., and *Chimes of a Lost Cathedral*

"In this important memoir, *Black Indian*, Shonda Buchanan explores a hidden tapestry of Americanness, as well as an inheritance of abuse and addiction. The family watcher, Buchanan confronts questions of identity and ancestry, asking every African American to consider the question of who we really are. Indeed, Buchanan circles through a host of issues revolving around the conundrum of growing up with multiple ethnic strands in a society that tries to box you in by race. This book will speak to anyone turning over stones to find lost grandparents and great grandparents, to mothers and daughters and sons and fathers, as well as to those determined to heal cycles of violence in their own families."
—Jeffery Renard Allen, author of the novels
Song of the Shank and *Rails Under My Back*

"Secrets have a tendency of dancing with silence. Shonda Buchanan's journey to discover her roots, to learn her identity, is not another American story, it's perhaps the first story. *Black Indian* acknowledges the past with all its implication of who we are as Americans. Our nation cannot walk a path of denial into the future. When we look into the mirror of history our features, our hair, and the essence of our blood and bone structure will provide us with the evidence and answers we've been waiting for. Shonda Buchanan has the courage to tell her story and the story of her family. Her story is our song. This book is muscle music. It can only make our nation stronger."
—E. Ethelbert Miller, literary activist, writer, and
host of "On the Margin" (WPFW 89.3 FM)

Black Indian

Black Indian

A Memoir by Shonda Buchanan

WAYNE STATE UNIVERSITY PRESS
DETROIT

Made in Michigan Writers Series

General Editors

Michael Delp, Interlochen Center for the Arts
M. L. Liebler, Wayne State University

A complete listing of the books in this series can be
found online at wsupress.wayne.edu

ISBN 978-0-8143-4580-1 (paperback)
ISBN 978-0-8143-4581-8 (ebook)

Library of Congress Control Number: 2019938102

Publication of this book was made possible by a generous
gift from the Meijer Foundation. This work is supported in
part by an award from the Michigan Council for Arts and
Cultural Affairs.

Wayne State University Press
Leonard N. Simons Building
4809 Woodward Avenue
Detroit, Michigan 48201–1309

Visit us online at wsupress.wayne.edu

For Afiya, Mama, Aunt Lily, and Rochelle
For RedBlacks everywhere

Some view our sable race with scornful eye,
"Their colour is a diabolic die."
—Phillis Wheatley, "On Being Brought from Africa to America"

"The only good Indians I ever saw were dead."
—Union Army General Philip Sheridan

She had some horses she loved.
She had some horses she hated.
These were the same horses.
—Joy Harjo, "She Had Some Horses,"
She Had Some Horses (W. W. Norton)

Contents

Author's Note

I WAS RAISED a Black woman in America, yet I was also fed stories of my multiracial heritage. This book represents my attempts to find that heritage, as well as to share the experience of growing up in a home and community that cherished these stories while also suffering from the loss of a multiracial identity. We were African American, American Indian, and white, yet unable to officially claim Indian or white status due to society's constraints, including lack of records, patterns of migration, erasure, punishment, and the labels of "Colored" and "Mulatto" and "Free People of Color" neatly in place. Historically, per the one-drop rule, a child with any "Negro" blood, or who looked "Black," legally had to claim Blackness as their identity. My book is an attempt to expand, reclaim, and celebrate the narratives of the African American experiences as well as the American Indian experiences. I have yet to fully research my white ancestry, yet I understand that several of my great-great-great-uncles chose to pass as white rather than admit any blood of color, Black or Indian. I want to make it clear at the outset that this is only one person's and one family's story. By no means is this representative of every or even any other Mixed blood or full-blood Indigenous American who lives on or off the reservation, with or without a tribal enrollment card, even if they do or do not claim their Black or white blood. I introduce social, racial, and cultural issues and explore their implications in relation to my family. This is not a scholarly book. It is a story, and I do not mean to offend anyone with it. I do know for sure that this tale is one of many others on the trail. There's also a pantheon of scholarly literature, legal documents, and subsequent documentation steeped in the Mixed blood discourse. My companion genealogy guidebook, *Let the Blood Tell: Finding Your Black Indian Ancestry*, lists a good number of the texts, research facilities, and genealogy sites anyone interested in this topic may consult.

As stated throughout, what occurs in this book is from the memory of the author, as well as re-imagined moments and dialogue as rendered by the author from recollections from childhood, puberty, and adulthood; from oral history, family interviews, documents and cross-checked memories, imagined moments, as well as extensive research incorporated from a multitude of documents. My opinion of a character or a moment is mine alone based on my interactions with the character or a recreated moment(s).

PART I

The RedBlack Heart

Me in elementary school.

My mother, Velma Stafford,
in junior high.

Me in junior high.

June 23, 2000

My family reunion looks like death, deep in the night sky. A shroud of swamp moss holding the moon's hair together. Indian ghosts and weeping willows borrowing our silence for their children's bones. Maybe it's the other way around. They grow. We grow. We return to them, forever bound together. I miss the moon in Michigan.

1

Wait

WAIT.

To tell you any of these stories, I have to tell you the first. The very first.

Somewhere in Mattawan, Michigan, there is an infant buried on top of a thirteen-year-old girl's grave. The infant, stillborn, was given a name anyway but the wind buried the syllables under its cool tongue. The child's sutured eyes and never-kissed lips greeted that 1950s winter sky, the color of heron wings, when her father—my grandfather—opened another hole in the mute earth and laid his second unforgiving child's body to rest in her sister's slender, waiting arms. Finally, someone to hold. Frieda shifted and yawned into the earth. Together there, my two aunts, the virgin and the infant, kept each other safe. They shared the secret of each other's bones.

And there were a lot of secrets.

Maybe I am the unborn child. Perhaps she returned in me to tell our story from my woman-child hands, Velma Jean's daughter's hands, fourth girl-child's hands, since we are, after all, the baby girls and at once the sixth seed. We both prefer the dent of rain in the earth to the din of voices, the fists, the liquor laugh-screams at family gatherings. Equally, we cherish our silence. And if I am her, what did I see hovering over the farm before the last mound of dirt covered me? What would I say first? Maybe something about the Potawatomi, Ottawa, and the Ojibwa building wigwams on riverbanks, before French trappers, missionaries, and settlers came. Something about Mama's sweet corn-bread and Daddy's cold beer. The five little burnished-yellow Mattawan fairies. Mulatto skin. Pocahontas eyes. I would take you to the fields, to Wolf Lake, to the bait house. Push you on the tire swing laced to the top branch of the weeping willow in the front yard; push you until you were dizzy, and then I would say it:

What I don't know I can't tell.

2

Mourning, 2000

"Hey Mommy," I say through the door crack. I cling to my nine-year-old daughter's hand. It is hours past midnight.

"Hello." Almost suspiciously, as if I bear more bad news under my blouse, in my airplane-tossed hair, my mother glares at me and cracks the front door one wedge further. I bite down on the useless *how are you?* when Death Happens, and there's no point in asking.

"Come in," she finally says and steps back. As we enter, the dank June humidity of the Midwest seeps in like a long-lost friend behind our bodies and luggage, palpable, leech-like. We pour in with it, the heat smoldering, the damp, hot darkness turning my daughter's once straightened hair into a black puff pastry. She doesn't know yet that pressing combs are useless trinkets in a Kalamazoo and Portage summer.

The city is a bowl-like valley "inherited" in bogus treaties from American Indians in the region, and all the moisture created by the sun pounding down on streams and lakes traps itself there until an autumn breeze out of Detroit by way of Canada wanders through, and suddenly it's winter. Then the soft flakes and high winds can curl up a blizzard in two seconds flat—one that stays for weeks, closing schools, bingo halls, and roads, laying over the mitten state like a foamy white blanket.

"Hey Grandma," Afiya says softly. Kind of ducking, my daughter almost tucks her neck into her shoulders like a turtle trying not to be seen; I recognize that tactic. I did it my entire childhood, but in my family, I could never hide.

I hug my daughter to me to assuage her nervousness. A warm bread scent exudes from the crown of her head. My mother mutters a faint greeting, eyes puffy but dry, then wordlessly ushers us through the dim living room. Her sheer, pale blue nightgown flares around thick thighs as she walks; curlers stick out around her head, making her look a little like a Martian. My mother's sallow face has sharpened with loss of her sister, my Aunt Phyllis, a middle daughter like me. But grief, for Velma Jean Stafford, turns into fury, into mirthless laughter: then a small storm.

Cautiously, I pad behind her: "Y'all staying in the star room."

Somehow my mother seems shorter in the four a.m. darkness, as if she is shrinking, disappearing before me. She is no longer the sparkling shooting star from my youth, no longer all legs, smooth banana candy skin and luminously long, black river hair. Somewhere between the raising of us hardheaded kids, taking care of other people's old folks at Matheson Nursing Home for the last twenty-five years, spinning Ray Charles forty-fives and making bologna sandwiches for us to choke down like wolverines, my mother has grown old.

Unfairly, I hold this mother up to the one who raised me—a young buttercup-complexioned hot mama from the seventies, who gleefully called to me to "shake that money maker" when I was a kid. In pictures, her silk go-go boots laced up her firm calves spoke of her go-go dancer days. The tight polyester pants or those seventies softball shorts flaunted her beauty, her defiance, her wide hips—and she had thighs for days, even as a child. Before she cut her tresses, her black hair staggered like a heavy blanket at the back of her neck—that "good Indian hair" that became a convenient synonym for "Mixed blood" and was followed by "What you mixed with?" and "What are you?" To which my mother replied, "Human."

"If y'all hungry," she says, in a tone that says, *I hope not.*

If my mother knew anything about being Indian, the culture and practices of any Indian tribe, she never told me. Our Indian heritage was oral history until I tracked it down to Sampson, Hertford, Halifax, and Greenville-Northampton Counties, all in North Carolina and on the cusp of Virginia. I had traced one ancestor, a Manuel, back to the Revolutionary War and thought about joining Daughters of the American Revolution just to shake things up. My great-great-grandfathers, George Thomas Manuel, Jeremiah Stafford, Sr., and Willis Roberts, Jr., were all Mixed bloods, Free People of Color, whose forebears had married full-blooded Indian women or who themselves were born into those tribes. While my mother always thought our Indian blood came from the local Kalamazoo tribes, instead we were migrants on the Appalachian Trail, of the Coharie/Neuse and Eastern Band and Delaware Cherokee tribes; on my dad's side I was Choctaw. But we didn't know any history: we didn't know our history. That was the Problem.

If my mother ever knew that Kikalamazoo was the original Indian name of Kalamazoo, meaning "mirage" or "reflection in the mirror or water," or any history of our family and the migration we'd taken from North Carolina, she never told a soul. But Mama kept all her secrets locked up tight anyway, her grin hard and bright as a swamp star in her face.

We shake our heads: "Just tired," I say. I wake with the rooster's crow no matter where I am in the world. Mama wakes between three a.m. and four a.m. regularly, as if she is still feeding hogs on her daddy's farm in Mattawan.

This big comfy house in Portage is the Waldorf compared to the houses we'd lived in, and most of all, to that farm where she grew up without running water, with a shanty-looking outhouse. With its modest backyard, close to the Kalamazoo county line, the Portage house hums with safety, unlike Southworth Terrace on the

Eastside where we grew up—we were card dealers, always trying to hustle her. Here, she is happy, but age and worry show.

Maybe it only shows when we kids come home.

I can see the outline of her squat body and imagine the patchwork quilt that we, the seven children born there, had made of her once slender body. All our lives, we were pretty damn sure our mother hated us a little for our constant hunger, our need to be held, and most assuredly, for each new stretch mark and each scar that ripped up her flat dancer's stomach. But maybe all mothers hated their children a little for this unintended slight; the first rupture started at sixteen and seemed never to stop. She almost died at forty, having the last boy. That was the year she cut off all her hair.

"Nite Mommy."

"Good night." My mother disappears down the dark hall, clicking her door shut.

Afiya immediately crumples into the soft bed, travel clothes and all, and is snoring in seconds. I change into my pajamas quickly and climb in beside her. In the dark, I look around the room my mother reserves for me in her new house when I come home. The star room, I call it, because the ceiling is lined with miniature luminescent crescent moons and stars that glow in the dark long after the light has gone out. It's an appropriate room for me, the baby girl, the dreamer.

"She so *special*," my sisters whispered behind my back when I was ten years old as I devoured book after book, starting at nine with *Harriet the Spy*, Ursula Le Guin, and Phyllis A. Whitney mystery books, then *I Am the Darker Brother*, with Harlem Renaissance poems by Gwendolyn Brooks, Richard Wright, and Langston Hughes.

"Um-hum." Bobbie Ann, the eldest, would roll her eyes hard until you saw the whites when she heard I had taken to reading in the bathtub atop a pile of blankets and pillows. "Touched. So backwoods. Just like her Mama."

The bathtub was the only place I could find peace when they played or fought and it often sounded the same. When they were playing, the house thundered with their pounding feet and laughter; when they were fighting, the house was a wolf den, and they, we, were a pack of wolves, fists and fangs forever bared. Reading was the only way I could drown out the constant backdrop of loud voices, or train whistles and steel wheels crunching rusty railroad tracks that crisscrossed Kalamazoo like a lattice.

To hear my family tell it, despite my two English degrees, I still had "not a lick of sense." Yet more importantly, I lacked an understanding of myself in a family who would kick you just as soon as kiss you. Blacken your eye as soon as buy you a Twinkie. Growing up I never knew where the laughter, pinch, or jab was coming from. We reenacted that enslavement love. That Trail of Tears love.

Caught in a nightmare, my lanky daughter turns restlessly and unexpectedly, flings out her hand and smacks me in the face.

"Hey," I hiss, blinking back stinging tears. "Move over."

Afiya's eyelids flutter. That over-hot bread scent oozes from her. In the soft dark, her oval face, more olive toned than brown, frowns up. In the half-awake, half-dream, she recognizes my voice, and the intention to push her off the bed if she hits me again, and she rolls back toward the wall. Her breathing evens and she lies still.

The house creaks and settles.

3

Ghost Whisperer

DAWN CREEPS THROUGH the sheer lace curtains, the color of blue corn silk. I must have drifted off; a full bladder presses my gut. I can hear my mother already up, before everyone, laying out her usual spread of solitaire. I wonder if she slept: maybe, our quiet-as-kept seer, she had a visit from Aunt Phyllis's ghost in the twilight.

Once she'd called me in California to smugly relay the news a week after my father died in 1996: "Your Daddy visited me last night. He said to tell you he's okay." *Even in death*, her tone said, *he came back to me. Not you.*

Like it was a competition. I could give two shit cents.

Me, I didn't want to see anybody's rattling chains, or deliver anybody's last words: there were gifts and there were *gifts*. As soon as I was old enough to sense the lingering spirits, watching me eat my Cap'n Crunch in front of *Sesame Street* when I was around seven or eight, I told our ghosts to keep that mess to themselves. I only wanted to dream about them. And we were a family of dreamers. Then I could wake up and say, "Well so-and-so came to me in my dream last night." The problem with that was sometimes it wasn't just the dead who came to call but the living who were about to cross over. Hard as I tried, I didn't have any control over that.

I hear Mama playing solitaire fast, snapping the oily cards on the table angrily, her sure hands manipulating their slender bodies. She sometimes finished a game in five minutes flat, rarely losing to herself. From my room, I hear the frustrated *flip, whisk, slap, flip, whisk, slap, shuffle*. "Shit," she mumbles. "Just my luck."

Then a soda can snaps open and the sweet acidic liquid pours over ice and fizzles. I tighten my thighs, holding my urine, not wanting to encroach upon her morning meditation with my footsteps, an intruding light, and the creaky bathroom door.

Solitaire is Velma's way of making sense of the world. Her way of making things come out balanced and in order or not at all. She has only the cards and her strategy to adhere to, nothing and no one else. She isn't a Stafford from the backwoods swampland of Mattawan anymore, not dirt poor and lettuce-sandwich hungry. For all Kalamazoo is worth, it's urbane in comparison to the two-story, 600-square-foot house and twenty-acre farm on M-43 where she grew up milking cows at five a.m., before school, and snapping chickens' necks for the supper frying pan under the judgmental eye of her mother, Dorothy. My mom is a city girl now in a big beautiful house. Good and proper. Not simply one of four golden-skinned girls who had been told all their lives of their "Indian, French, German, and little bit of Black" lineage.

Nobody used the term American Indian in our family, it was always "Indian," and we knew that meant "our people." In family pictures, Mama and her sisters looked like little Black Indian fairies or waifs without traditional dresses. They were clad in thin cotton dresses and pinafores, white socks, and shiny black Mary Janes, their braids silk licorice rivers down their backs. But one of them is gone now.

Solitaire Velma can do.

Anybody's gambling she can do. Play the Michigan Lotto for a hundred dollars' worth of hunches and random license plates and restless dreams, which she does with nearly every paycheck. Gambling is her only addiction, but solitaire is her reprieve. It's just a game, but she has control over it. Balance. This morning of all mornings, she needs that.

Her husband, John Cloud, tolerates Lotto tickets stuffed in my mother's purse but he gives her a kind of balance too. He is a kind, lonely widower, a handsome brown-skinned man who was my mother's grade school sweetheart. He'd tracked her down three years earlier and "courted her" properly. Taught my mother that not all men wanted to "shuck or jive" or hurt her. He'd bought this house for her on the outskirts of Kalamazoo and furnished it. He'd bought her a couple of cars. *He didn't hit her*. He'd persuaded her to trust and love again, coaxed her. *He didn't choke her*. The son of a reverend, John Cloud even had her going to church. *Church*. When I first found out, I gasped in disbelief. "What do you do there?" I laughed.

"Pray, dummy." She looked away. I stopped laughing.

Even though my dad was a preacher, I didn't live with him growing up, so I wasn't raised in church. Yet I couldn't imagine my mother sitting quietly in a hard wooden pew, as some sweaty panderer in a black polyester robe talked *at* her. Growing up, I didn't have to go to church on Sunday like other little girls unless I was at my father's house, and I *hated* going to church with his family because his fat wife pinched the blood out of my arm if I fell asleep. Of course I fell asleep: I was bored to no end.

In my mother's house, none of us kids had to go. For something to do, I was in and out of summer Bible camps she sent me to, and sometimes I'd go to church with my friends; I asked Mama on and off if she would go with me. No and no. After a while, I stopped asking. I felt a little like a grateful heathen until I decided to go to church myself at sixteen; then at eighteen I stopped again. I didn't like to pray in a box. I didn't like listening to an interpreter. I started carrying church in my heart and prayed on my own. My memory of religion was my evil stepmother's claw-like hands; my memory of religion in our house was Mama's snarl: "God ain't done shit for me. What I'ma go to church for?"

My sister Rochelle remembered it differently. Apparently, when I was a baby we ate and slept in church, "twenty-four, twenty-four," and Rochelle hated it too. That must have been when my father was trying to become a preacher, and maybe that's why I only like to hear the choir sing because the sermons put me to sleep.

When I was growing up, we cleaned house on Saturday, and instead of sitting up in some stuffy room full of hot worshippers, we rested on Sunday.

Like God, we did not go to church.

Something had happened in the past, maybe in a church, that my mother kept hidden from us. But because the question, like many of my questions, made her snap and snarl, I let that curtain fall shut.

"What do you do there?" I had asked as a joke, but when I saw how it hurt her that I questioned her faith, I stopped smirking. What an asshole I was for trying to take that away from her. I was happy she'd found religion after all these years, along with her peace of mind. For a while she and my Aunt Lily were both Tina Turner–style Buddhists, the chanting kind, and then they were Buddhist Christians. And I think they just dropped the Buddhist over the years. Who was I to judge. I had started on what felt like the path of my ancestors, attending African gatherings in L.A. and sweat lodges regularly in the California mountains. The first time I participated in a West African dance class, I got what the babalawos call "mounted" by a spirit. One moment I was dancing to the African drums and the next I couldn't breathe because my body didn't feel like my own. It was crowded. I burst into tears and had to sit out the rest of the dance class. I felt like my, or someone's, ancestor was welcoming me back to the circle. I was a seeker and believed in that old timey religion from both my African and Indian lines. I couldn't judge my mother's path at all; she had gone back to the Baptist church and that was fine by me. We all needed to believe in something.

It took her almost fifty-five years to get here: back to God; to that fingerprint-smeared glass table in a perfectly tiled kitchen, with cream latticed curtains lingering against windows that framed a large, still backyard that the cicada serenaded in loud drones; to the two standing grandfather clocks and a dining room with all eight chairs around the table; to a man in the bed who loved her.

The bathroom can wait.

I stare up into the darkness, faintly able to make out the shapes above me. Hot, I reach up, give the ceiling fan chain a quick tug and instead mistakenly flick on the light. I yank twice, the fan whirs, and the room is Plato's cave again. The stars and half-moons hum glow-worm yellow, reminding me that I am still a child in my mother's house. Even though I have my own daughter, and at that moment her thick breath does a snag-mock whistle in my ear, I am still the baby girl, sixth child of seven, the fourth girl child, and therefore not special at all.

Aunt Lily's voice chimes a sleepy "Good morning" as she joins my mother in the kitchen. Their sounds murmur against the kitchen's noise as the house wakes, the refrigerator grumbling, the floorboards creaking, the hogtied snores of my brothers in the basement where they slept getting fainter.

"Is it?" Mama quips. Flip, whisk, slap, shuffle.

Aunt Lily snorts a response. "You want coffee?" she says.

"Nope. I'm fine."

I imagine the sharp look she cuts the back of my mother's head with—*The fuck you are. No, it is not goddamnit. Our sister is dead, but you can be an asshole if you want to because you're in pain. I'll allow that. This time.*

Aunt Lily knows my mother, who hasn't spoken to their sister in a full year, is living all her regret in the hours before the funeral.

Velma is eating it for breakfast. Crow pie mixed with regret. I always wondered why people wait to tell it, to say, *you hurt me, you fucked up my life, I love you so much, I'll always love you.*

I think my mother could see in my wet eyes when I was born that I didn't know how to *keep my mouth*, the way she would say it—I often felt like my stomach was on fire if I didn't say the thing burning in my mouth. My mom, on the other hand, cherished her bitter silence against her two eldest sisters. My family was glad that I lived far, far away. L.A. to them was like Oz; I was the Black Indian Dorothy who'd been tossed into the rain clouds by a tornado and we all liked it just fine. I hated keeping their secrets and secret grudges; I wanted *The Brady Bunch* but instead I got *Good Times.*

"How 'bout some eggs?" Aunt Lily persists. "You should eat something, Velma."

"Nope." Flip, whisk, shuffle. "I'm *fine.*"

Aunt Lily is a thinner version of my mother, high cheekbones above the pronounced Stafford chin, pillowy skin the color of autumn's first leaves, unrepentant curly black hair. Always able to laugh, she would muffle a teenager's giggle at something acerbic my mother said: most likely, someone's reputation shredded on the clean kitchen floor. Even at fifty-five, my aunt is the queen of giggles, polar opposite of my mother, the purveyor of frowns. Having learned her cuss words honest, right on her daddy's knee, Aunt Lily has a mouth like a pirate; she is always quick to crack on someone who deserves it, her tongue sharpened on years of telling her alcoholic husband just what he could do with his "sorry, drunk, lying ass."

Aunt Lily's strong chin puckered in or out in every family photo depending on the battle she had just finished or was about to start. But a gentle teasing at the corners of her mouth held her smile steady, ready to make everyone else laugh. She was at once our family comedian and keeper of our memory. I distinctly remember, in a photo dated June 1962, after the birth of her first son, how her eyes had grown wary. Still alluring yet aching, holding summer secrets close to her chest. She'd changed; life tasted different, her eyes said, as an adult. Her skin was glowing, but her coltish eyes were penetrating with an unspoken cotton sorrow.

Every time I think of that photo, the quiet, yet constant pain behind my aunt's eyes when she was young, I compare that version with the aunt I see and know now, my aunt the slayer, Lily, the truth talker, and wonder how anyone could even think of tussling with her.

A sharp stomach pang brings me back to this moment. I can't hold my pee anymore; I hurry to the bathroom. Then instead of going back to bed, I head to the kitchen. To my mother. She doesn't look up when I enter. Her head is lowered, brow furrowed in concentration. I walk over, lean down to kiss her head, hugging her from behind. The back of her neck is an angry pink; she'd just gotten a haircut. Her short black curls are wavy and soft under my lips. Ignoring me, she melds the cards like a Las Vegas dealer.

"Morning Mommy. You not eating?"

No answer.

A fresh, sweet shampoo scent immerses me. I tighten my embrace, pressing hard enough for her to hear the blood in my ears rushing through my body, knowing she is full of water unshed as of this moment. Her sister's death must feel like the loss of a finger she never realized she needed until it was gone.

Then, because I'm not going away, Mama half encircles me with one arm and continues dealing her game out with the other, flicking down cards with her thumb. Stoic. Terse. Eyes dry. Whereas all my life I was sensitive and had approached puberty like a leaky faucet, Velma was the Mojave Desert. She was always the strongest of us. Efficient in emergencies when broken bones or blood was involved.

"You sleep alright?"

"Yeah," I lie.

Selfishly, confusingly, I still want her to be the strongest woman in the world even though I hate her for that strength. Her anguish, like her love, has the silence of trapped water, and I got the hell out of Kalamazoo the first chance I could because I always felt like I was drowning.

Kalamazoo was not big enough for me, my Mama, and my Mama's ghosts.

After that everything I did was California's fault. Getting pregnant at twenty when I was the "smart" one. *That damn California.* Not marrying the father. *That's what them Californians do.* Going back to college. *Oh, you think you smart cause you in California?* When I locked my "good" Indian hair and now resembled a Rasta: *Look what that damn California did to Shonda.* To them, in my crazy California Sanskrit shirt, with my soft writer hands, I would always be the baby girl.

No living uncles, no grandparents, and now only two aunts; an intra-racist great-aunt; and a tight-lipped mother, who used to allow us kids to play hide-and-go-seek and truth or dare during the hot summer nights, our screams pulling down the crushed red summer sun, the light snuffed out by our urgent night-coming-down-soon whispers. Fireflies gave up their wings for our pleasure on that ground, for our pounding feet ruining their moist flower beds. The waist-high grass that Mama let grow wild on South-worth Terrace clearly defined our country sensibilities.

There were times when childhood was magical to me, running through the grass like it was a jungle; firecracker smoke and sulfur on the Fourth of July; fish fries and cleaning greens on the front porch while the neighbors looked down their apple pie noses at us. Our white house, shutters trimmed in black, sat in the middle of our property, which felt like the biggest house on the block when I was shorter. The edges of the yard were bordered with what the

Michigan Chippewa called sugarbushes, towering maple oaks that dripped sticky sap, as well as massive pine, birch, and crabapple trees. One summer, Mama let the grass grow at least three feet high and someone reported us to the city. *Not long from the swamp*, I'm sure the younger and hipper of our neighbors, or the old Polish immigrants, snickered. We didn't care. Kalamazoo, Decatur, Ypsilanti, Mattawan country.

"You know you got some Indian in you?" my mother proudly crooned every six months or so when we were growing up. How did she know? Her Aunt Katheryn, our family historian, told her; Mama's father told her; her cousins and uncles told my mom and aunt stories about being from a tribe in Mattawan, but later her dad said Oklahoma, yet none of them did the research. My research uncovered our route: we were migration trail transplants from the Eastern Shores that lined the edges of the first counties that formed the Union.

My mother's great-grandpa Manuel married Ida Mahoney, and Ida's mom, Mariah (Anne) Peak(e), is listed on a family photograph as "full-blood Cherokee." But a later pedigree chart from my Great-Aunt Katheryn lists Mariah as both Delaware Cherokee and Pequot Indian, born in Oklahoma. The Manuel men were full and Mixed blood Coharie/Neuse Indians from Sampson County, North Carolina. They'd either married Indian or black, or other Mixed race women like Ida. My Great-Aunt Katheryn was the first to handwrite a family tree that showed names, dates, and ethnicities in her spider-like scrawl, and I traced the rest like an explorer, using her genealogical treasure maps.

My mom's grandmother, Caledonia Frances Stafford Roberts, a Roberts by birth, was one-fourth Cherokee. Caledonia, also known as Callie D, was a descendent of the Roberts Settlement, one of the first Free People of Color settlements in Indiana in 1830. Theirs was a Mixed race, bi- and triracial community of light-bright people who traded with the Quakers. Roberts family lore has it that the patriarch, James Roberts, born in the mid-1700s, was the son of an American Indian mother and free African "servant" father who was never a slave. Descriptions of James, a Free Person of Color who owned and sold over 700 acres of land between 1765 and 1809 in Northampton County, North Carolina, confirm his ethnicity. While the family reported James's mother was Cherokee, she could very well have been Tuscarora, Nottoway, or Meherrin, as those were also predominant tribes in the area at that time. Because of shared experiences in colonial America, interracial marriages between African Americans and American Indians in the 1700 and 1800s were the norm, despite prohibitive "anti-miscegenation" laws.

Little did my mom or her sisters know that when their grandmother's (Callie D's) grandfather, Willis Roberts, Jr., left Indiana for Michigan in the early 1850s, he was one of the first to stake his claim to "unspoiled" farmland in Mattawan. There were only a few "of color" Mixed race farmers in those parts then. And who wanted that swampland anyway? Farmers did. Willis came just on the cusp of the 1854 Census, which lists fifty-four "free black" families moving to the state. As FOP or Free People of Color (a term that originated in the 1800s to encompass Black, Indian, and white interracial families who were never enslaved), Willis and his wife had their hands full trying to build a farm. Free People of Color also encompassed full-blood American Indians who had either decided to leave or were forced off their tribal homelands before they were renamed reservations.

Before deciding to leave North Carolina because of the Southeast's onslaught of new race codes and restrictions whittling their freedoms, my Manuels, Staffords, and Robertses owned hundreds of acres in North Carolina and on the border of Virginia. A few even owned their family members as slaves to keep them out of the hands of white slave masters because "property" was a concept respected in the Antebellum, unlike free papers, selfhood, and Indian sovereignty. James Roberts held two slaves who were most likely family members. Conveniently, the term Free People of Color eventually shortened to Colored as the years wore on to replace Mulatto without regard for blood quantum. Willis Roberts, Jr., my fourth great-grandfather, once called a Free Person of Color, and then a Free Black, was listed as Mulatto on the 1860 Michigan Census.

My Robertses and Staffords are listed on the Guion Miller African Eastern Cherokee Rolls, a collection of transcribed interviews and recorded letters from 1908–1910 from people who, wanting to receive reparations and land allotments promised (in exchange for already stolen lands), asserted their Eastern Cherokee Indian blood. Ironically, having already left the reservations, they couldn't prove it by U.S. government standards. Many tribes would not open their records to help prove Indian status of those who'd abandoned the reservations. If your family wasn't listed on one of the federal rolls, like the Dawes Rolls, you were ass-out in the wind.

No reparations for you.

Because many were illiterate then, most of our history was orally passed down from generation to generation, however one of the patriarchs, Elijah Roberts, was educated and mindful enough to keep records. In fact, since 1765, most of the Roberts children were educated and had several years of schooling. When I finally saw pictures of some of the Robertses, eerily, many of them looked so light they could easily pass for white. Same for the Manuels, and one of those great-great-uncles did decide to pass and never spoke to his Mixed race brothers and sisters again. When I was teaching in Bath, England, in 2008, I found out that we, the multicolored darker-skinned spawn, were never invited to those Roberts family reunions in Indiana. They had their own church and everything. But they didn't care about my mother's convergence of Indian blood flowing through her veins. *She* was the right color, translucent as a blinking star in the swamp-black sky, but her kids, especially me, weren't light enough: we were all the shades of the coming night.

We didn't care: no one could take the country, the indigenous, or the Black out of us. Mattawan or North Carolina, wetlands was in our blood.

4

High Yellow

"Where are the pictures, VJ?"

VJ is Aunt Lily's nickname for my mother, Velma Jean. Still playing solitaire, my mother grunts at me, pointing toward the guest bedroom. Excitement tickles my palms as I retrieve and set the plastic green container in the center of the kitchen table.

"Phyllis was just like Daddy," Aunt Lily says, looking at a photo of her dead sister at sixteen. From the slant in Aunt Phyllis's full lips, I can tell the girl in the photo was full of self-knowing about her own shattering beauty. What she didn't know was that her features looked similar to those Spanish drawings by the Europeans of the first encounter with "Natives" of the Carolinas and Virginia. For ignorant bullies at school, or catcallers, they were half-breeds, high yella gals, redbone, milk-in-the-coffee girls.

"Uh-huh. Ornery," Mama comments, licking her thumb and snaking a card off the deck.

"Remember that school, VJ?"

"Uh-huh." My mother stops and stares at the cards like a Gypsy reading her crystal ball. "Moore School. That old, one-room schoolhouse."

I choke a little, desperately hoping they can't hear the sound my eyes make popping out of their sockets. My mother tossing out a fact about her childhood is simply unheard of. I'm used to her litanies of who she can't remember in which photo and why. I am always attempting to piece together our story; I stopped and started several family trees for lack of help and interest, especially from her. Mama's "help" could be summed up in six words: "You ask too many goddamn questions."

Mama is like her father too.

It seems as if her childhood had never happened. As if my grandfather's tight-axe grip is still choking her all the way from the grave. The gaps in her memory make it seem as if she'd skipped her own childhood. But I've persisted, refusing to believe that my mother's memories have sealed themselves up like two swollen eyelids after a fight, protecting the eye from what it couldn't see—the next punch.

And here she is, her memory easing into gear like a well-oiled ten-speed bike, comfortable and safe with her little sister next to her.

"Boy, I used to kick that old teacher. She was mean to me." My aunt is still indignant after fifty-some-odd years. "She was *always* picking on me and I was the *littlest* out of the whole school." Aunt Lily picks up a picture of Frieda, her favorite sister, who died at thirteen. Her eyes mist over with memory.

Then she drops Frieda's picture a little too hastily, shoves it under a pile, and picks up one of my mother.

"Yo' Mama wouldn't come inside the school, though," Aunt Lily crows gleefully. "She hated school. Just decided one day she wasn't gonna go no more."

In the largest class picture, all the nonwhite kids are see-through pasty, high yellow, or ruddy faces from farm labor. These terms that categorized your Mulatto heritage, no matter how you got it, and depending on who said it, could be a compliment or a cuss.

"Look at you guys." I gawk at their checkered, high-collared dresses and black, silver-buckled shoes, worn down so much in a couple of the photos I can see where the sole was about to flip up. You can tell by their shoes who was really dirt poor. All the girls are shiny and pretty like fresh cornbread, yellowish and tan hues that, growing up, I never associated with being Indian. When you're a child, you don't see color. You just are who you are, how people see you: the baby girl, the tallest boy, the best spitter, the fastest runner.

But in Van Buren County, which was made up of four "major" cities, seven little villages really, including Mattawan and Paw Paw, when the high yellow folks, Colored, and freed slaves started cutting down trees to erect homes in the early to mid-1800s, things changed. Some of those folks you couldn't even tell if they had one drop of black blood they were so white-looking, and that was a Problem. Some white people claimed not to mind the light-skinned, white-featured, Free People of Color living next to them, but they did if they were marrying white women.

Then disappearing into white society. Never to be Black or Mulatto again.

The beauty of being a "settler" was that there was a lot of fertile Potawatomi land, but the Problem, for white settlers, was the "gall-blasted Indians." Then there was the Harriet Tubman Problem—her exploits from the South hauling escaped slaves to freedom. Migration of white settlers was good: Black Indians, freed slaves, Free People of Color looking for freedom, and Ottawa, Potawatomi, and Ojibwe or Chippewa who wanted only to be left alone to their ceremonies and hunting—Kemosahbee Problem. If the indigenous tribes were allowed to keep their hunting and ceremonial grounds, well then, what land would the settlers have to settle on?

These "worries" were addressed in many ways.

Burning crosses on front lawns and white sheet meetings, riots, massacres of Indian villages, land-thieving, land squatting, bogus property line claims, smallpox blankets, burning courthouses down full of land deeds, birth certificates and bonds, and of course, out-right trickery. Then there were also the "right to patronize" signs that read, "No jobs here for Coloreds, Indians, Negros or dogs."

My mother's father, Clifford Gaylord Stafford, used to piss and moan because he couldn't get hired for looking too Black, but when he sat down in a bar, he looked white enough to warrant a bottle of Jack Daniels or a can of beer. This was just one of the reasons he hated Black people so much even though he was half-Black himself. He could spend his money to drag himself more in debt, but because of his indeterminable race, he was on the last hired, first fired circuit, just like the rest of them "goddamn Black ass niggers," he'd say. Being an Indian who didn't know the name of his North Carolina tribe, my grandfather had no inkling that the Potawatomi Indians of Michigan were discriminated against also. In truth, he wouldn't have given a damn anyway. No loyalty. But in 1864, a gang of Potawatomi were deftly rooted up like turnips and heaved into Indian Territory in Oklahoma, though many made their way back.

Like most of those who got the short stick of life because of their race, Grandpa Stafford hated those brown parts of himself because whites told him he was not their equal. He hated himself because darker-skinned Blacks ostracized him too. He had a Hitler complex. The Indian Removal Act, Jim Crow, and *Gone with the Wind* did their jobs on him. He saw how whites saw him, too, and didn't want to be associated with Blacks or Indians, but his difference wasn't on an ID or a tribal enrollment card in his wallet, it was stamped on his face.

This smattering of communities, sprawling farmland, fragrant cattle ranches, and miles of cornfields and apple orchards, pocketed with lakes, ponds, and streams, held whites, Blacks, Mixed bloods, and full-blood Indians alike, even if the Indians were damn near invisible. Whether they were indigenous to Michigan or like my people forced to migrate, they were subsumed by one side or the other, white or Black, in an attempt to quell confusion surrounding the question *what are you?* And to keep the past quiet, many of the

Indians and Mixed bloods, like my grandfather, answered, "Whatever will get me by, get me the job, keep my family fed."

Despite the hard memories, my brother and I had always wanted to buy the farm back in Mattawan from Mr. Kovach, the blueberry farmer who slid in on a Stafford family feud and bought it for eight thousand dollars. I shit you not.

Sitting with my mom and aunt, looking at childhood photographs of their young, wary faces, fills me with a sense of wonder and curiosity. For a moment, I can forget about the reason we are here: the funeral.

"Who's that?" I point. "That little white girl."

"One of the cousins. I don't know," Mama says. "She ain't white."

These burnished-faced children with milky-brown-skinned parents. I've never seen most of the pictures that are scattered across the table. In several shots, their saffron faces attempt to blend in with the translucent white ones, and possibly would, were it not for that thick, wavy hair twined in Pocahontas-like plaits and swinging restlessly over their shoulders. In each photo, there is maybe one darker-hued face that dots the rows of boys and girls dressed in patched up slacks, overalls, and thin corn silk dresses. They were farmers' children, and children of railroad workers and paper mill recruits. They hunted possum and squirrels, plucked eggs out of chicken coops at four a.m. and crawdads from the river banks. They looked like willow trees with roots deep and wet in the land. In each photo, my mother and aunts produced painfully shy willow smiles for the camera.

"Yo' Mama would sit outside on the playground, on that merry-go-round," Aunt Lily says, turning to my mother. "Remember, VJ? Looking at the school with a smirk on your face, swinging your little legs."

Though they are smiling, I can tell it's hard to talk around the lumps in their throats.

Aunt Lily points to one photo of my mother in a bonnet, a child of seven or eight, her face crinkled defiantly at the photographer.

"Mommy, why you do that?" I ask.

"Cause I felt like it."

Yes, I think, she would do exactly what she wanted to do. She always had and always would.

"Boy, Yo' Mama was always ornery," Aunt Lily giggles again. "Defiant little witch."

It's true. In every photo, the way her chin tilts up says, "try me." Her defiant black gaze tells the lens that she can take a punch. Maybe more. With a huff, Mama pushes her worn playing cards aside like a memory. And the ritual is over.

She hands me a bottle of nail polish, a soft lilac pink.

"Paint my nails, Shonda."

The pungent enamel scent seeps into the air with each careful stroke as they talk up Aunt Phyllis in porous tones. Applying the polish to my mother's pinky nail, I look at her hands, knuckles thick and knotty. More like my sister Rochelle's hands, but somewhat like mine also. Pinching Mama's cuticle away from the nail, I realize that I am a woman sitting across from a woman, next to another woman, my aunt. I am not, and will never be, their equal in status, not having survived what they survived, but I am equal in gender and motherhood.

It is not quite morning. We exist in the unnamed minutes between twilight and dawn, and as we talk, I'm suddenly no longer a child. As they decide which photos to give away, which to keep and which to give to the funeral home for the photo collage, they have quietly let me into the circle of Stafford women. It's a moment I cherish like pearls on brown skin. I hadn't thought I'd ever get here.

As if challenging my revelation, Afiya is standing at the threshold of the kitchen, sleepily wiping her eyes. "Hey, little girl."

I motion her in. She runs over quickly to hug each of us, then beelines for the bathroom.

Aunt Lily is standing at the kitchen sink now. Her breakfast dishes clink as she places them in though she tries to move gingerly, but I can tell she is pissed to the highest pisstivity about something. She has her daddy's square chin and now it juts out like a fighter's to hold back the sob lodged in her throat: "I hate that people think they got to go to the *Black* funeral home just because *they* Black. Harper's don't know what the hell they doing. When you see your Aunt Phyllis just be prepared."

"It's disgusting," my mother nearly snarls.

Blowing on her nails, my mother pushes the cotton balls and nail polish to the other side of the table with the heel palms of her hands and deals herself another set, holding her nails carefully up and away from each other like MLK church fans.

Flip, whisk, slap. Shuffle.

5

Powwows

IF WE WERE farmers again, or fishermen and women on the Neuse River in North Carolina, instead of the nomads we have become over time, having sold all of our land—if we were real farmers, we'd be in the fields plowing. Maybe barbecuing slabs of beef and pork carcasses behind Grandpa Stafford's house like we used to in Mattawan. Maybe we'd be braiding each other's hair under a weeping willow. Possibly shifting in lawn chairs, the backs of our legs pinched, pink and hot from the flecking metal or worn plastic. Maybe we'd be snapping peas we'd grown, sitting in a circle, gossiping about old times. Or shucking corn husks from a pile of cobs that the adults had sent the children to pull from the erect green stalks in our porous garden.

Instead, my family flows like a river toward a squat brown building that held a harvest we'd like to give back. The moment I step out of the unflinching, butter-hot sun, and into the dim funeral parlor on the Northside, perspiration drenches me. Pools under my arms. My upper lip feels slick and heavy, harnessing all the dank moisture of the day. A lake of sweat is cradled in that tiny half-moon crescent that used to fascinate me as a child, when I had nothing else to do but stare at myself in the mirror. But today, at thirty, I am drowning in my own skin. What did I expect from Michigan. I long for the solitude of the star room in my mother's house, and the sound of my mother intuitively flipping cards at the kitchen table. Or to be in L.A., anonymous, where no one sees the swamp behind my eyes. Instead, on this sweltering day, I am burying an aunt.

"Hey, Shonda." Debbie Kay nods stiffly at me. She is Aunt Phyllis's youngest daughter. Debbie Kay's butterscotch skin gleams with sweat as beads drip from her upper lip and forehead. She squeezes her children's shoulders protectively. Around eight or nine, both the boy and girl squirm and crane their necks, interested to see all the people whose blood they share but have never met before. She keeps them hidden from us, just like I keep my daughter in California, hidden from them.

Debbie Kay has lost much of the weight that led her brothers and mine to torture her growing up. But her thick, black-rimmed glasses attest that she is still the same old nerdy Debbie I once beat in a cussing contest.

"Mom-*ah*," her boy complains. I don't know his name, have never been told he'd been born. She doesn't introduce me to them.

"Hey, Debbie," I reach for a hug, but she ushers her children quickly past me. I am prepared to console her with, "I'm sorry about your mom." But she wants nothing to do with any of us. Not even California me. She is as ready as I am for "it" to be over and done with, so she can go back to building a safe life for her kids without the past hovering over her, even if it means walking away from a body in the ground. Even if that body is her mother's.

That's when I know I am home. Not in Los Angeles, not cheerily biking the Playa del Rey beach bike path where I spend my weekend mornings. I'm not writing at the local bed and breakfast, The Inn at Playa del Rey, looking moodily out the window.

I am Back Here.

Where my black skirt creases in between my thighs and at the back of my knees like country attic cobwebs. Where the humidity parts my scalp in six sections, coaxing sweat in two loping paths down the nape of my neck, two lines past each temple, two into my eyes like welcome-back kisses. I know I am Home by the tense faces and tears. Pent-up jaws and scowls. As if we've been rehearsing all our lives. We know how to do this: to lament. It's in our nature. I know I am back in Kalamazoo.

"Mama." My daughter tugs my hand. Her olive, heart-shaped face turns up innocently. "Who was that?"

"A cousin." Someone I used to play with.

But I don't blame Debbie Kay. I hesitate to introduce my precious daughter too, because after the mourning maybe they will attempt to feed her meat, teach her cuss words I was forced to learn, invite her someplace where a fight would break out and I wouldn't be there to drag her away; maybe they'd try to claim her as one of their own. They would ignore my protests to keep her innocent. They might try to subsume her, get her high, tickle her till she pees on herself, laughing and crying at the same time. A lioness kind of mother, I couldn't let that happen. I might have to murder a family member behind that shit. Then we'd be having two funerals for the price of one. I had fought too long and too hard to leave the violence I grew up with behind. No one in L.A. knew what our hard love looked like.

"Did someone find the preacher?" I overhear one of my cousins whispering as they hurry into the main room.

The second set of funeral doors directly in front of me are propped wide open. The thin brown carpet is worn down to the color of a deer's trail. To my left, a smaller hallway leads to a cavern of the mortician's private chambers, chilled rooms where he carefully pries organs from the contents of breathless, ashened bodies like distended pearls from clam shells. To my right, another doorway leads to a bathroom that I will never use because all my water is seeping from my pores. About five paces in front of me, my mother, usually as ornery and piss-stain evil as the day was long, shakes as she walks in. She looks as if she is crumbling with each step. Clad in tight gray slacks and gray jacket, her head, arms, and shoulders sinking lower and lower toward the floor as she moves.

I open my mouth to say something, like "Mama, sit down. Do you need anything? Can I get you some water?" Then I close it, piercing my lips tightly. My tongue is a thick book in my mouth. If I opened it, the words I want to tuck in her ears would simply scatter like pages in the wind before I could identify which ones I want to catch and show her.

All at once, the presence of kin at this funeral, of my mother, sits on my chest. Blurry, crimson eyes and smeared lipstick, hands choking tissue. I am laden with the same feelings of inadequacy and ineptitude as I was when I was a child, and my mother would catch me playing alien or jumping off the porch with an umbrella for that one crystal instant feeling of flying. Through a barrage of awkward stutters, I'd try to explain to my mother why I believed in fairies and unicorns, life on other worlds.

"Girl," she'd shake her head. "You are one strange child."

Touched.

The hardness of her misunderstanding face; her small, crinkled nose; her alert, predator eyes are forever set in my mind. I was certain then, as I know on this blistering day, that there was and would always be a chasm yawning between her knowing of the world and mine. I don't know how to make small talk with anyone in my family. I always have questions about the past. They hate that.

Someone coughs politely, a *please move forward* sound.

"Excuse me." Someone else brushes past, smelling of stale cigarette smoke.

Somehow word has spread that I am Velma Jean's youngest daughter, Phyllis's niece, and soon people begin to embrace me with hugs reserved for handling cotton balls, teacups, and babies.

"Boy, your daughter sure growed up. She tall as a weed."

I nod politely and hug my daughter closer to me.

"Yes, she sure is tall, ain't she."

"Sure is," someone else beams.

Holding my daughter's clammy hand, I nod my thanks at the good conversation and inch closer toward the main room.

When my elderly Great-Aunt Katheryn walks in, she is so frail any feeble breeze would topple her in a cloud of dust. Her showy gold bracelets and rings would be the only identifiable trinkets on top of her heap of ashes.

Standing in the back, my nephew Jason, Rochelle's son, looks ready to bolt. He's close to his running buddy's apartment. Possibly, he'd thought he could make a quick trip and return before his mother noticed. Instead, sulking at his mother's determined look, he hunches his broad shoulders and drags his feet over to Rochelle. They walk past me into the room. My daughter and I follow.

6

Mothers and Sons

ALL THE FAMILIAR ingredients of a funeral are present.

The customary, yet suffocating tension that death breeds. Cheap, drooping flowers. The curious, surprised ones who want to see how well we mourn. Programs with Aunt Phyllis's face grace ash-blue covers signifying the occasion. But here, commonplace ends and my family begins. Hardly anyone wears black. We are clad in T-shirts, jeans, dress shirts, slacks, pantsuits. Kmart special tennis shoes on the kids. J. C. Penney loafers and high heels on adults. We are cracked, tattered, and Midwestern wind-blown. The no-show singer, I learn later, had been booked by Debbie Kay's sister, Jo Ann, the eldest daughter. The singer, supposedly Jo Ann's good friend, was too cracked out to show up. And we all knew she was just contraband anyway: a prop from Jo Ann's own exalted career with heroin and other such drugs.

"Jason," Rochelle vehemently motions to her son. They have somehow gotten separated. He grimaces but lumbers over to her and flops into the seat. Earlier that morning, at Mama's house, a tornado began brewing between them. I reflexively crossed my fingers that'd I'd be gone before that shit hit the fan.

When Rochelle entered Mama's house hours earlier, her twelve-year-old son, Rodrique, and Jason, sixteen, scooted in sheepishly behind her; my mother's left eye narrowed and started to twitch.

"Hey Mama," Rochelle smiled nervously. She was pretty in a bright top, tight blue jeans shorts, and red lipstick. She didn't often wear lipstick. The gap between her top teeth flashed when she smiled. Six-feet-something, Jason had grown into the Addams

Family's Lurch. Looking like a mini-hulk, he had to turn almost sideways to get into my mother's front door. He tried to hide behind his Mama, like he hadn't caused everybody the worst kind of grief these last few months for running away from Rochelle's house where they lived in Alabama. She'd only moved there to get Jason away from his yeasty hood friends, but he hated the South. Somehow he'd gotten back to Kalamazoo and hopped from one family member's house to the next, each one eventually putting him out for his attitude, his laziness, or his mouthiness. Rochelle was angry at everybody. Popeye, our youngest brother, offered Jason the last place he could crash.

"Hi," Mama snapped at Rochelle and clamped her mouth shut, making her cheeks puff out like she'd swallowed a lemon. I looked between Mama and Jason, who avoided her eyes. I stepped between them.

"Dang," I said. "What y'all feeding these boys down in Alabama?"

Jason folded me in a tight, hot embrace. "Hey, Auntie," he rasped, voice brassy and much deeper than I remembered. I counted the years I'd missed of his life in inches. I'd been in L.A. for over ten years now, but still I was stunned that I couldn't put my arms easily around his body anymore, his chest a small mountain of muscles and flesh.

Mama refused even to look at Jason. Worrying Rochelle to death was tantamount to kicking little dogs because Rochelle was a recovering addict, and any little stress sent her reeling.

My daughter came over to stand next to me. "Hey Jason," she said.

"Oh my God. That's Afiya?" He hugged her. "I'm have to kill some niggas behind her."

"Hey, man. Words." I hugged Jason tightly again. "Dang. You all big. Voice all deep. You taking care of Yo' Mama?"

I knew he wasn't.

"You know she be trippin'," he joked, then dropped a bomb. "I'm not going to the funeral. I don't have the right clothes."

Was he talking to me or to himself? In the middle of our laughter, the air suddenly drew up tight like a storm was coming. I turned, feeling the heat of Rochelle's gaze. Her eyes narrowed to slits, nostrils flared, as her face woodened into an African mask. Jason grinned, faking a punch at her, but his grin held a lifetime of hurt. *His Mama using; his Mama in the streets; his Mama in recovery* was in that carnival grin.

Something was happening here.

"I'm not going," Jason repeated with that secret smile of his.

Instantly, I was jolted into a deeply buried memory: Rochelle eighteen, living at her boyfriend's parents' house. The boyfriend, Philip, was laughing, but then started yelling. His once handsome tawny face was now a ruddy, contorted, over-fried egg, and he was punching Rochelle. "I told you don't do that," he barked as he punched.

I was screaming because that is the normal reaction when a dickweed is smiling one minute and then punching your sister in the mouth the next. First Baby Jason attacked his father, hitting and pinching him around my attempts to pull them apart. She was only eighteen. And Jason, my sweet, two-year-old nephew, ran to the corner of their bedroom biting himself, gnawing on his own arm in silence. But there was a ghastly smile on his face too. Someone threw a lamp or a broom.

I realized it was me. I was throwing furniture and screaming too.

Philip ran outside, laughing. Suddenly, we are all outside except Jason. Rochelle, sweaty and bleeding, was scouring the yard for something under the pretty fall leaves. Finally, with a grunt of satisfaction, she jerked up Philip's daddy's wood chopping hatchet and slung it over her shoulder like a gladiator. "I'ma bash your goddamn head in you ugly mothafuckah if you ever hit me again."

I snapped back to Mama's house, in the living room, with Jason over six feet tall, over two hundred pounds, towering over everyone except Popeye, and smiling that fucking smile, and Rochelle, a small fire gurgling in her throat, clenching her fists. I heard clearly in my head, *I don't know how to fix this. I never know how to fix this.*

Jason sat on the couch and leaned sideways.

"Mama." He exhaled for effect, then enunciated each word. "I. Do. Not. Have. The. Right. Clothes."

He couldn't stop the small quiver of his lips from going up. I couldn't help but smile at his stupid smile, but I lowered my head when Rochelle's eyes grew country-beefsteak-tomato-round. He walked out of the room to my room, the star room.

"Ja-*son*." Rochelle's voice skipped three notches to that helter-skelter, fingernails-on-chalkboard level we were used to. As soon as her voice reached that pitch, my daughter, who'd been sitting on the floor against the couch watching us like we were TV, got up and hurried out of the room. I heard the basement door close and knew she'd be safe watching real TV in my Mama's basement.

Rochelle followed Jason. I followed her. "*Don't* argue with *me*! Jason, you are *going* and that's *it*! And stop smiling that dumb-ass smile."

He looked like his father when he smiled.

Standing in the corner, his lower lip inflated into an inner tube. A soft mauve hue spread across his brown cheeks in embarrassment. "I am almost a man," his crowded eyes say loudly to his mother and then to his brother, who'd been pretending to look for socks in his bag. Then Jason looked at me. I looked away and down.

He would have to learn it on his own. How cavernous and hungry our family was. How deep and wide our anger and resentment went beneath the ground for generations, then how our love snapped back at you quick and stinging like the skinny rubber bands we used to pull off *Kalamazoo Gazette* newspapers and sneak-attack each other with, as if it was a fun game. It was a known fact in my family that we wouldn't be allowing him room to live his own life any time soon. We didn't let you go down quietly either. You'd be buckshot by our gossip until you either set your priorities in order or left town or died. Most got tired of our mouths, deciding to just up and die.

My priority had been to get the hell out of Kalamazoo as soon as I could vote, but I could tell Jason one thing, that even if he left the wet, peeling roads of Kalamazoo, even if he could by some fluke of fate escape the waiting black earth, the ghosts would come for him. No one escaped heritage or past.

Instead, I said, "Jason, just please do what your mother says."

It was his turn to look away. Rochelle left the room.

They loved each other. They will crush each other.

THE FUNERAL HOME is at least a thousand degrees and everybody's damn near swimming in their clothes. As if that's not enough, when I look to the front I see Aunt Phyllis's oyster shell of a body from the corner of my eye, and the barely solid feeling in my stomach dissolves to mist. I might throw up. *Sweet Je-sus*, it's open casket.

"Why is the casket fucking open?" I whisper under my breath.

The mortician proves *not* to be a good makeup artist. Once an ample woman, my aunt's skin drapes loosely around her cheekbones, displaying the effects of how fast liver disease and aspirin on an empty stomach can siphon a human body. Around the hollow, numb parts in my chest, the sight sickens and angers me as much as it had my mother and Aunt Lily.

I am not prepared at all.

Pretending I think we've arrived too late to properly see the body, I step out of the viewing line and firmly steer my daughter into a third-row seat behind my mother and her husband. When my Aunt Mildred, the oldest of the Stafford sisters, pours her body into the chair next to mine, a sour Johnson & Johnson talcum powder scent, combined with the day's heat, lays its fingers around my throat. Old woman smell, combined with the pools of Avon perfume soaking behind her ears, clashes in my nose.

"Hi, dear," she says. She is my least favorite aunt.

Aunt Mildred's sallow face sags under seventy years of a flint-snap judging glare. Her spiteful ash-black eyes scared me as a child, even when they fogged over at the oddest moments, but that didn't stop me from tangling the skinny teeth of silver combs in the river of blue-black hair that poured down her back. She was my living doll.

Once in her home, while she was attached to an oxygen tank, sad plastic tubes sprouting from her like spider legs, Aunt Mildred pulled out one of the oldest pictures of our family on the Mattawan farm. Our ancestors, about thirteen of them, gazed stoically back at the camera, standing in front of the very first clapboard house built on the land. From adults to children, they were decked out in homesteader's clothing, complete with pitchforks and puffed out skirts and ruffles on their sleeves. The oldest of the girls, Aunt Mildred actually remembered some of them. I'd never met any of them. Looking at the photo, less afraid of her but still wary, I'd asked, "Why did Grandpa Stafford cheat on his wives? What do you remember about him saying we were Indian?" Before my eyes, my evil aunt turned into a little girl and smiled a little girl odd smile: her eyes grew unfocused, almost hypnotized. "Daddy wasn't flirting with any of those women. He told me he was just trying to make them feel good about themselves. 'Wouldn't any woman want to have a nice compliment?' he'd say."

I see the same hard but dislocated look she always had, ready to turn us to dust.

"Hey Aunt Mildred." I choke back a tingle in my throat. I pray that time speeds up. That I won't sneeze. That this will soon be over and I can go home, to *my* home, Los Angeles. Where I am the daughter of no one. The niece of no one. Where I am only "Yaya Afiya," Yoruba-speaking Nigerians say, mother of Afiya.

But there she is, Aunt Phyllis. Supine, face mottled. Arms crossed over a motionless chest. Her once legendary crow-black Stafford hair now lays like limp bacon across her skull and does nothing to disguise the trauma her body has experienced. The gaping casket lid reminds me of how much I hate funerals. It reminds me that open casket funerals are a stupid American custom. Making me feel forced to peruse the body like disposed goods. Making sure the participants are buying into their own misery. Getting our money's worth of new stockings and shoes, as a fresh wail rips through the crowd because Death is near.

Although I recognize this ritual is sacred, I don't need to see the body; I know the person is dead if there aren't any sounds coming out of the hull. Still, watching my mother's cheeks burn fuchsia as she sheds her water, wrenching her gaze back and forth from her sister's face to her own lap, I know I have been defeated by time, by disease, by distance, by my life. Most certainly by our legacy.

All my aunt's stories have gone with her to the grave, lost to her daughters and me, the niece who needs them. Tears run hot and sour into my open mouth.

"It's okay, Shonda." Aunt Mildred pats my arm. Her touch is clammy. Afiya keeps her eyes down and leans in closer to me, her body shivering like a puppy's. "You okay?" I ask. She nods, but I know she is not okay. I should not have brought her.

The casket sits by itself in the front of the room like a lighthouse as we wait. That must be it, I think. We can go. I rouse Afiya, prepared to stand. But the thick pause reminds someone of the minister. Hands signal and heads turn. Furious whispers. Reverend

Underwood nearly leaps out of the audience. Nervously adjusting his tie, he asks, "If anyone else wants to speak, please let me know."

No one rises. It's hot as all get out in that musty room. There's an embarrassing pause. Clearing his throat, the reverend launches into an impromptu, highly unprepared sermon.

"I'm told Phyllis McMillan was an amazing woman," he says. The three-piece suit he's decked out in makes sweat beads march down his face. "She took care of not only that lovely grand-daughter, but she made other kids in the neighborhood feel like she was a second mother to them. Now that she's gone, don't mourn her. Funerals are supposed to make us reflect on the love that existed, not what was lost. And she had a golden reputation as a crossing guard."

Aunt Lily sucks her teeth. I can tell she wants to snatch a knot in his ass. His stupid words rub her like sandpaper. As he talks on, her mouth tightens until it nearly disappears from her face. I can hear her thinking, *Niggah, if you don't shut the hell up with yo' shit for brains.*

"And furthermore, as I was asking around about the Staffords, I found out I'm yo' cousin from my daddy's side of the family. We related by way of the Underwoods."

I glance around. That last nugget hits the crowd like a dud. People stir but not quite. Except for Aunt Lily. Hair cropped short against her head, chin angled out rigidly, she rolls her eyes hard. Her body stiffens as if holding in a whiplash retort that would scour him clean of his Blackness. I can almost hear, "He can keep that shit to his-self. This ain't the time or place for no family re-union, dumb ass."

But it's supposed to be one, I would remind her. I am supposed to be returning for our second real family reunion in a decade, not this funeral. Over the years, my two eldest brothers, several cousins, and I have flung ourselves out of the Midwest and across the country.

It took my sisters longer to leave, but at some point we all returned for a spell, for vacation, or like now, to bury someone. It seemed that every time I came back, my mother and her sisters had moved further and further away from each other, like the constellations in their own separate part of the night sky. They probably haven't all been in the same room together in ten years, until today.

Only three are breathing.

I look around. Our skin tones are the shades of a Kalamazoo autumn field, from the most golden of leaves, to muted pink-skinned peaches and ripe plums, to bright yellow corn cobs and their wafer-like silken husks.

How do we know we are American Indian? My Great-Aunt Katheryn M. Manuel wrote on the 2002 Manuel family genealogy that my great-great-grandmother Ida Mahoney's mother, Mariah (called Anne) Peak Mahoney, was Cherokee and Delaware Pequot Indian from Ohio/Oklahoma. Aunt Katheryn also penned that Mariah's husband, James Mahoney, was "multiracial." But Mariah's parents' race isn't labeled on the chart. Many more early records exist that state my ancestors are American Indian, Negro, Mulatto, Colored, or White, but none of them say African. Later, they all mostly say Black.

One lists a great-great-grandfather as a Freeman, so he could have been a former slave or just a Free Person of Color who was also multiracial. Multiple family members somehow showed up a different race or ethnicity every ten years on the U.S. Census, as if they didn't just live the last ten years of their life in a whole other social class. Because that's what passing for white or Indian was back in the 1800s, and still is—a way to leave social ostracization behind. To change your life. To live a better life, not just an exotic life, because you were lighter. To feed your family. Hence, we have multiple "light-skinned" Blacks ignoring the one-drop rule and claiming another race or ethnicity, simply because they could.

And yes, because of racism, prejudice, and discrimination, a sense of privilege came with passing or claiming Indian blood, but only after American Indians had been defeated across the country. Before that, being one was dangerous. But we were not "claiming" it. Our records said so. Our DNA says so.

And we were dangerous.

That inherited anger, the drinking—wherever it came from, enslavement or stolen lands was our ruin.

I look at my family in that funeral home: we didn't feel exotic.

My mother, her sisters, and their kids were certainly not the "privileged" generations, and neither was mine. Something had broken somewhere. If that Indian mystic quality, or our whiteness, was supposed to make life better, when was that going to happen exactly? Our Blackness and our Indianness, not our whiteness, were undeniable in our bloodline and our faces, on my face; our blood was at war.

I continue to gaze anywhere but at the casket, taking what little comfort I could from the presence of my sisters, brothers, and cousins I haven't seen in years. We look tired, beyond mourning. Sated. Life has worn my family down and apart like brittle wishbones.

My Aunt Lily always says, "There's something under this ground. I used to think Michigan was cursed because we could never catch a fucking break."

The land. It didn't matter that it was Indian land: that Kalamazoo's white "founder" Titus Bronson basically stood on a mound in 1834, looked around and said, "open for business," and promptly auctioned off parcels. It was inconsequential that Kalamazoo is a Potawatomi word meaning either "reflection in the water" or "boiling water," also "mirage," referring to the bubbling eddies on the Kalamazoo River down the street from us, which smelled like shit mixed with more shit for years because Eaton paper mill dumped their factory trash in it.

That the entire state of Michigan, derived from another Indian word, "Michi-gama," loosely translated to mean "Big Lake," was once populated by vibrant, friendly nations, such as the Ojibway/ Chippewa, Ottawa or Odawa and Potawatomi or Anishinaabe, did nothing to deter the later removal and routing out of everything Indian. City officials and football teams did keep the cute-sounding names of most of the towns and high school mascots. Consequently in Paw Paw, where I went for fourth and fifth grade, one of seventeen "civil townships," or more accurately, little back-road towns with big Indian names, I never saw a Paw Paw Indian.

None of us could catch a fucking break.

Amid the folded tissues in our hands, the cotton shirts, slacks, blue jeans, and rouge eyes, there are other things present. Resentments. Grudges. Things, history, rummaging past our ankles on the cold floor, things that only we are familiar with, having grown up with lakes in our backyards, cornstalks, horses and a farm to straddle in the summer. The dense scent of a swamp. The hint of moth-winged winters. Salt licks and palomino horse hair. Woodstove smoke.

A fresh backwater breeze.

"I didn't tell her goodbye," my mother suddenly wails and breaks down in one cavernous sob, her body heaving. She can't stop shaking. Her thighs strain against the seams of her gray pantsuit as she rocks, her entire body shuddering and pitching in the chair as if she's been possessed. Her anguish sets off a fresh siren of moans and chairs creaking across the room.

"It's okay, Velma," John whispers, trying to hold her steady. At fifty-nine, her wail sounds of all the unspoken things, the rift of their silence, their harrowing childhood.

Last summer, my mother had refused to invite Aunt Phyllis to the only reunion we'd had in years. As the clock ticked on, and no other cars drove up except my brothers' and sisters' and Aunt Lily's, I turned to my mother.

"Mommy, did you tell Aunt Phyllis and Aunt Mildred we were having this?"

"What I'ma call them for?" she quipped, her stance and angled chin challenging me to pick up the phone that sat on the kitchen counter inches away from us.

"We getting older, Mommy," I said quietly, backing down. "We need to see each other."

I knew she'd cling to her favorite epithet, "fuck 'em." She didn't need them. Fed up with the arguments and misunderstandings, she'd closed her circumference. Let sleeping dogs lie. Now, the sorrow marauds my mother. Rides her like a black-eyed tornado. She looks as if she were about to explode or disappear in the center of it.

Aunt Lily, the baby girl of her sisters, now fifty-five, holds my mother's trembling hand. Aunt Mildred looks on bleary-eyed, her once flawless skin washed out and puffy around her mouth and eyes from salty tears. In appropriately hard-backed mourners' chairs, we sit two seats away from and behind my mother. The back of my mother's neck glows a ruby red just below her hairline. She's just sheared more of her wavy hair off. Once long, her tresses have become an unwanted gift of her heritage. After she hit forty, my mother's hair never reached below her temples. Now exposed, vulnerable to us, her ears burn away their normal yellow hue to conch shell pink, then poinsettia red.

As if no one else has anything to say about Aunt Phyllis's life, her granddaughter, Brandy, skin a well-oiled Barbie doll brown, gets up and hogs the rest of the show.

"My grandmother was," Brandy pauses, surveying the crowd meaningfully. Her chest heaves under her tight lavender dress. "*She* was always there for me. The *only* one."

Through drawn, painted lips, Brandy reads a kind of eulogy, chewing her words down to the gristle before she spits them out.

"My grandmother was the *only* one who loved me and took care of *me*." Brandy stabs Jo Ann, her mother, with a hateful look. In a tight white miniskirt, brown top, and calf-high white boots, Jo Ann hovers near the front of the room, looking hungry-dog skinny, beaten down by life. Drugs have turned her skin into a pot-marked road. She avoids her daughter's eyes.

Just before she died, rumors surfaced that Aunt Phyllis had begged Dennis, her youngest son, to speed up his house search for her because she was terrified of Jo Ann moving back to Kalamazoo. My aunt dreaded the havoc she knew Jo Ann would carelessly inflict on her finally quiet, alcohol-free life. Some said, quiet as kept, that my aunt gobbled down aspirin so she would die before her daughter arrived. Looking at Jo Ann's dazed, dry eyes, my heart cringes. I don't want to know if the rumors are true.

Slender in her favorite dark blue dress, Afiya adjusts her steaming head on my shoulder. "You okay Mama?" she asks quietly. Am I? But I nod, grateful.

I tune Brandy in again but am confused as she mouths more saintly words about a woman I never knew. In my view, Aunt Phyllis was hellfire in a handbasket. I try to catch my eldest sister's eye. Does Bobbie Ann remember this aunt? She is forty-one and remembers everything. She is also the most stoic of the mourners. That's her *modus operandi*—the toughest dike in Kalamazoo. As the first child, Bobbie Ann constantly had to fight the next two children, both boys, to prove that she was just as much of a man, if not more, than they were put together. Her reputation around town was solidified due in large part to a legendary left hook. Today, her purple lips are puckered, eyes watchful. Making sure everyone else is handling their grief, she sucks hers into her cheeks and patrols the room, rather than crying. Her body, a hulking square of flesh, is ready to catch the ones who will eventually fall. When she finally sits, Bobbie doesn't look at me. I think she'd barely been breathing.

"And she was beautiful," Brandy continued.

When she was younger, my aunt was light-bright pretty. Older, Aunt Phyllis was a scowling woman who could occasionally turn on a kilowatt smile, particularly later in life after she'd stopped drinking. But mostly, I remember a woman with breasts the size of watermelons, which she always threatened to smack against your head if you acted up at her house. Even the *thought* of my aunt's breasts squashing against any part of me made me queasy. Consequently, when I visited her on the Northside as a kid, I ever so quietly sunk into the couch against the back pillow, watching television until my mother picked me up after she got off work or out of Bingo. Probably Bingo.

"And my grandma is the one who I will always love."

Having finished her eulogy, Brandy begins reading a poem through gritted teeth while choking up. Her wrath illuminates her like a brown orb. She hates everyone in this room for allowing her grandmother to die. Brandy chokes back another sob.

"It's okay, honey," my mother calls quietly. "You don't have to do it."

"No. Leave me *alone*." Brandy's eyes spit daggers at us. I don't recognize this cousin. When my real cousin Brandy was five, she was mute to the world. She never uttered a sound no matter how much candy she was plied with, but instead watched her crazy-ass, crackhead mother rip a hole in the earth with leveled, crow-black eyes. Brandy watched Jo Ann slip and ooze her way in and around Kalamazoo in tight minis and tank tops for a fix.

I recognized Brandy's silence as a survival skill, as self-protection from the drugged-out men who hung with her mother and leered at her. That ghetto addict life. Brandy's watchful gaze disappeared several years later and was replaced with a hurricane fury. Having inherited her mother and grandmother's Stafford temper, not only did Brandy cut you with those eyes, but she fought with knives.

"No. I'ma do dis for my grandmother," she growls at my mother.

Though I know I would never do it, the desire to sock my cousin right in her eye for disrespecting my mother crosses my mind. My sisters shift in their seats. They would do it. I know they are thinking of the consequences of bopping Brandy on her head, that it wouldn't serve a purpose. Brandy is as drunk with grief as the rest.

No one has asked my mother or the other sisters to speak, and now, like a slow dance when the song fades, it is over. The grief seeps out of my mother and she rises, limply making her way to the front door, out of the funeral home. Into the sun. We file out to the waiting cars. One of them holds my aunt's empty shell, others the would-be farmer's daughters. Still other cars hold their seeds, this small town's embittered harvest. Funeral or family reunion, you always returned home.

Now there are three sisters. Everyone that day knows there are three.

7

One Flew Over

"GOD-*DAMN*-IT!"

The shout booms from the living room. Clenching my eyes shut, I turn over and shove my head under the pillow. When the yell bounces against the walls again, I sigh and pull on a pair of black biker shorts and a T-shirt. I emerge just in time to see my sister Rochelle slam-dunk the cordless phone on Mama's glass table, making the decorative rocks in the glass bowl shudder like Jell-O. In the same tight blue jean shorts and faded red T-shirt she'd slept in, Rochelle anxiously paces from couch to front door to couch again, biting her bottom lip. Thinking, calculating.

"I *cannot* believe this." Rochelle's words punch through clenched teeth. The perfect gap in her mouth, geometrically centered like an open doorway, flashes when she talks. Whenever Rochelle is excited, she peels whistles through that gap without warning, making the nearest person's heart leap out of their mouth. She can probably break a window with the ear-numbing pitch. She suddenly stops mid-stride, checking her cell phone. No messages. Her lips are a compressed, tight stitch in her face. She fumes, wiping sweat off her wide forehead despite Mama's air conditioner on blast. Back to pacing. Rochelle pats an itch out of her scalp, her permed hair and bun. Chicken-bone-skinny from ankles up to waist, she has lost weight since the last time I saw her. Her brown cheeks are ruddy with agitation; her usual full-lipped, contagious smile is gone. Beads of moisture reappear of their own volition on her temples, slipping down her cheekbones.

I flop down on my mother's scratchy brown couch. "What happened?" I force my calm, clinical voice into the angry air.

Despite the ruckus, my youngest brother Popeye remains asleep on the floor, his mountainous frame hulked by the door like a hibernating bear; one muscular, tattoo-riddled arm is folded beneath his head for a pillow. He is our bear cub, the youngest and physically largest of us. At 6'2, three hundred-some-odd pounds, his hugs are smothering. Popeye, and now Jason, are the proverbial town giants with cotton candy hearts. They could swat us down like African flies if they wanted to, but in the end they hugged us, no matter how much we women yelled.

He sleeps peacefully; he is used to the spontaneous shattering of things.

My daughter is not. She pokes her head out: "Good morning?"

I shake my head at her but say, "Morning love." She disappears back into the room. The only violence she's ever experienced has been well-deserved spankings. She has never seen me fight with a man who loved me. We live in Los Angeles, two thousand miles away, for this very reason. My little apartment is a violence-free zone, the walls decorated with African masks, pictures of dark-skinned African women, and American Indian rattles. My childhood was like living in a not-so-funhouse, where, because of the sudden violence, I was distorted in every mirror. *I am only home for my aunt's funeral*, I think. *I only have one more day in Michigan.*

Fuming, Rochelle spits out her words: "*Jason* said he can't go to work *because I* took his clothes *from* Popeye's ex-girlfriend's place *and* he doesn't have the *right shoes* to *wear*! Come to *find out*, he's going to get *fired* if he doesn't show up 'cause it'll be his *third time* being *late*."

I sigh. Everybody but Rochelle knows that her son Jason, a seventeen-year-old "playa," would rather have his thumbnails pulled out than flip patties at Burger King out on Stadium Drive. His undercover bouncer's job pays him twice as much in less time and reputational harm.

"We can go get his clothes and take him to work," I offer, a stupid city reflex. Always too helpful.

Rochelle whips her head around to stab me with bulging eyes: "Really?"

I immediately regret my words. Unintentionally, I implicate myself in her one-woman war party with the "we." A tense spiraling knot forms in my chest, which I quickly identify as remorse, or, in the favorite Midwestern Kalamazoo parlance of my grandfather, the feeling of "what a dumb ass" that I didn't stay in bed. Didn't ignore the familiar tightening, the dwindling of oxygen, the yellowing of the sky. I knew from childhood what the coming of a storm looked like.

I'm doing exactly what I said I wouldn't do—getting pulled in, against my will—but I don't know how to stuff my words back down my throat. It's my turn to break out in a sweat.

Everyone is prepared for storms in this rural township except me. In case of tornadoes, nearly every neighborhood block lined with drafty two-story houses has basements to retreat to—in the country, about twenty minutes outside Kalamazoo, they call them cellars. If a storm jumped our curbless sidewalk, or hopped a river, and happened to rip a house or barn from its foundation, all the barely surviving mom and pop corner stores would still have their wares tucked neatly below ground. Dusty milk cartons in the refrigerated case, gum-stained floors, and musty onions in wooden bins would be gone, but the people would hunker down under a washtub or hide behind a scrub board. Save themselves.

Me, I don't know no better. My sister is pissed to the highest pisstivity; you can see the steam emanating from the crown of her head. Even the squirrels and possums my grandfather loved to skin and eat knew when to hold their breath, scamper for cover. Hide. Me, I'm up shit creek without a paddle.

Rochelle scoops the car keys from the couch before I can backpedal. Without waiting for a reply, she says, "Come on." Showerless, we race to the door. The second we step outside, the June humidity cloaks our bodies like Cling Wrap, pushing moisture between every available crevice: fingers, necks, toes. We jump into my mother's pitiful blue Lumina, dynamic duo to the rescue. I start the clock ticking; from this second until I get on the airplane, I have to make it out of Kalamazoo, with my daughter and my scalp. I have to make it out alive.

Wait. Stop. Rewind.

I WAS A Buchanan, half sister to the Bynums, the first five kids in our family. When we were younger, they were famous for and cock-proud of their polyester Soul Train jumpsuits and the spongy six-inch afros that reeked of seventies discos and strobe lights. Growing up, both my light-skinned, handsome big brothers, Tyrone and Loren, were constantly pestered by neighborhood girls who wanted to be seen walked home by them, down Southworth Terrace, or East Main Street. The Eastside was Bynum territory and they knew every road, roof, hiding place, basketball court, and weed house like the backs of their hands.

When my big brothers and sisters walked up and down our block shoulder to shoulder, we actually took up the middle of the street and the sidewalks, and sometimes, where there was no sidewalk, the rising mounds that edged our neighbors' front yards. Maybe having no curb on the sidewalk lent them this sense of possession. And because Southworth was a narrow street, mostly populated by elderly, soft-skinned immigrants—Russians, Poles, Yugoslavs, and other European Jews having escaped Hitler—cars rolled slowly by us. Those poor old folks didn't know what we could do: all tan- and brown-skinned and loud-talking. We turned out to be kindhearted kids who shoveled their sidewalks in the winter for a few dollars and raked up their sepia maple leaves in the fall. One thin-veined immigrant, a sweet woman, would stuff us with vanilla wafers almost every time we passed her house, calling out to us with an accented, "Come here, you, child," because we always looked so hungry.

To the other neighborhood kids on the next blocks over, the Bynums were nuts. Their kin-to-them-crazy-ass-Staffords' reputation for being skillful fighters was widely known. Tyrone thought he was Bruce Lee and would break out a Bruce Lee Kung Fu cry in every altercation. He used to practice with his black nunchucks in the yard and all over the house until he clocked himself in the head and grew two lumps the size of chicken eggs on his temple. Everyone knew that we were really Staffords and Manuels, that our blood percolated with country willows and swampland, and therefore we were prone to stomp a mud hole in your ass first and ask questions later. We were the Waltons with loaded double-barrel shotguns. Being the baby girl of this clan came with instant protection and wide berth for me in school.

Racing down Oakland Drive at a breakneck speed to take my recalcitrant nephew his work clothes, Rochelle glances at me sideways. Nervous, she wipes perspiration from her face. She wants a cigarette but knows I'd pitch a bitch-fit if she smoked one. Grandma Dorothy's cancer killed her. Rochelle wants, I can tell, to feed her anxiety and anger the way she used to years ago—a hot silver spoon pooling with perfect crystal, with mind-numbing liquid.

But she is clean now. Today. This week.

"Is that too much air?" She flicks the switch off for the fifth time.

Still, she needs something. To say something. Do something. We are doing fifty-five in a thirty-five-mile zone, flying down Oakland Drive, a one-lane hill, like witches on our brooms. And because this is my life in Kalamazoo, I turn off my worry button, because this is Normal here. Turning off the worry button is what you do if you don't know whether or not you're going to die soon. But she loves me, respects my locked-vegetarian-spiritualist lifestyle, and defends me if someone (always Mama) cusses and pulls at my locks, saying, "*you ruined your Good Indian hair.*" Or when Aunt Lily says: "When you gon cut that shit, nigga?"

I followed my big sister like a hatchling, and Rochelle raised me like a protective barn owl in a den of hungry wolverines.

When my mother worked graveyard shifts at her nursing home or had debilitating migraines, Rochelle poured my bowl of Cap'n Crunch and helped me button my coat in the winter and sent me off to school. She, not my heavy-handed mother, combed my hair all throughout elementary and middle school, pressing the straw and dirt out. This was a kind of ritual in my family—placing the burden of raising the youngest daughter on the next oldest daughter. When we were younger, Rochelle tried to rebel: "I don't want Shonda to go with me. She *always* goes with me."

"Take Shonda with you or you staying your skinny butt home."

I was the tattletale, so Rochelle couldn't get into nothing Mama wouldn't know about later. I waddled after Rochelle all over the Eastside, head down and mostly in a book. Rochelle, beautiful Rochelle, thick black hair pulled back in a bun, wide gap-toothed smile with a single dark shadow that twinkled in her mouth like the North Star. Heart big as Lake Michigan. She didn't have a chance. She should have listened to her dreams—not the bad dreams but the good ones. Not the dreams where monsters chased her down, but the dreams of her being a famous, well-off cosmetologist, being called by her nickname, "Hollywood," and living there too.

But that hadn't happened.

"How's your boyfriend?" She fiddles with her lighter. "Whatshisname?"

"Who?" I suck my teeth. "This sister is about to be single. He ain't man enough. How's your husband?"

"Who? Girl, that shit done come and gone. He couldn't *handle* all this."

"Honey, you still crazy as all get out."

We burst into nervous laughter, our relationships frayed, lives tattered. But it feels good, like old times. Rochelle protected me as much as she could when we were growing up—though our family possessed tremendously effective Inquisition-like tormenting skills, our only true inheritance. She quietly ushered me through my own thirty-yard dash as a teenage alcoholic, the summer before I left home after high school, without a word to Mama. Rochelle would break someone's face for me.

Now, I wish I could protect her like that.

"Sister Floozy." Sweat beads mow down her brown face. *Here it comes.* I don't want the laughing star Rochelle to fade out. I felt her absence in so many ways in Los Angeles, missed her especially when I wanted someone beat up. She was everyone's favorite sister and friend, who would, and had, give you her last of the last: a dime, swallow of soda pop, a cigarette.

I know things have happened since we last saw each other, things that she keeps locked deep inside.

"What am I going to do about Jason?" she says.

Rochelle had only been in Mobile for a year.

"I don't know. Let him figure it out, Roach." I try to soothe, smooth out the rough creases of this moment. I can feel the wind from the storm whispering behind my ears before it hits me.

"Shonda," she rumbles like a volcano, churning and full of its own cayenne-red blood. "I gave *everyone, every one* of y'all mothafuckas a place to stay when y'all needed it! I *never* turned anyone away and they just *used* me and took my shit and ate my food!"

It's as if she's been waiting one thousand cold, hard years to erupt, to scream this at the top of her lungs. Her words shell out. The syllables dissolve into incinerating lava. Several layers of the earth's melting skin froth out of her mouth, a harvest of an almost incoherent rage at everyone for turning her son away, talking about him behind his back, not giving him whatever he needed to live. Something she's done for all her sisters' children, even me and Afiya for a few months when I returned home nearly eight years ago. She has a right to be angry. All our nieces and nephews who've run away have all ended up at her house, even our brother Popeye. Given her leniency with everything from boyfriends to weed to food, the nieces and nephews were careless, thoughtless. They took everything Rochelle had to give like cacti hoarding water. They sucked her love dry. They lived off her, ate off her plate, had sex on her couch, and rarely said thank you. A recovering drug and alcohol addict, her hard life can be seen on her cheekbones and thin hands; I sense the weed and alcohol ebbing and flowing in her veins. And despite it all, everyone knew our beautiful sister would never let any family member go hungry or homeless. She'd been there. Done that.

But in the process, they, *we*, had driven Rochelle slightly crazy. And now, I am staring at the madwoman, her mouth open like a dragon's, breathing up hot, singed stars. Rochelle's need to be loved, to be mothered, made her open her home, but her need to be the one to give everything to everyone had ultimately worn her down. And she doesn't know how to say it. Instead, she becomes the storm:

"I have taken care of *your* children!" Her eyes are blazing black lava orbs. "Done *everything* for them and now no one wants to take care of my son!" At the end of her sentence, she breaks into heavy racking sobs.

The car swerves.

Suddenly, familiarly, I disconnect. I float up from my adult body and back to the dank moisture of a childhood day, the heat bubbling up from the dew-drenched afternoon, lying in bed on the first day of summer, my limbs nearly wooden from excitement. I don't have to worry about My Death yet. I don't have to hold a sister's membrane falling out of her ears. I don't have to keep a car on a road. A warning buzz croons in my head, and I snap back, aware that another sharp move might plow us into oncoming traffic.

"I know, Rochelle, slow down," I murmur, trying to talk us to the speed limit, one eye on her purpling face, the other on the passing cars. What do they think of us? Two Black women, one gesturing erratically, tears scalding her swollen face; the other covertly keeping an eye on their headlights as the windows slowly fog up, as if doused with smoke from a magic trick gone awry. In the accident report, we'll be called "two African American women dead on the scene," while my grandfather, when he died, in a car crash, with his ex-wife who was white, was referred to by the reporter as "Caucasian man and wife." No one will mention that we have American Indian, Irish, French blood, too. That we are half-breeds. Mixed race seeds. Descendants of Free People of Color. Black Indians. No one will honor our bloodline.

"All my time using drugs, I have *never* stole from none of y'all!" Rochelle's lungs are heaving. As if in a cartoon, I imagine them bulging out through her chest on one side, smashing her heart against her rib cage on the other. "I have never taken a damn thing from any of you! I'm proud of that. And now, none of y'all is helping my *baby!*"

"I know," I say again. The temperature jumps: I imagine this is what it feels like in hell.

"*No*, you *don't* know!" Rochelle shrieks, voice hoarse. "You could *never* know."

A fresh set of tears break as she palms her wilted head and drives. She is the shrill voice of everything our family lost on the long, hard road from North Carolina to Michigan; she is every broken bead, every shattered piece of pottery, every forgotten dance. I can smell her salt. At that moment, Rochelle is Hemingway's Pilar, the dauntless Spanish Gypsy, the metaphorical pillar who leads her husband's rebel camp in a secret mission to blow up a bridge during the Spanish Civil War. Rochelle is Lot's wife racing away from her fate, away from Sodom and Gomorrah, even as her bones shrivel into salt, and we both know if Rochelle looks back at the crumbling city that was her life, back at the trail of our tears as Black Indians who've sacrificed our children in order to save ourselves, if she turns the car an inch any other way than forward, we will die.

"I have done everything for everyone in this family and no one has done *shit* for me." Rochelle's palms slam the steering wheel. Hot, wet salt escapes her eyes.

This day after Aunt Phyllis's funeral, watching Rochelle's strong hands pound the steering wheel, I know these words have been inside her for years, creating a life of their own volition. She's waited to see me, this day after so many years have passed, since I've been grown and living a safe distance away from this kind of anger, to say everything she's wanted to say since the day my mother made her take care of me as if I were her own. Rochelle knows intuitively that she was sacrificed at the crossroads.

Months ago I'd offered my one-bedroom apartment in Inglewood to Rochelle like an oasis. Afiya and I would make room if she could only see fit to let Kalamazoo go.

"Come live with us and see something other than that crazy place."

That is all I could do, I thought at the time. Living in Los Angeles, two thousand-some-odd miles away, I reason that I can't really help in the way that Jason needs it or Rochelle wants it. But that isn't true. We've failed her.

She simply needs more from us. She needs my sisters to give Jason what she had given their kids—a safe place. She needs their children to say thank you. She needed my mother's love when she was younger. Instead, I was pawned off on Rochelle while Mama ran after her married boyfriends, worked graveyard shifts, or spent days trapped in the house when her migraines blinded her. We've failed her, I say clearly in my head. If I say it out loud, she will deny it, because, as a sister should, she loves us desperately.

How did Rochelle get here? Pulled under the water as a teenager, a part-time party girl, into Kalamazoo's budding drug culture, and then, years later, tossed up on the shore as an adult: withered and battered as any shipwreck.

I fall silent and erect the wall that separates me from *mania*. Retreat into my safe garden with a fountain and a swing. It's the one thing I know to do best when confronted with the dragons smoldering in one of my people's wombs, when it bellies up, lashes out, regardless of who stands in its wake. Sensing my withdrawal, Rochelle clamps her lips together. Then she abruptly changes the subject.

"Fuck." Rochelle slaps her forehead. "Even if we take Jason his clothes, he's going to be late for work and get fired anyway. Fuck the dumb shit."

She jerks the car off the road and onto an exit, and then beats a trek to Burger King. Our thighs stick to the dull red vinyl seats at the fast food restaurant. We plead Jason's case to the stony-faced manager, a twenty-year-old white woman who could give a shit that Rochelle's world is crumbling.

Rochelle: His great-aunt just passed away and he's having a hard time dealing with it.

Manager: I don't know. He's not enthusiastic about his job.

Rochelle: My son's a good boy and he just needs a chance.

Manager: He's got to be here by noon.

Rochelle: Thank you. Thank you. So much. He'll be a good worker.

After this lie, Rochelle and I jump back into the Batmobile, capes and breasts flapping, smelling like garlic and salt. We race across town to Seville Apartments, where suspicious heads peek out of door frames, watching us from curtainless windows. In the dim hallway, shadows, dust balls, and the dank, pissy odor of soiled Pampers ether up like smoke from the dirty floor. Through the murky heat, at the end of the hallway, Jason stealthily whispers to another boy his age. Encased in darkness, the other guy's face is a smudge. When the boy sees Rochelle's face, he takes off the other way, leaving the door flapping back and forth.

"Who was that?" Rochelle fires her question at Jason before we reach him. Even I, the square, recognizes that body language, knows the young man was looking to buy or to sell.

Jason parlays her question with his own. "Why yaw here?" he asks, but when he hears our case, he pulls up like a quarter horse, flatly refusing to jump. "I can't go to that job no more, anyway, because I have to work the late shift and the bus doesn't even go out there at that time of night, *Mama*. I was gonna quit anyway."

He has his plans all figured out and Rochelle is putting a wrench in the whole thing, trying to control it.

"*Get* in the car, Jason," Rochelle orders through her teeth. We speed back to Burger King. Jason's job gives him the day off, first to buy the regulation shoes from Kmart, and second to mourn his great-aunt's death, but he is not pleased. On the way to my mother's house, Rochelle and Jason argue, ignoring me until they need me to co-sign.

"Ain't that right, Auntie?"

"Right, Shonda," Rochelle says. "In one ear and out the other."

"Jason, why don't you just listen to your mother?" I am weary and sticky. A puddle is gathering between my thighs and at the back of my neck. My body's tangy funk is wafting up, exacerbated by the humidity.

"She don't listen to *me*." He pokes his lip out, wiping his hands on his shirt.

"I do!" Rochelle interjects and then grows quiet when she realizes she's made his point. Nervously locking eyes with him in the rearview mirror, Rochelle shoots her next question out like a knife from her sleeve: "Popeye said you selling dope. Is that true?"

Jason's mouth flops open. His eyes grow big as onions in his face.

He will break her if he's selling drugs—they both know it. If it's true, he will have betrayed everything Rochelle fought for in several rehab programs to get clean, be sober, to expunge her record and raise her two boys. All the hours she's spent telling some circle of strangers about our mixed-up family and her miserable place in it. About our mother's neglecting to teach us what it meant to be women and leaving that job up to the world. About her sons and her great wall of Greek shame. About the wheel we are spinning on called family. I know all this so badly my left eye starts to pound with the knowing. His answer means everything to her. And I will hate him for hurting her, my sister who raised me. I will hate him with the hate someone reserves for strangers who harm the person you love the most in the world.

Lie, lie, I chant under my breath.

Jason recovers quickly and hoods his eyes. "Ma, why would I do that? Popeye is the one selling."

"Jason," she pleads, voice strangled. "I hate when you do this."

"That's a lie." He slumps against the back seat. "Popeye's lying on me."

"Don't lie to me, Jason." She grits her teeth. After a few seconds of silence, Rochelle drills him again, question after question, then cuts him off before he can get his words out. When he responds, she blows up again.

"See, Ma. Man, you never listen to me." Jason shakes his head, smiling that dumb half-smile.

"I do. I always listen to you," she cuts in again.

"Rochelle, let him talk." I muscle the window further down. "Listen to what *he* wants."

She gouges my sentence: "It doesn't matter what he wants. He don't know."

"See." Jason holds up his hands in defeat, and then drops them in his lap and looks out the window.

"Rochelle, you're not listening to him."

"Why should I listen when all he does is lie?"

8

Afro–Native Assimilation Blues

As the lore goes on my father's side of the family, my great-grandfather, Grandpa Tone, had two wives in Okolona, Mississippi. He had an African wife and a Choctaw wife, who lived down the street from each other with their own separate families. These two sets of families produced two different but shared bloodlines. My Uncle Blue told me at my father's funeral, "Grandpa Tone spent half his time at one house with the African family and the other half at the Indian wife's house."

Those were the days. No one asked them for tribal enrollment cards or a blood pedigree. Was Grandpa Tone a slave or a full-blood Indian? No one knew. But I have his story.

Sometimes Black folks give me *the look* when I say I am American Indian as well as African American. It's simple, I think. Fifty-fifty, like two sides of a coin. "Girl, please." I get the neck roll and the corresponding roll of the eyes. "You know you Black, heifer." Or, "Everybody got some Indian in them. Don't get uppity."

Everybody got some Indian in them. Not everybody.

And not as many as we think, according to historian Henry Louis Gates, Jr.'s work in genealogy where he basically says very few African Americans possess American Indian ancestry based off the sheer disproportionate ratio of Africans to Indians in the New World. But my RedBlack friends disagree vehemently with Gates's hypothesis.

Vehemently.

At one panel discussion at the Hampton Public Library, I heard the following comments:

"He's only going back so far. He's got to go back thirteen or fourteen generations on both sides. He's got to check *all* the bloodlines."

"Gates is a literature professor, not a genealogist."

"Who does he think he is, trying to negate the oral history of half the Black people in America?"

Maybe not half, but a good number. Many African Americans self-identify due to family legacy, or census records, or war registration cards that note "Indian," as in the case of my fourth great-grandfather, George Thomas Manuel. I see us at powwows. I see us at the family reunions we used to have. I see us at ceremonies, gatherings, Bear Dances, Sun Dances, and sweat lodges. I see us in the grocery store, at writing conferences. I see us. I see me.

In Black families, especially those termed light-skinned or Mulatto, those whose ancestors were slaves or bought themselves out of slavery, who had children with Indian or white women and men, people often could only trace their history through slave master records, court deeds (if the courthouse records hadn't been burned on purpose), and sometimes freedman's papers.

Tragically, for American Indians who kept oral traditions and communicated via images and symbols, their only "written" records were "ass out," as my grandfather would say. Europeans didn't understand and therefore did not *value* signs, symbols, and other identifiers of tribal importance. Tribal Councils at first didn't see the need to keep written records, until Chief Tecumseh created a Cherokee language in relation to English. Tecumseh realized that his people had to prove who they were to be counted or validated in white society. And then he assumed a written language would protect them, but he was wrong. Even though their ancestors had roamed the land for thousands of years before Columbus, nothing would protect them from the British, Scots, Irish, French, Dutch, and Portuguese who descended with greedy, land-hungry eyes.

Because of colonization, unless a bond deed, land deed, government recognition of land, or a literate, educated family member kept records, American Indian tribes could be forced off their lands. A Free Person of Color, like my Robertses, Manuels, and Staffords, who actually *wrote down* their history in Bibles, marriage licenses, crop records, birth recordings in church ledgers, and journals and letters to each other, was able to buy, keep, and eventually sell their land. My Great-Aunt Katheryn wrote our pedigree, which showed that a fifth great-grandmother, Mariah (Anne) Peak(e), was full-blood Delaware Cherokee and Pequot Indian. Because I don't want to be considered a "hobbiest," I keep my aunt's family chart, my grandfather's Social Security card, and my family trees with me. But it becomes tiresome to have to prove the oral history—what I know is in the blood—again and again.

There is so much proof. History shows how slavery and indentured servitude allowed space for the intermingling of races and the mixing of ethnicities, like the Scotch-Irish, and the Africans and Catawba Indians of the early Carolinas, in Catawba Indian territory, before the state lines were drawn and redrawn. In the South—Mississippi, Kentucky, Tennessee, North Carolina, Virginia, Georgia, and Alabama—anywhere plantations bred their own work supply, ex-slaves ran away to nearby tribes and disappeared. Some Indians who escaped the Trail of Tears in 1828–1832 were hidden by Free People of Color and became family.

Before the Five Civilized Tribes—the Cherokee, Choctaw, Creek, Chickasaw, and Seminole—were forced to leave their homes and tribal lands in the Southeast, many had assimilated in order to save themselves, to keep their land. They cut their hair and wore western clothes and adopted white ways to make whites feel "safer" around "Native" Americans. They owned hundreds of slaves, who walked with them during the Great Removal to Indian Territory in Oklahoma and Alabama.

Slaveholding Indians? I never learned about that in school.

Black slaves suffered too on that grueling and deadly trail, along with their owners. Of the over 60,000 people on that "Great Walk," 4,000 deaths in the Cherokee tribe alone were recorded on "The Trail Where They Cried," but some say the numbers are higher. How many of those were half-breeds, Mixed bloods, both Black and Indian? Soldiers assigned to that horrific task of removal reportedly suffered their own trauma, horrified at their role in these senseless deaths.

When U.S. president Andrew Jackson signed the Indian Removal Act in 1830, it was the end of the age.

I often wondered, were any of our family members on that trail? If they had been, we'd never heard it.

For years after the first cargo ship arrived on the shores of Jamestown in 1619, carrying nineteen enslaved Angolans (who incidentally could be baptized out of slavery in those early days), runaway or newly baptized Africans were found, befriended, married, and subsumed into tribes. Blacks and Indians married and, like Abraham, begat. Indians, indentured white servants, and slaves shared the same burdens: forced labor, servitude, low wages or none, demeaning and pitiful lives. Horrors upon horrors that they never told their children about. But they commiserated. They licked each other's wounds and tilled the earth together; created communities, like the Roberts Settlement in Indiana; traded stories and medicine with each other and the Quakers. They, as a friend of mine says, made relations and babies and disappeared into the swamps, forests, and dense brush. Or they hid in plain sight.

Casting a blight on this tale is the record of how some members of the Five Civilized Tribes owned and mistreated their slaves. In 1833 the U.S. Census showed that among the Creek Nation's population of 22,694, they held 902 Black slaves. The 1835 Census showed that among the 16,542 Cherokee, they owned 1,592 Black slaves. The numbers of slaves owned only increased until the end of the Civil War, when the tribes had to grant their Black or Mixed blood slaves full tribal rights and citizenship. Cherokee bands who owned both Black and Indian slaves sometimes exhibited the most anti-Black policies, passing laws that prevented Blacks and Cherokee from marrying, as well as Black slaves from owning property. The Chickasaw were reportedly the most vicious slave masters, treating their Black slaves just like the white plantation masters, who likened their slaves, and even their own Mixed kids, to animals. After the Civil War, the Chickasaw were the only Indian tribe that did not immediately free their slaves. Beatings, rapes, and sales were unfortunately sometimes as horrible in slave-owning tribes as they were on any white chattel slave plantation. Which, considering the history of the colonization of North American Indian tribes starting in the 1500s, was a tragedy and a failure for full-blood Indians as a whole.

Despite this, mingling and marriage occurred. Some slaves became tribal members when they married full-blood American Indian women or men; other slaves became relatives when they were adopted into a tribe by members. The latter happened when slaves showed their strength, tenacity, and bravery, or when slaves ran away to and were hidden and subsumed by the tribe. Others were simply adopted and ceremonially made brothers, aunties, sisters, or cousins. Reportedly, several of the Buffalo Soldiers, Black men who fought "out West" for the Union Army during the Civil War, stayed there, and married or coupled with Indian women.

The Lumbee Tribe of North Carolina claim the largest population of African American Indians, embracing and representing the darkest of Mixed and full-bloods without apology. Not so for other tribes like the Croatan, who, under threat of losing their Indian status because there were so many Mixed race families in the Carolinas, developed the document "George Edwin Butler, 1868–1941,

The Croatan Indians of Sampson County, North Carolina. Their Origin and Racial Status. A Plea for Separate Schools." This document traced the Butler and Maynor and several other bloodlines to show they had "no Negro blood," in order to keep federal monies flowing to their tribes to build and maintain their schools. Separate schools. Separate lives. But at what cost? To distance themselves from their Black cousins, these Croatan claimed descent from the lost colony of Croatan Indians, also called the Roanoke, on the border between North Carolina and Virginia.

In the 1880s, they were granted the status of full-blood Indians; they left us behind.

I feel as though I'm always apologizing to some Black people, who think that by claiming my American Indian side, I am trying to distance myself from being Black, when the exact opposite is true. Conversely, I feel like I'm also apologizing for my African blood, my locks, and cultural status to tribes who essentially "card" at their powwow. Then there are those Mixed bloods who *only* want to claim their Indianness, or their Indianness and whiteness.

I'm both, I say to the doubting eyes—all of it. *Pick one*, their eyes say back.

Not dark enough for Black folks. Not light enough for full-bloods and white Indians. Skin two, three shades darker than Sacajawea, the Shoshone Indian princess. Than Pocahontas.

It was years before I realized that I was not only attempting to follow my own family's breadcrumbs, I was tracing the kith, creed, and ethnicity, and very origin of the beast—the ugly history of racial formation in this country.

I NEVER SAW a real tipi until I was sixteen and visiting a Michigan reservation for a high school program. Those Indians looked Mexican to me. Maybe I looked Mexican to them, too. No dream catchers on their walls, or mine either. Come to think of it, there were no feathers, and no one was wearing a buckskin hide or looking majestic on a horse. There were no horses, even. I'd grown up riding horses bareback. There were several rows of nondescript white buildings and some sad-looking trailers. Our host was a white-looking tribal representative, who talked about being a recovering alcoholic. He looked like my super light cousins. There was no playground; no colorful anything to speak of. It was a sad place.

Maybe our farm in Mattawan looked like that to people who visited *those* Staffords in the sticks without totems or medicine. A bunch of bedraggled light-skinned Mixed bloods, legally Black or Colored but who "looked" Indian. We weren't purposefully bad people, but my elders did give a different ethnicity every ten years. We were suspicious of stupid census takers who could never place us neatly in a box anyway, so why try?

That box made us lose our way.

Racial categorization, slavery, and assimilation made us a little crazy.

The removal of American Indians from their homelands, all the way up from South Carolina, from the Midwest and the Great Plains, did us in.

When I first started my research, I'd somehow gotten ahold of my great-aunt's notes. Mostly for health reasons, I was told, she'd written down the births, deaths, and marriages of all the kin she could remember. Her handwriting was as spidery as a web on the white sheet, a kind of nervous scrawl of numbers and names of people I never knew. Though I could read most of it, on the last page her handwriting faltered and was cut off at the end of the family chart. She wrote: "Race Line: Spanish, German, French, Indian (Cherokee, Tribe out of So. Dakota or Oklahoma)." The last part, the "Tribe out of So. Dakota or Oklahoma," concerned me most. Which tribe was it? And then the name she'd scrawled looked like

"Deksea" or "Neksio," but I thought "Neusiok" or "Neuse," because those words referred to a tribe that lived on the Neuse River in North Carolina until they were pushed off by settlers and trappers and eventually merged with the Coharie and Tuscarora.

The day after my Aunt Phyllis's funeral, I called Aunt Katheryn to get clarification on what she'd written: "Hi Auntie. This is Velma's daughter, Shonda."

"Hello, I know who you are." I could tell by her lukewarm response that she barely remembered me and wouldn't bother too hard trying.

"I was wondering if I could talk with you about some of the things you wrote down about Grandpa Manuel and some of the others." I readied my pen.

There was a pause: "I'm not going to talk about my family to you."

I hadn't expected that. I broke out in a sweat because suddenly I did feel as if I was an interloper looking in, outside of the line of Manuels she belonged to, keeping the name because she never married. For me, our language functioned as a record.

When my tawny-skinned, six-foot-three grandfather whooped and hollered in a drunken daze around the house and farm, we all looked sideways: "Crazy damn Indian." When someone's hair was long, soft, and beautiful as a black river flowing down their back, we said, "She got that good Indian hair." When we needed someplace to sleep, someone would say, "Just make a pallet on the floor." What the hell was a pallet? My friends laughed at me. A place to lay your head, I'd say, blushing. After years of saying it, I finally looked it up in the dictionary: "a small makeshift bed." Its origins, for us, were North Carolina by way of the French and British, who transported it to Jamestown. Mustard-gold-bellied robins, we brought that word to Michigan like a seed in our mouths. The word "piddling" too. If someone was moving things around the house, unable to sit still, they were piddling. The first time I heard that word outside of Kalamazoo, I was talking to a friend who was born and bred in North Carolina.

"What you doing today?" I asked, as I washed dishes. She responded, "Oh nothing, just piddling."

I rocked back on my feet. How had my Midwestern colloquialism gotten into her North Carolina mouth? The dictionary lists "trifling" and "shiftless" as synonyms but also, circa the mid-1800s, British: a cross between "piss" and "puddle," which came to mean "pathetically trivial." In my upbringing, we said things like "Well as I live and breathe" and "Gallblasted, if it ain't so and so"; we said things like "She crazy as the day is long."

Though we didn't have tipi poles, didn't know the names of our tribes, my family had carried North Carolina with us in our language, in our very mouths. We have our pictures too. I've got Great-Grandma Peak's picture and Great-Grandpa Manuel's picture. We have Aunt Katheryn, who will soon celebrate her eighty-eighth birthday. She'll never die. Evil never does. But I've got her family records. However, her memory stops with her great-great-grandfather, Ephraim Manuel, born in the 1790s, and his son, Peter A. Manuel, born in North Carolina in 1839, who fought and died in the Civil War, July 29, 1864. Peter and his brother Daniel were listed on the Colored Soldiers rolls for Michigan Cavalry. But the word "Colored" was an invented term that, from the late 1800s to the 1960s, meant everyone not white. With the egregious 1924 Racial Integrity Act, the term "Colored" reinforced the "one-drop" rule, meaning if a child was born with one drop of Negro or American Indian blood, they were Colored and not white. Now legally, bindingly, punishable by law if disobeyed, Colored meant all Negro, all Black, all Indian, all Mixed bloods; even if you were white and Black, you were still Negro. That shit was Merlin the magician math. The word itself was magic trick, no, it was an axe that cut every North American tribe down at the knees. The word erased them. Crushed them. Disappeared them. From 1924 until today, American Indians have struggled in and out of local, state, and federal courts to reclaim their Indianness. In their own country. Go figure.

But I've got Grandpa Tone's Mississippi love triangle tale. I've got family trees and tombstones. I've got oral history and memory.

There's an African proverb: "If the lion could speak, the true history of Africa would be told." Perhaps if the buffalo of the Plains or the waterfowl of the riverways and tributaries of this land could speak, the true history of the Indigenous American would be told.

But who or what will tell the Black Indian's history?

9

Country

MY MOTHER LIVES in the suburbs now, Kalamazoo's suburbs, but it's really another township, called Portage. Every front yard's wide, fawning lawns are well-manicured and cut regularly. The backyards have swing sets ordered from Sears. Bikes lie carelessly on the grass. The houses sport American flags and wind chimes and other emblems that symbolize suburbia. The Michigan loyalists drive Fords or General Motors cars, trucks, and family vans—probably first editions fresh off the car line, parked on the dirt curb or in every other driveway. Shaded by towering oak trees, their leaves shimmering in the sultry afternoon breeze, the houses are all "nice" in the expensive sense of the word.

She has escaped the country for good.

There are no other Black people in her neighborhood—a far cry from our old Eastside haunt that had slowly been overrun by Detroit and Chicago drug warlords.

Almost before the car stops, Rochelle yanks the key out of the ignition and retreats into my mother's suburban house. Sticky, the new late-morning sweat on my forehead drying on top of old early morning sweat, I inhale. Just breathe, just breathe. Jason's own breathing sounds labored, abnormally loud in the back seat. I think it's over, but he knows better.

Seven seconds later the front door swings open. Moving like a mountain off its range, Popeye's normally ruddy brown face flushed the color of crushed grapes, he exits my mother's front door, fists clenched. When I see his face, his pierced lips, I jump out of the front seat and inch between Popeye's hulking form and Jason's door. Popeye reaches around me and calmly clicks open the back door, a silence made louder by his gentleness; he can take the door off its hinge if he wants to.

Like a sheet flapping on a clothesline, I waver uncertainly between the car and Popeye. He ducks down to eagle-eye Jason. "Did you lie to Yo' Mama?" Popeye bellows hoarsely, his body trembling with rage.

Popeye gently shakes the car frame: "Did you tell her I lied on you? You *know* I know you sellin'!"

Slouched in the back seat, Jason slowly shakes his head. I peek down at him out of the corner of my eye. I can't *believe* Jason is smiling, but it's his nervous-twitch smile, his hiding-fear smile, his I'm-about-to-get-pulverized smile. His voices-in-my-head smile. A salty scent wafts from the car's interior, the ink of a petrified animal.

"I'm not selling," Jason snort-laughs. "I don't know who keeps saying that."

Popeye's hand grips the car door: "Get out of the car, Jason."

"Nope, I'm not getting out." Smart boy.

"*Get out* of the car, *boy*!" Popeye's tongue gnashes against his teeth. "I'ma teach you not to lie on me."

"Popeye, we don't need this at Mama's house. Just leave it." I pull on his arm. It is on fire. I am a flea on the back of an elephant as it walks across a desert. There is no water there.

"Pie, Mama is gonna be pissed we showin' out here," I tug. No luck.

"Get out of the *muthafuckin'* car. *Boy-I-will-hurt-you*." Popeye's words are bricks, rocking the Lumina with each utterance. Spittle slaps me in the face. "Don't you *ever* lie to your mother. *Ever*."

"Pie, the neighbors are looking." In their slacks and loafers, some have come out of their houses. Someone has just parked a nice, trusty silver Ford truck across the street. We will, no matter where we live, always give our neighbors a show.

I push Popeye back with my hips. A couple of my fingers disappear in his soft flesh. "We don't need this. Let's go into the house."

Rochelle stomps out the door and pulls Popeye inside, hushing him, finally realizing the spectacle we are making for folks who haven't even paid the price of admission.

After a quick look to assure that Popeye is gone, Jason follows. I stay outside and rock on my mother's porch swing. Just breathing. One more day. Twenty-four more hours before my plane leaves.

In the ground, the roots of the willows drink deep.

Inside, the smell of fried eggs and ham permeates the rooms. Good, people are finally eating. Rochelle is sweeping the kitchen floor because cleaning is her meditation.

"Don't sweep my feet, Auntie!" my daughter says, trying to get a cup for water. Afiya grabs the handle and spits on the broom bristles. I taught her that because my mother taught it to me.

"I just need to clean up before I eat. You know I can't stand a dirty kitchen."

Afiya returns to the table and flips cards. Solitaire, her favorite game. She reminds me of a miniature Mama. Rochelle fidgets in the kitchen now that she's washed all the dishes in the sink.

"What do you want for breakfast?" she growls, glowering first at Jason, then me, then Popeye, daring us to say we aren't hungry. I've forgotten that it's still morning. We haven't eaten or showered.

Sweat rivulets drip from Rochelle's face in sheets as she pulls the first things her hands touch out of the refrigerator, slamming them on the counter. Eggs, butter, mayonnaise, hot dogs, bread. She cracks the eggs open with an expert vengeance and scrambles them hard. She is trying hard to please Jason, her stiff back says. To be there. Be a good mother. To listen. Like a good mother.

She didn't want to argue with him this time. But it is hard to move past their old pattern. This is what the children of addicts do, with the subtle sleight of hand that only our children, parents, and lovers can have over us; Jason uses her addiction, her failure, against her, molding her into the ugly-beautiful clay beast she already thinks she is. They move like seagulls on the hunt, my sister and nephew, walking in and out of the room: swoop, fall, clutch, leave; swoop, fall, clutch, disappear. The bitter ardor of mother-son-mate bonding. It is as though this conversation, this dance, is one they've been having since he could talk and walk. With her manic, posturing, emphasizing the first syllable in his name; him laughing, smiling nervously, pouting, huffing angry words, mumbling to himself, and then the secret smile appearing again.

Recognizing this tune, I sit on the couch. My head buzzes.

I wish Mama would come home from shopping. I wish they would freeze. Stop moving. I want to leave, just take a walk, but I can't. My protective wall creeps up again, knowing I am powerless to stop them from their circling. I wait.

"Mama, I want to go back to Star's house."

"No, Ja-son. You're going to stay here for awhile."

"I want to go. Ain't nothing to do here."

"I'm here! Damn! I ain't seen you in a while. You don't want to spend time with me?"

"Ma, it's not like that, I just want to go."

"Where you got to go?"

"I just want to go, Ma. I can walk."

"Ja-son, you aren't going anywhere. What do you want to eat?"

"Nothing."

By this time, she's half-fried a skillet full of bacon. Over her shoulder, I peek in the skillet. The scrambled eggs look brown, almost burnt. I want to put my arms around her, but I know she will just cry, leaking all over me. Don't touch me, the back of her neck says, don't touch me or I'll scream.

Popeye and I hover, interjecting comments they ignore. Jason rolls his eyes off to the side and smiles, that secret smile that steadies him while it ingratiates or irritates others. The grease snaps in a moist spot and settles as Rochelle turns off the electric eye under the skillet, leaving the eggs in the pan and tossing the bacon strips on a napkin-covered plate. Deft and swift, then choppy, her movements mimic how her mind latches onto something she wants to say but doesn't. She works quickly, as if breakfast is the key to everything, as if eating will make the unpleasant things dissolve and we'll all awake in another skin, another family. Furtively, Jason nabs the cordless phone from the couch. Rochelle hears the dial tone.

"Who you callin'?"

"Nobody. Star. Philip. I'ma call my dad to come get me."

The words enter as neatly as a paring knife, like he's planned—Hamletesque—slipping through her rib cage, poised just before her lungs and heart. Rochelle slams a pan down, nearly foaming at the mouth. She stomps back into the living room.

"Ja-son, you better not call him! What that mothafucka got to do with this? What has he ever done for you? Not shit! You better not call him!"

"I'm just playing Ma." He laughs, smiles at his pretty secrets. *"I'm not calling him. I'm just joking."*

"You better not call that no good for nothing punk ass bitch!"

In the kitchen, I saw into a fleshy cantaloupe rind and scoop out the thick orange flesh with a spoon, pretending engrossment with each mouthful, attempting to stay out of Rochelle's way. But I can't. I want her to see me, a reminder. I want Rochelle to walk away. I want her to let go of everything she was ever taught, learned in the streets, or missed learning from Mama and my aunts. *Leave Kalamazoo behind*, I whisper into her back, *leave Kalamazoo behind.* As I chew and swallow, I pray fervently that the anger evaporates and that she'll break the violent cycle of her life. Of our family. I want to say all of these things, but instead, I roll my eyes up silently and close them to show my adoration of the fruit, as Jason punches out another number on the phone.

"Stch," he sucks his teeth and leans back on the white couch in the living room with his arm crossed over his head.

The living room is my mother's dream concoction: a sparkling glass table, two towering daffodil lamps on either side of the couch, reminiscent of the Dick Van Dyke show. A glass bowl of peppermints on the glass table. A pretentious grandfather clock leaned across the room, clicking and whirring its concepts of time at us. Mama's four grandfather clocks—two wall, two standing—are my mother's prized possessions. Jason has no idea of the things my mother suffered to have that white couch for him, and us, to sit on. The couch belongs in the house that belongs in this neighborhood that belongs in this suburb, with that even lawn and rust-resistant mailbox by the side of the road. Despite not knowing what goes on behind anyone else's walls, at that moment a feeling of betrayal creeps through me.

We do not belong. We loud. We Black. We poor. We elephants stampeding.

We anger blowing cannonball holes through each other's hearts. Our madness does not belong there. Jason scratch-whispers, scratch-whispers conspiratorially into the phone. He says "Mama" a couple of times and the word "trippin'."

"Who is that?" Rochelle demands.

"Nobody.

"Who the hell you talking to about me?"

"Nobody, Ma."

"Who is it, Ja-son?"

"It's Philip. I'm just talking to him to—"

"What?" She is shattered. She rushes over and tries to grab the receiver. *"Get off the goddamn phone!"*

Yesterday, I took Jason aside and assured him that once he completed his GED at the continuation high school, he could come to California, and I'd help him get a job and enroll in college. "You can live with me until you get yourself together," I told him, ignoring the nagging warning that my life would change with him in it; he'd hurt my feelings like he'd hurt everyone else's.

"For real?" he asked. "California." His eyes whirled like an owl, calculating, planning his escape. He could get out of trouble with everyone and leave behind his mother. Enthusiastically, he agreed.

Now, he is the last person I want to come to California or anywhere near me. The hope I had for him slithers out of me like air from a stepped-on doll.

"Jason," I say, deflated, not believing he has the audacity, even secretly marveling at the stupid bravery it takes, to hurt my sister like that.

I REMEMBER ONCE when we lived on Southworth Terrace on the Eastside, and Eddie Moore, a loping, slope-headed thirteen-year-old boy, pushed me down in his backyard, and then slapped me. He was always picking on me, but that's the first time he hit me. I got up, brushing the dirt off my clothes without a word because he was huskier than my slip of an eleven-year-old body. Everybody was afraid of Eddie and the jagged scar on his face. But when we ran home, my best friend Jayda blabbed. She slammed the front door open: "Big Eddie hit Shonda," she yelled to no one in particular.

"Shut up," I said, and ran upstairs. She was hot on my trail.

Rochelle was in the bathtub. "What's going on?" she yelled. Jayda said, "Big Eddie, the dude with the scar on his face, he hit Shonda." My chest tightened when I saw Rochelle's face turn to granite. A cold, hard, murderous anger.

"Oh no he didn't," she yelled. "Where he at?"

We backed out quickly as she emerged from the tub with a great whale-like whoosh. She dressed swiftly, wordlessly. Jayda chirped happily. *A fight.* Braless, Rochelle descended the stairs in twos and fled out the side door. My sister's breasts swayed with each hard step in a long-sleeve, tie-dye blue shirt, hair a floppy Medusa-coiffed afro as she marched down the street, left fist holding up her loose blue jeans at the zipper, while the other was balled like a claw just behind her right hip. I saw the Stafford twitch, my mother's twitch, in her eye. Right then, I felt truly sorry for Eddie. Wished, for his sake, he hadn't picked on me. That he had known who I was.

"Did you hit my sister?" she barked, when she stepped up to his back-porch steps. He looked down at her first. Then, sauntering down the three cement steps, Eddie sized Rochelle up, being big for his age. They were the same size. Though she was fifteen, I could see he was thinking maybe, because she was skinny, he could take her. He smiled a crooked smile. Eddie's mouth had a permanent crooked twist to it, a facial birth-defect I now know, which made us brand him Eddie the Monster after the guy on the TV show. That's what I'd called him, and if I was Eddie, I might have smacked me too. But I was the Bynums' sister, a Stafford's daughter, and he'd just moved into the neighborhood. He didn't know yet that no one messed with me, not until Rochelle's right fist snaked out and cracked the good side of his face, bringing him down in one blow. He cried out, writhing in the dirt when she drop kicked him.

Nimbly, she rescued a loose board from the ground, and when the nail flashed in the sun, I cried out: "Rochelle, there's a nail. You gonna kill him." Either she didn't hear me or she didn't care. She clobbered him three solid times with that board, the nail connecting once with his thigh. The entire left side of his mulberry-hued face was covered in a fine light sand, crusting around his mouth. I smelled his fear, brackish under his cheap Kmart cologne, over his grassless backyard; he was mocked by the thick green brush growing earnestly a few yards away. By this time, like bees shaken from the hive, other kids had homed in and gathered around. Their voices rumbled behind us. I wondered where Eddie's parents were.

"Rochelle," I sniveled.

"Shut up," she snapped. "Sock him in his face."

She penned him to the ground with her knee, her blue jeans hanging dangerously low. I couldn't do it. With all the blood I had seen in my house, I hated fighting unless I was cornered. Having watched my brothers and sisters rearrange each other's faces regularly, I was scared of their anger, of my own anger.

"If you don't hit him I'ma beat you up," she ordered. I finally, half-heartedly, tagged him on his lopsided, dirty cheek and felt awful for weeks. But nobody messed with the Bynums or their relatives on the Eastside. This was our territory. Our mother had taught us well what it meant to be dominated and to dominate. Having survived her tyrannical alcoholic father, and a husband and boyfriends who tried to rub the pretty face off her with their bare knuckles like you rub yellow off dandelions, my mother knew what it was like to be down and stay down. Whether he knew it or not, Eddie had learned one of our family truths. Someone was always on the bottom, someone else on the top. We were never on the bottom. Eddie and his family moved away some months later.

STANDING IN MAMA'S kitchen, it is hard to fathom that Jason is challenging his mother, our most fierce warrior. My sister, this woman who's defended me even though her pants were about to fall down, even though she looked like a wild woman, even though we'd disturbed her peace that day in the tub. What is he thinking, I wonder? I wish I could sit him next to me in a dark sweat lodge and hold his hand and say, "Jason, just listen."

Jason cocks his head and smiles absentmindedly; he knows his mother has fought with nearly every man she's chosen under our family motto, an unspoken dictum, an anthem for the functionally insane. Knows that she has lived most of her adult life addicted to drugs and on the bottom, knows that Rochelle would walk to the end of the earth without shoes for him. Family is everything for Rochelle. Even if it takes you down with it. But Jason presses the button to hang up the phone smirking, mumbling secret words and rolling his eyes as Rochelle paces and rants.

"Let me take him to Star's, Rochelle," I interject, already formulating the lecture on the way, outlining the main points in my head with a bright blue highlighter—*responsibility, understanding, learning to listen. Don't hurt your mother. Never hurt your mother.*

"No!" She yells at me for the second time that day and possibly the second time in my life. "He's *my* son. I'ma deal with it! He's my responsibility."

"Fine." I raise my hands. Afiya's slender body slips past me to go to the bathroom. Our lives are nothing like this in Los Angeles. She's never seen adults argue with their kids like this except in the movies. I've screamed at her sometimes, but this, I know she can feel, is different. This is the light of dying swamp stars.

The toilet flushes and the door opens. Though Afiya's form is hazy out of the corner of my eye, I feel her moving like a good ghost behind me by the hair standing up on the back of my neck. She trots downstairs to watch TV in the basement.

"Jason," I say. "Just listen to your mother. Just shut up for a few minutes and listen."

"He don't know how to shut up," Popeye chimes in. Though he is defeating the purpose, he is right. Jason never knows when he needs to take a break. It's his trademark. When he was younger, he was cute, funny, good at sliding, and when he made us laugh, we let him slide. Like we let any comedian slide. But today, his arrogance gnaws at me. I don't consider that he might be mentally ill or emotionally traumatized from his childhood, his adulthood. The thought never crosses my mind that he needs a shrink. We don't see therapists.

The stress of the weekend, my aunt's death, Rochelle's blow-up in the car, Jason's disrespect—it all boils inside me. My anger rises like a log-cabin fire in my heart, and I try to put it out. My head is pounding. I am hot and tired. So tired. I want to hide in the star room, climb in bed with a book and sleep until morning, until it is time for me to leave. But Rochelle is seething too loudly for me to even close my eyes. *If only Jason would just be quiet*, I think, *everything will calm down and I can rest.* I lull myself with the thought of a cocoon, craving the border of a blanket under my chin. *Then Afiya and I can leave.* I rock myself with this, mentally putting entire states between us and Kalamazoo. I can leave them behind again.

"Jason," Popeye says. "Be quiet."

"I'm not saying nothing," Jason says. "I'm just sitting here."

"Jason, please shut up," I say.

"I ain't sayin—"

"Then just shut the *fuck* up!" I yell, the words bouldering out of me. Rochelle whips her head around, stunned. On guard. The silence in the room is maroon, air as congealed as neck bone grease in a pot of cold greens. Jason opens his mouth. And closes it. I turn away.

"All I'm saying is—" Jason mumbles. In two moves, I shot-put throw my cantaloupe at his head and lunge from across the room like a gargoyle, leaping over my mother's fingerprint-free glass table. I crush his shirt in one hand and ball up my fist, wanting to plunge it into his precious, startled eye and make him stop hurting his mother. I know he is just a boy, but I want to teach him manners, a lesson. I want to control him, dominate him, make him shut up, like I've learned from watching my brothers and sisters and the men who maimed my mother. That's what worked in my house. A fist in the face. A black eye. The leaking of blood.

Caught in the very element I am trying to avoid, I have become a sinister thing. Entrapped in the ruin of our family history. In that hot, white light, I hate him as I would an enemy. Indolent, Black, Indian, depressed, with undiagnosed mental issues. A boy and a man. He is a product of ours and I am a product of him. I loathe him as much as myself. My grandfather. I am my grandfather. My mother's abusers. I am a Stafford and a Manuel. I am wild. Black Indian. Multiracial.

My assimilation is showing. An inheritance of anger. Of violence.

In that moment, I am certain we are ruined: the incessant, decaying ruin of ancient cities, where moss invades the mouths of idols and once polished ruby eyes fog over with neglect because people have lost faith in their gods. Yes, we are ruined.

Still in the alleviated space of time, the day on him, the heat, creased silk in his eyelids, two-day-old Walgreens cologne. Calvin Klein, I think. I want to hug him quiet. It is not even me doing this. No, it is me. As if I've slept-walked up a mountain and am about to fall over a cliff, I jerk back and awake. Ashamed, I release his shirt. In that instant of gaping quiet, Rochelle and Popeye are too stunned to move. Me, the pacifist. Me, the I-don't-eat-anything-with-eyes vegetarian. Me, the reader and writer who hides away in her room, reading the day away. Like puppets on a stage, they lurch into action.

"Shonda, no!" Popeye tucks his arms around my waist, lifting me like a feather away from Jason. I burst into embarrassed tears.

I almost made it.

"I *hate* this family!" I shout so hard my heart muscles contract. "I am not a part of it anymore! I *hate* this shit. I hate all you crazy muthafuckas."

I stomp around the house yelling and finally skid down the basement stairs, trying to escape the person who'd climbed out of my skin and threatened my nephew, trying to hide from the thing that had risen so easily from me. Popeye follows, watching me. When Afiya sees me tumble down the stairs, she jumps off the couch and watches me warily. Her arms are close to her sides, but her hands flower out at the bottom daintily, and when she sees her escape route, she makes a clean break for the stairs. My throat burns like I've swallowed a cup of acid. Popeye grabs me and holds me tight because by now, as I prowl and rant, he knows I want to break something in Mama's nice, clean house. Her old records on the counter. The glasses in the china cabinet. Something that could crash and shake and burst into a million splintered pieces, like my heart. He crushes me to his massive chest until I push away.

"I don't belong here." I shake my finger at him. "*You* mothafuckas is crazy. I am *not* a part of this *fucked*-up family." I announce this as the baby girl who didn't get her way; who grew up in hand-me-down Goodwill clothes, ate bologna sandwiches and hotdogs for dinner; whose family's poverty had bent all of them so close to the earth we became gnarled trees, fighting for root space on barren ground. Caught in a migration web we didn't spin.

Did my mother know it would be like this when she birthed us? We women, howling.

10

Retreat

QUELLING MY DESIRE to break something in my mother's basement, I push past Popeye and stumble up the stairs to the star room. Afiya is lodged at the kitchen table. She glances up, then quickly bows over a row of cards. Solitaire. Something she can control. Flailing by, I see the fear lurking in her eyes. Her trust in me shaken. I'm imperfect, fallen now.

"Shonda, you okay?" Rochelle halts her pacing in the living room, her face knotted into an anxious bow.

I pack my little black suitcase as fast as my hands will move. I refuse to enter into the bond with my sister or my mother, with any of them.

My daughter and I are *leaving*.

The word "leaving" leaps out of the headache in my left eye. I toss clothes and toiletries in, mashing everything down until I am forced to sit on the lid to zip it.

"Hello?" I call the airline. "Is it possible to change my ticket to fly out today on a red-eye, or even at midnight, at one in the morning without paying?" No.

When the airline refuses to change my ticket, I lie on the bed like a blowfish, inhaling and exhaling, practicing the yoga stillness I learned in my class. I stare at the plastic stars and moons on the ceiling—no longer cute—concentrating on the least amount of breath I need for another eighteen hours, to stay alive in Kalamazoo.

Connecting the shapes on the ceiling, I try to stop my mind from thinking, but the words "alcoholism," "addiction," and "violence" rattle around in my brain. These are just the symptoms of our illness. Our secrets. We perform the duties of the living: we talk, stinging people with praise; we laugh, forging bonds with calculated jokes and breaking them in the next instant. We loud. We ragged and beautiful. We tender and mean. We tight. But there is an oppressive silence hovering over us. A desire to be gone, to disappear into this silence that we keep locked up and protected. We look at each other, but we don't see ourselves. We never name the depression that links us, leaving us ravaged in places language cannot name.

Rochelle doesn't realize that what she practices is ancient, something southern and foreboding. Something came to this land with the settlers and the trappers. The slaves, Free men and Free women. With our grandfathers and grandmothers. The Mulattoes. Rivers of silence. Years of blood-brother silence. The secrets in the land, warning us not to tell the other what happened, how we got there. Only we don't know what really happened. So how can we tell? We don't know. We only know what we do to each other, but we are still keeping the coven of silence, no matter the cost.

Fifteen minutes later, the afternoon light shifts in the room when Jason enters quietly. Is it still only the morning?

"Auntie, I just want to say I'm sorry for making you mad."

I ignore him and busy myself with the shadows of leaves, the sunlight patterned through the window.

"Well," he turns to go. "I just wanted to say I'm sorry."

"It's not your fault. I'm sorry." I don't look at him as I say this.

"I was just . . . I don't know. I'm just sorry. But nobody listens to what I want."

"Jason, what happened isn't all your fault, but your mother loves you. You can't hurt her like that. You gotta respect her. If you don't, everything you do is not gonna work. It just ain't. Not until you respect her."

He huffs, fiddling with the lint in his pockets, shoving his eyes down. I want to hug him, but I don't.

"Well, anyway, I just wanted to say I'm sorry and, you know, I love you." He shuffles out, his heavy footfall saying, *Auntie don't understand me neither*.

I've never seen her do this before, but when Rochelle enters, she is actually wringing her hands like one of Macbeth's Witches Three.

"Shonda, you don't have to leave, I'll leave." Her mouth is sucked up into a dried apricot seed. I shake my head, unable to talk. My throat sandpaper thin. My skin a damp kiln. If I open my mouth, I will unleash a monsoon of fire tears. Not the sensible leaking that my eyes are doing now.

I don't know how I end up there, but I find myself outside in Mama's nice suburban backyard, barefoot, gripping the cool arms of a lawn chair, trying to garner some peace or at least sympathy from the towering oak trees, but they sway impartially, half in, half out of the sun. My eyes are still leaking; I can't turn them off. I'm adding moisture to a land where the willows are already weeping.

I think back to Aunt Katheryn's phone call after yesterday's funeral. In a shaky voice, she informed me that she'd notified the Better Business Bureau, reporting Harper's Funeral Home for their terrible administration of Aunt Phyllis's funeral. Adding insult to injury, besides the disorganization of the service, Harper's boys had lowered the casket into the grave with the grace of a rhinoceros while people were still standing there, still preoccupied with the "ashes to ashes" part. Horrified and livid at the sight, my mother and aunts had bolted away from the group of mourners like stallions, high-stepping over the soft clods of cemetery dirt.

"They know it was disgraceful," Aunt Katheryn said. "You don't handle someone's dead like that."

I hear my sister Tina's car pull up and the front door slam, then some mumbling and then quiet. My eldest sister Bobbie's car pulls up shortly after. More mumbling.

Soon, my mother's car pulls into her garage. Even though I don't see her, I know what her face will look like as she enters, sensing the tension in the air. I hear Mama: "Why y'all so damn quiet?" She pushes the back screen door open and stands next to me.

"What's going on, Cisco?" she asks. I recognize the "mother-daughter-talk" tone from my favorite TV shows, not that we've ever had one.

"Nothing." The gnats are starting to tickle my ankles. I sink my feet deeper in the grass, needing to feel the earth, something solid, unmoving. I want her to go away, leave me to my deflation and the scent of pine trees wafting across the lawn, mingling with the woolen wet odor of my locks. Anger can be exhausting in itself, but family anger depletes you like you've been seer-sucked, and you don't know why you're so weak until you see the wet, globby, red body latched on your heart. There is next to nothing left after you've run up against someone you love.

"They told me what happened," she says, looking across her lawn. "But that Jason is just plain hardheaded." She is trying to make me feel better by blaming him, but I can't let her. We're the adults; I am the adult. He's the man-child.

"Mommy, it's not his fault."

"He just keeps yakking—"

"We're all fucked up. I'm fucked up, too. Jason is fucked up because Rochelle's fucked up because Grandpa Stafford fucked you up. It's not Jason's fault. He's just a product of us."

She falls silent. I have never spoken to my mother like this, but I want her to know that I know things. I know things I'm not supposed to tell. Things a girl-child shouldn't know. I no longer want this burden of memory. Of violence. But that's the crow's call: you can't pick and choose your memories; your memories choose you.

The silence grows louder, pressing me down like a large, wet hand, pressing more sweat out of me. I wish she would go back in the house.

"I hate this shit," I say. "Why can't we be like the fucking Brady Bunch?"

"Well, they were all fucking each other," she says matter-of-factly. Against my will, I crack a smile.

The next morning, I repack. Outside, before we pull off, Afiya and I are embraced in bear hugs. Jason hangs back and then meanders bashfully up to me. I pull him in lightly, softly wrapping my arms around his meaty frame. Later on the road, my face is pressed against the window of John Cloud's Suburban. Words stream from his mouth as he whisks us down I-94, closer to Chicago with each rotation, and I nod and smile as though I'm there with him. But as the road disappears under our wheels, I am already in LA in my mind. My daughter and I are safe.

TWO NIGHTS BEFORE, my daughter and I were catching fireflies in the backyard. Enchanted, Afiya ran across the moist grass. We had the Pacific Ocean but we didn't have fireflies. Because I could catch them so easily without hurting them, almost a reflex from years of doing this, I was like a goddess to her at that moment. I felt magical too. The slick grass between my toes, the feeling of snapping my hand out into the darkness and coming back with light, these still held power over me. My body cut the air like warm butter and I remembered how we'd play hide-and-seek (which we called hind-go-seek) on warm summer nights like these, our voices chiming with childhood rhymes to see who'd be "It." The seeker.

Afiya hadn't grown up with these memories, but she was one of us. A little version of me, smelling musky-sweet as a wildflower, her scent gently piercing through me like a ghost's longing. Earlier, I'd poked holes in the top of a glass jar and she carried it smashed against her chest like it was a treasure box, just like I did when I was her age and my mother had ventilated mason jar tops for me, caring that I cared if the fireflies lived or died.

Fleetingly, watching her chase their glowing bodies around in the darkness, I'd wondered if I could ever bring her to live here, in Kalamazoo. As John spirited us to the airport, I realize that vulnerable, wildly sentimental moment was nothing but self-denial, innocence, or ignorance, because I had promised never to live in Kalamazoo again after I turned eighteen. I had vowed my daughter would never purposely live within the confines of this backwoods, hick-country town. I don't hate Kalamazoo and Mattawan, but I desperately resent the hardness between the soft spaces, the maples and oaks, the train tracks that were their lifeblood in the 1800s. I hate the Kalamazoo River and the hospitals that cured or killed the dead.

And I resent my grandfather's weak, bitter struggle with manhood. His un-knowledge of our past. He was a lousy farmer. He was a horrible father and husband. He beat my mother. He had no memory of what we called the Red Road, no African spirituality of the Orishas of West Africa. Our family was ritual-less: we practiced the ritual of violence. Clifford Stafford not only drank himself into several holes and inflicted every failure on his family, but he also betrayed us. He betrayed my mother's trust. Now, though I love her, I feel Mama has betrayed us too, not with violence but with her indignant silence.

"Mama, how many did you catch?" Afiya hadn't mastered the reach, gentle clutch, shake. "Like this, Sweet," I tried to show her. Reach, gentle clutch. Shake to see if it's there.

"Mama, look," she giggled a few minutes later. "I got one." She held it for a minute and then got freaked out by the lightning bug's sticky feet crawling against her skin and let it go, but she wasn't afraid anymore. She launched into her *Mama, look, Mama, look* chant each time she caught one. I knew that excitement ebbing across the yard from a bodiless voice against the darkness. That fuchsia energy was mine. Last year at our family reunion, Aunt Lily had finally got off her chest that I used to be hyper like my daughter.

"I couldn't stand you by me sometimes." Aunt Lily's eyes had grown big at the remembered panic. "You'd be jumping off things, saying 'watch me, watch me!' I was like, get this child away from me. Shit."

"Uh-uh, Aunt Lily. Not me."

"Uh-huh. I'd call Velma and tell her to come get you, too. So fucking hyper."

I'll call it brave instead.

My daughter is brave like that. Aggressive. She challenges herself, pushes herself to do the thing that no one would expect a girl to do. At nine, she had decided she wanted to hang glide off the bluffs above Playa del Rey. Remembering my aunt's words, I realize where Afiya might have gotten it, this non-fear. Now, after having seen and heard the walls of our vices crumbling, having witnessed her mother turn into a Gorgon, I think now she has a sense of the other possibilities adulthood might bring.

In the morning, before the sun saw us, I escaped Kalamazoo. In truth, I was always leaving. But this time, as the car speeds down I-94 toward Chicago O'Hare Airport, the golden ears of oak and birch trees waving on either side of the spinning highway, I chant under my breath, "I will never live here. I will never return. I will never live here. I will never return."

On the airplane, I catch my reflection in the oblong window, floating in the clouds as they turn a muddy amber against the afternoon sun roasting Chicago. The exhausted face of a young woman stares back with confused, innocent, coveting eyes. The things my mother had suffered in her childhood and later, as a wife, were somehow normal to her, subconsciously. That "as is" love had been passed down. And that's why Rochelle and Jason, our family, loved as if love were a hunger. As if wearing each other down like blocks of salt licks, shattering ourselves and each other, were all we knew. Where had it all begun? Assimilation? The Trail?

My daughter's teddy-bear-brown hand is so small, so trusting in mine, as her eyes widen when the plane's engines burst to life. As she prattles, she grins at me over the noise, reassuring me that now, even though she is afraid, everything will be alright. I grin back, her excited fear less real than the other fear I saw in her eyes back in Michigan, at my mother's house the day before. What had I brought her into? Reflexively, I tighten my grip on Afiya's hand.

"Not so tight, Mama."

"Sorry, baby." I loosen my grip.

Something deep in me, a quiet betrayer of the code, always sensed there was a different way to live than how I grew up. Beyond the oppressive heat of the landscape, beyond the ghosts, beyond ourselves, there had to be another way to do this. I knew it like little kids know the ice cream truck is around the corner before they hear the music. The knowing vibrates in me like a live wire.

Because the chasm of our legacy is much too wide, gaping, and hungry for me, wanting me to join in, to be devoured or the devourer, I fold the rivers and lakes, push the sweating tombstones, mosquito nests, and manic laughter into a small prism and bury Kalamazoo underneath my tongue. I bury it right next to my Aunt Phyllis in the family cemetery. That's where bones belong, not in my hands, not in my mouth, not in my mother's living room. I have fallen out of love with the weeping willows. The spring dew can keep her cool, crisp kiss. The Mattawan sky, her bouillon stars. I've escaped again, but barely. *I mean to stay away this time, too,* I tell the young woman trapped in the small airplane window, mocking me with barnyard eyes.

Not last night, but the night before, twenty-four robbers came knocking at my door.

The kissing sound our soles made on the damp grass catching fireflies the night before hums in me. The mirth of my daughter's laughter over the crickets rushes to my head.

I got up, let 'em in.

I cling to that moment of our laughter when we raced across the wet grass, as if scattering liquid green fire out of the ground, gently plucking flames from the air. That night, the fireflies rose for us, bobbing in their yellow finery as if they held the last bit of magic in the world. My daughter too was a firefly, innocent, darkbright, and beautiful.

Hit 'em in the head with a rolling pin.

Untouched by us.

I cared if she lived.

11

Something Wicked

WHEN WE DESCEND on the excruciatingly slow escalator at the Los Angeles Airport and the crowd opens up, my boyfriend, Charles, waves hesitantly.

"Eh, well, hello Queen. You look shell-shocked." He hugs me, then Afiya. "What hit y'all?"

It's true. My daughter looks shorter somehow. Her hair escapes from her bun. I could use a bottle of wine to anesthetize the feeling of giddy loss buzzing in my brain, but the granddaughter of an alcoholic, I only rarely drink.

"Everything." I hug him. "Everything hit us."

I climb into the front seat of his old-school Cadillac and clamp my mouth shut. Grateful to have landed and passed off her nutty mom to an adult, Afiya immediately nods off to sleep. Looking sideways at me, Charles picks his words carefully.

"So, do you want to talk about it?"

He's intuitive like that, a sweet, unfocused man with a tremendous caretaker's spirit, but I shake my head.

How can I tell him about my family? Charles, who claimed his own Black and Indian heritage through his Alabama ancestors, is the one who took me to my first sweat lodge in the California mountains, but he doesn't really know us, me, or them, at all. He doesn't know what it's like Back There. Home. We are wolverines in a cramped den. Elephants on a bridge.

A free-spirited herbalist who plays drums, Charles loves me, but while he sees history as the colorless past, I see history as a lesson with teeth. We are the pages ripped out of history books.

According to historians Williams Loren Katz and Jack Forbes, we are the pages that history was written on. This country has done incredible damage to North and South American Indians, Caribbean American Indians, and Black people who are/were either fully African or in any way Mixed. The founders of America worked diligently, patiently, like spiders spinning constitutional webs toward the erasure of indigenous tribes. It is a fact that this country has killed and/or sanctioned the killing and removal of Indians from their homelands on over a hundred recorded documents. We know this.

What is often unknown is that through the 1924 Act to Preserve Racial Integrity, concocted in the Virginia Bureau of Vital Statistics under control of Walter Plecker, eugenics was born and became official policy. Plecker threatened all his employees with jail if they allowed dark-skinned or mildly dark-looking Negroes to write "Indian" as their child's race on birth records. Plecker's Mad Hatter reasoning was that those Negroes who claimed Indian could later claim white, go to white schools, and then marry white and be subsumed into white society. It was a valid assumption. One of my great-great-uncles did it. But the Racial Integrity Act, clearly white supremacist in nature, bulldozed over everyone's prior race or ethnicity: you were either Colored or white in Virginia. You had no tribe except in memory.

Because of this, Mixed bloods (or Mulattoes), American Indians, Blacks, *and* whites who claim Indian blood, have fallen apart and away from each other so that we are divided, splintered, and forgetful. We ourselves have forgotten that our blood carries the truth. Even in documentation of the founding of the Coharie tribal school, there are sentences like "there is none nor has there ever been any Negro blood in our tribe." Mainly because Blacks were not allowed an education, a kind of Negro blood hunt ensued in some tribes, to extricate any half-breeds from their schools or make them deny ties to Blackness. And because of these kinds of divides, we remain a racial invention on a sheet of paper; we checked a box on the Census that represents only half of what we are. Not the whole. Colored or white.

Despite hard, drawn-out battles to reclaim tribal names and lands, American Indians have finally been recognized by state and federal offices after years of disenfranchisement. After years of fighting, pillaging, recovery, and meager reservation life, a tribal enrollment card can feel like gold in your lint-filled pocket. Because of this restructuring of tribal homelands and brainwashing, some, not all, card-carrying Indians feel that lighter-skinned or darker-skinned, non-card-carrying Indians water down "recognized" tribal needs, issues, and activism. "Recognition" (from the very entity that disrupted tribes in the first damn place) has allowed tribes access to federal monies, the right to build casinos, and the right to reclaim land that was taken and is now parceled back out like candy canes from the culpable candyman. But the terms "recognition" and "tribal cards" smack of another era, of other evils, like Stars of David in Nazi Germany and the Freedom papers Blacks had to carry in the Antebellum South. Tribal enrollment cards would not be necessary if all treaties were honored and if tribes were not forced off their lands. If families weren't split apart because of racial classification.

From the late 1800s to the 1930s, repercussions against tribes possessing "Negro" blood occurred all too frequently. Some tribes were targeted by the government. If they had too many Black-looking kids or wives hanging around, or if they were educating Blacks—even if they were your kin—funding would stop. Imagine that. Other Mixed tribes lost their status. To my mind, tribal intra-racism was an injected virus, a cancer. It caused further rupture and self-imposed erasure. It caused Black-looking or Mixed blood Indians to be refused the right to marry, to receive an education, to receive land, and, in contemporary times, to dance at a powwow without your enrollment card. This virus, this mental illness, American racism and prejudice in tribes, was the same as whites against Blacks in pre–Civil Rights times. Cousins, aunts, uncles, sisters, and brothers fighting for scraps at the federal government dinner table. Fighting each other for the right to be counted the real American Indian. To remain Indian.

The iconic image of Nez Perce Chief Joseph comes to my mind. Not the noble one that western myth purports but the one of him at the end of the trail, bent over his horse, exhausted from fighting and running from the U.S. Calvary. As the story is told, Chief Joseph famously refused to live on a reservation after he was notified his tribe would have to leave their ancestral lands. Starting in Oregon in 1877, Joseph and his tribe of 750 tribal members gave chase across the plains, fighting the U.S. Calvary, racing toward Canada's safe borders. He finally surrendered in Montana, but because he and his people had resisted so skillfully and bravely, he remains honored for his prowess. But for many of us, the image of Chief Joseph on that horse, head bent, defeated, was the image that represented 300 years of resistance and then, finally, defeat. Rendered by some unknown artist, this picture can be found on keychains, leather pouches, wall art, wood carvings, and drums. It pervades our American Indian psyche, symbolizing our internal exhaustion from the onslaught of settlers, land thieves, murderers, soldiers, and squatters, all complicit in the erosion of not simply a tribe but an entire culture.

IT TAKES ME three days to finally tell Charles some of what happened; I can't tell him everything, the yelling, the storms. I don't want him to see that violence in me.

"That's unfortunate, Beloved, but you're still here."

I am still here. Aren't I?

When I wake up in my apartment, I welcome the cool silence. The peaceful calm. I roll over and pull my journal from the pillow and open it, writing everything down. I want a record. I write: "I am still here." On my way to work, blasting Sade's "Your Love is King" on my car stereo, the Los Angeles sunshine envelopes me like a friend who's been waiting a long time for me to come home, though it has only been days. I feel like an adult, sane. Not afraid of what the day will bring.

This was why I put a country between me and Kalamazoo. My sanity.

I shower, dress, and go to work. I meet with the editorial team at the magazine where I'm an editor, answering calls from writers and drafting several stories for the next issue. My daughter is actually excited to go back to Orville Wright Middle School. When I pick her up, she is waiting for me at the curb. She climbs in our white SUV and chatters about school, about failing a math test and what her friends did to the substitute teacher that day. She tells the story of someone locking him in a broom closet as if she hadn't laughed at that, but I know my daughter: she has a class-clown streak. I know she laughed.

"Uh-huh. I'm getting you a math tutor, okay?"

Afiya rolls her eyes. "Can I go to a slumber party at Sidney's on Friday?"

"Who's gonna be there?"

"Just the usual, Natalie, her sister, Gabby, and I can't remember who else."

I cut on the car radio and Destiny's Child's "Say My Name" croons out of the speakers. Afiya sings along in a strong, willowy voice.

"You should think about joining choir," I say for the umpteenth time. Afiya rolls her eyes but says, "Maybe. That choir teacher is crazy though. For real. I'm talking super dramatic."

We drive down Manchester Boulevard in silence. I turn up a steep hill toward the Pacific Coast Highway. In Playa del Rey, we lived so close to the beach we could walk or bike there in minutes. I spent nearly every Saturday and Sunday biking the path from my neighborhood to Manhattan Beach or Santa Monica. I had gotten extremely lucky landing an apartment for half of what it normally cost to live in this safe, multicultural community because the owner was a millionaire who worked in my magazine's building,

I park at the curb. The ocean is a blue blanket stretching into the horizon. The sun spins cords of soft gold into the water's reflection.

"I just want to make sure you're okay, sweetie." I'm trying to do damage control.

"What do you mean?"

I don't know what I mean. I just know I want to protect her, but from whom? What?

"Your family is crazy," she laughs a little. "Did you really throw a cantaloupe?"

I had thrown a cantaloupe, hadn't I? Where had she been?

"Well, nobody's perfect, even your dad's crazy family."

"Ma, please." She hates when I talk about her dad's family. She is tight with those cousins who'd escaped South Central for San Bernardino: those cousins can do no harm. My family, however, probably could. "I'm fine," she says.

I'm fine.

My mother always said that just at the moment when she was the least "fine."

WHERE'S THE PROOF? I am constantly asked. *What are you?* Classmates have fingered my "good" hair and pointed at my toffee-hued skin. "You're not really Black," one former friend told me years ago when I was nineteen or twenty, comparing my slender nose and skin tone to her beautiful thick features and rich kola nut skin. I knew I was not fully Black, but for her to say it set me apart from the Black race, the Black fight, the struggle of my Black people. I love my Blackness, my Africanness. My connection to Africa. I love the dopeness of our culture, our music, our artistic expression and scientific inventions. Our culture could be appropriated but never owned. I love and appreciate my American Indian culture in the same way. The dancing and drumming fills me with a sense of belonging. I feel blessed, not cursed, to share both.

But my Aunt Katheryn and her Manuel kin are from the old-school light-skinned crew, they are the wooden splinters of the Racial Integrity Act: the darker the berry for them didn't make the juice sweeter. Their minds are stuck in that tragic Mulatto trope: their light skin *did* make them better than us, than me, who got my darkness from my father's side. But if you asked any of them how and why, they probably couldn't explain it.

It's equally strange and hurtful to hear some full-blood Indians make jokes about us Mixed bloods. *What's wrong with you? You think you know what it means to be Indian?*

Maybe I don't, but I know my history.

Andrew Jackson had a plan for nonwhites and the nonwhites' possessions. Andrew Jackson's plan, along with his all-white administration, was to *take* Indian land. A proud white supremacist who was also friends with Adolf Hitler, Walter Plecker had a plan to keep pure-blood whites pure blood, to stop intermarrying and to reclassify all nonwhite people as Colored, especially Mulattoes and multiracial Mixed bloods. It seemed like such a good plan, no wonder the rest of the nation bought into it. Why not? I can see them slapping each other on the back. Why the *hell* not. Plecker aimed, in essence, to erase any trace of individual tribes, tribal affiliation, and Blackness, and, more significantly, to not let biracial couples' miscegenated products leak through and claim whiteness. "Negro,"

"Indian," or any Of Color-looking babies all became Colored. Probably a few swarthy Italian babies were suddenly Colored too. Eventually, all Blacks and Indians bore the label, though it stuck more so for Blacks.

The social implications of erasing heredity lines between Blacks and Indians were as much a public policy of eradicating the Indian himself. Mulatto, Chino, Sambo, Quadroon, Octoroon, Mestico, Redbone, High Yellow: the power of naming and renaming worked like a spade to dig up the roots of families, nations, and entire linguistic groups and tribes. Thus robbing them, us, of an original identity.

But they couldn't stop it. The mixing of races happened everywhere. Black slaves ran away and married into a tribe (African *or* Indian) and birthed little half-breed, Mixed blood babies that were very much, as much as any full-blood, a part of that tribe. Buffalo Soldiers married full-blood women and were welcomed into the tribe. Indian women and children were stolen from their homes, from river banks, and from their villages by bushwhackers and sold into slavery, according to *Black Indian Slave Narratives* by Patrick Minges. Slave masters put the captive American Indians to work as slaves next to African and Mixed white and Black slaves. Why would a slave owner bother to differentiate between a dark-skinned Indian and a Mulatto slave if it were easier, because they were property anyway, to lump them all together?

Yet despite the unrelenting misery, in some moments of our migration, Michigan was good to us and held precious, coveted dreams laced in its soil. Southwestern Michigan was the last outpost on the Underground Railroad before Canada. For escaped slaves, Black freedmen and women, Mulattoes and Indians passing for white (like my grandparents' siblings), it was the land of hope, and they made desperate lurches at that freedom. With the help of Harriet Tubman, who has a commemorative statue in Battle Creek, not ten minutes from Kalamazoo, slaves built new lives. With the help of sympathetic Quakers and random whites who were disgusted by slavery, or disagreed with it, many of Michigan's founders of color either were cargo on or conductors of the Underground Railroad. We saved each other. We hid each other. We made babies.

Yet land was always the ultimate goal—all of it. So was erasure. E/race/sure. Erase/sure. Erase us for sure.

I REMEMBER BECOMING aware of race. And with that knowledge, like many kids, the Andrew Jacksons and Walter Pleckers, I did a terrible thing. I was eight or nine, and in the second or third grade. Mrs. Redmond, a pear-shaped white woman with freckled white skin and a pageboy haircut, was my favorite teacher then. Mrs. Redmond's class was small, the walls lined with encouraging phrases like "You Can Read."

But also, taped just above the chalkboards and along each wall were the pictures of every U.S. president. We had to memorize their names, starting with George Washington. I hated how those white men leered above me, judging me for all that I was and, in their eyes, was not.

One November day, the iciest day of the year, I was helping Mrs. Redmond sweep the classroom during recess when we heard a commotion outside the door, then a terrified scream. In the next breath, a young white teacher's aide rushed in, holding Raoul, the only Hispanic kid in our entire school, by the shoulder. He had a weird smile on his face and as he turned, blood gushed out of a dime-sized jagged hole in his left temple. "I was pushed by another boy," he said apologetically to me or to the glaring presidents.

The young teacher tried to stay calm, but her voice was a whispering screechy sound. "He hit a chunk of frozen ice. Mrs. Redmond, Mrs. Redmond, he's bleeding."

The boy who'd pushed Raoul was pale, a white boy shrunken with fear: "It was an accident. I swear, it was an accident."

In a class of over twenty kids, more than half of us Blackish, Raoul always seemed to be just the cool kid: he wasn't labeled anything.

Mrs. Redmond turned slowly, maybe thinking he'd cut a finger, and then blanched. "Ohmygod, ohmygod, ohmygod," she repeated coolly as she dialed the principal and then 9-1-1. Just under the sharp, efficient haircut, her ears glowed Christmas-bulb red. More blood slid down Raoul's cheekbones and pointy chin: the hole looked big enough to put two fingers in his head. Mrs. Redmond rushed over and swung Raoul into her arms and left. Raoul was in class the next day, showing off his bandages, boy bravado in his high voice.

Mrs. Redmond nearly always maintained her teacherly calm. Especially the day Steve Brown, the boy we ruthlessly teased for being a Jehovah's Witness, dropped his mental marbles. That day Mrs. Redmond, a genuinely kind woman who really *looked* us Black kids *in our eyes*, asked him to put down the scissors and join our reading time. "I'm not finished," I think he said, cutting paper.

"Please join us in the reading circle, Steve," Mrs. Redmond repeated. He ignored her. Smiling, she went over and gently laid her hand over his, showing him how we put scissors down. Steve, a beautiful dark brown–skinned boy with a perfect oval head, dressed in his usual slacks, a long-sleeved shirt, and polished brown Stacy Adams, went berserk. He snarled and launched himself at her, fighting her like a man and tearing the sleeve of her nice teacher's blouse in the process. Her normally pink ears flared scarlet with surprised anger. We kids froze and as one Did Not Breathe. We were in a kind of vice-grip awe that one, he'd hit a Teacher (*who taught us things*), and two, she didn't shake him until his teeth rattled out of his perfect oval head. That's what our parents, my grandfather especially, would have done had we dared to look as if we wanted to show our asses like that. The principal appeared as if he had been there the whole time, but maybe he'd heard the screams or someone else had. Steve was removed from the classroom. Frazzled, Mrs. Redmond regained composure enough to say, "Kids, let's have a recess."

The word "recess" was like the phrase "ice cream truck" to us. Whatever had just happened was forgotten and we ran for the door.

Steve did not come back to cut anything for weeks. When he did, no one teased him anymore that he wore dress slacks and church shoes to school. No one, to my knowledge, ever asked him what had happened.

But they sure were talking about him behind his back. They talked about me behind my back, too, and sometimes to my face. I didn't look "fully black." "Is that your real hair?" "Why don't you press all the time?" The day I came to school with my hair pressed, with my mane flowing down to my polyester pants like a horse's tail, I suddenly had all the popular girls as my friends, and they fought over who could play in my hair like I was a life-sized Barbie.

"Are you mixed with Indian?" Dee Dee Cross asked me.

Before I could answer, someone cut in: "Of course she is, you see her family? Duh. She got that *good* Indian hair."

When I got home, my mother barely let me put my books down before the whipping started because my *good* Indian hair was in knots. I didn't care, though. That five minutes of fame, when I was otherwise ignored, had been worth it.

But my mixed Black and American Indian was different from Nigel Lockett's mixed Black and white. Somehow, his mixed gave him more status and swagger; my mixed came without pedigree and was only mysterious and cool to the kids when I looked to them like Pocahontas. A creamy-skinned boy, Nigel's mixed came with a nice house, two parents, brand-new tennis shoes, crisp blue jeans, Polo shirts with baby alligators on them, and good lunches in a shiny Spiderman lunchbox. My mixed came with a regular-sized house, one exhausted nurse's aide single mother, hand-me-down Kmart shirts, high-water pants, already scuffed tennis shoes, government cheese, and lukewarm school lunches.

I'd had a crush on Nigel since kindergarten. But he never looked at me.

He only liked the white girls and Yvonne Gibson, who was light-bright pretty; the slightly darker-skinned Black girls collectively knew we didn't stand a chance with him.

One day, in my Curious George treks around the Eastside, I turned down a well-kept street that I had never been on. The houses were majestic to my eyes, brick and wood, with manicured lawns and expertly shaped hedges. It was as if a new and improved version of my street had been magically dropped into our community, like Dorothy's house in *The Wizard of Oz*. My imagination knew no bounds, then. And oh look, a pretty white woman coming out of her front door, probably a fairy godmother.

Oh, there she is kissing a Black man; he gets in his car and waves at his son, my classmate, Nigel Lockett. The fairy godmother was hugging Nigel now, and handing him something, maybe his lunchbox. It suddenly struck me with a terrible glee that Nigel was mixed *like me.*

Although he wasn't Black and Indian, he was Black *and white.* It was the '70s and Black Power permeated the air. I was a kid, but I saw the smug pride of my brothers and sisters when they sported their Afros and Black Power–fisted ebony picks in their hair. No one wanted to be white when the fine Smokey Robinson and the Miracles oozed from car speakers as we drove around town. No one claimed to be mixed anything when we learned to do to the Bump or pretended we were the Jackson Five. "Black Power, baby," my brothers and sisters would say in passing to their friends when coming or going. "Ungawa, Black Power."

But Nigel was white.

My new knowledge gave me a terribly sweet sense of power. I had something over him. I just didn't know what it was really. The next day in class, I looked at him, unafraid, hopelessly enamored, but knowing he would never give me the time of day, and I started humming my song in my head as I added up my math problems and practiced my long O's and S's and D's. D's were my favorite. N's too. As in Nigger. And I hummed until the bell rang for recess and sang a little of it on the playground to the shock of my schoolmates. *Hmm, hmm hm, hm, hmm, hmmm. Ni-gel is a nig-ger.* It had such a swell ring to it. The alliteration of the "n" thrilled me. I sang in my head until, after we climbed off the bus at the end of the day, it burst from my mouth: "Nigel is a nigger. His dad is Black and his mama is white. Nigel is a nigger."

He was hanging back with his friends and couldn't hear me, so it didn't matter. I sang, skipping along East Main Street toward my street, Southworth Terrace. I was giddy in my newfound knowledge that a boy I had a crush on, who ignored me, was not better than me. He wasn't better than any of us.

I never stopped to think that it was none of my business, that maybe he was embarrassed, that his desire to keep quiet about it was for the purpose of protecting himself. I felt somehow betrayed that I got nothing as a biracial girl and he seemed to get everything. Maybe because I knew his family had money and mine didn't. He always had clean, new-looking clothes and good lunches; and I didn't. Maybe I just desperately wanted him to like me back. Maybe I was possessed. But I could not, for the life of me, shut up. Someone must have told him about my serenade.

"Nigel's coming," someone yelled. I saw a scuffle and a sea of kids parted like, you know, the Red Sea, and he darted out of it toward me. I took off. I was scared shitless, laughing out of sheer terror of what he was going to do to me when he caught me. I was the fastest runner in my age group on my block, but Nigel was faster.

"I'ma kill you. You better shut up, Shonda."

He chased me, ran me down like the dog I was. For some reason, I couldn't keep the words from coming out of my mouth as I ran.

"Nigel is a——." He caught my arm and threw me down on my back. He straddled my stomach and raised his hand. He'd been trained not to hit girls. He hesitated until I laughed. Laughed like the dolt I was as he slapped me hard. Then for good measure, he spit in my face. I didn't care. I laughed like a big dummy. Kids are cruel. I was cruel. He was cruel too.

At that moment calling him the worst insult I could think of was instinct, but later, years and years later, I realized he hated his black-white self a little too, more than he hated me. Maybe as much as I disliked myself for not knowing what or who we were, because we didn't look Africa Black. Our skin tone incriminated us. Our high cheekbones and our soft spongy hair set us apart.

I was light brown, my sisters and brothers were mostly high yellow, and my mother was nearly as translucent as a star. Me and Nigel weren't what our history books termed "niggers"—Black slaves in a cotton field—but somehow we were tainted with the heritage of that word. My mom hadn't really taught me to be proud of our Blackness. The multiracial and Indian part, yes. But being proud of my Blackness—that I had to learn.

I didn't care about any of this then. I just knew that even though I had a crush on Nigel, I hated him a little too. Since first grade, he'd done stuff to me as part of a group of what we called "mannish" boys. The term "mannish" meant a boy or girl trying to be grown, too sexualized at a young age, talking back or just bad.

What some of my male classmates did to me and a few other "early developing" girls would be considered sexual abuse. Because my breasts were growing and my behind was rounder than other girls, they chased me down the street. On the playground, they pinned down my struggling limbs and felt me up, rubbing and pinching my butt and my developing sore breasts, because that's what they thought men did, or maybe they saw men do this. Nigel was one of them, those big-headed boys who kept touching me until I stopped struggling and heaved shuddering tears. I had no control over this moment. Then they stopped and ran away laughing, as if they'd gotten away with something. They had. I felt so violated. When it happened at school, I had cried and cried in Mrs. Redmond's arms, heaving up my tears like a sacrifice.

"There, there." She gave me a tissue and dried my tears. "Who did it? Who was it?"

I looked at her and shook my head; I wouldn't tell. I was ashamed. What would happen to them anyway? We all rode the same bus home. I had known these boys all my life, and suddenly they were strangers. My ripening body made them little monsters.

I became meaner at school. I started chasing the boys and twisting their arms behind their backs if I saw them messing with any of other the girls. I shoved them, bit them. Cut them with my laugh when they didn't get something, a math problem, right. I made my best friend Cindy Kozminsky hit her own boyfriend, Ricky Cook, in the face because I saw him hit her earlier. I remember her crying and running away on her tippy-toes. I had a serious irrational crush on Ricky too, but I didn't care.

Harassing Nigel, demeaning him with the "N" word, this word that no one was supposed to say, a word I heard stabbing the air only in serious anger, was one way to get my revenge. To hurt him as badly as I could. He could spit in my face all he wanted but I knew what he was.

I had totally forgotten about this day until I came to wonder if I'd ever discriminated against another biracial person, or effectively dismantled another person of color like my brothers and sisters did when they called someone an "African Booty Scratcher." Or told a Yo Mama joke, like "Yo Mama so Black somebody thought she was a skillet and tried to fry an egg on her face." I wondered if I had ever made another person feel like she had three heads, like I felt when someone asked me, whether with innocence or malice, "What are you?"

I was the light-brown-skinned girl with long, soft, flowing black hair that wouldn't stand up in an Afro and tangled at the neck and edges if too much moisture was in the air. I was the daughter of a woman who was part Cherokee and Coharie Indian but who didn't yet know her tribes; I was the daughter of John Buchanan, who said we were Choctaw and Black from Okolona, Mississippi, but he didn't have any proof. No evidence. This was my oral narrative.

I was Me. I was Nigel. I was everyone who ever felt they had half a face, half a life, half an identity, no tribe, no connection to a nation, felt themselves sliding between race and ethnicity. But in my attempt to navigate the racial expectations of others, to get out from underneath that biracial microscope, I had betrayed the one person who should have been my comrade.

Maybe I was a little monster child who just couldn't handle the fact that a boy did not like me. And I was also the girl Nigel had physically harmed. I was both.

I know that people, since the beginning of the first cave drawings, have found ways to differentiate and separate themselves, the smartest from the slowest, the weakest from the strongest, the babymakers from the hunters, and though these are labels that don't always stick, many do. And somewhere in there, in my most terrible moment of isolating Nigel by calling him the cruelest name I could think of, I wounded myself too. In the name of intra-racism, I exposed our self-hatred.

I was the daughter of my grandfather after all, complicit in the act, the game of self-erasure. Nobody I knew hated himself, and everyone else around him, more than Clifford Gaylord Stafford, who could pass for white if he wanted to, and who married one white woman after divorcing my grandmother, and another one after she died.

Walter Plecker's grand design, his hateful pogrom to erase ethnicity in every person of color, lumping us all together like fish heads in a pile of fish heads, like shit on a stick, became one of America's most divisive surgical tools that resulted in this fallout. The havoc he wreaked with his desire to keep whiteness all white smudged the lines between Indians and Black Indian and Black families. Made us afraid to claim our darker-skinned brothers and uncles, made us kick our Blackest-looking nieces and cousins out of Indian schools because educating them was a crime. Was it a game to white, slave-owning land stealers who had nothing else in the world to do but break us apart and move us around like pieces in a jigsaw puzzle?

However they accomplished it, Blacks and their Indigenous family members were no longer together. No longer relatives, no longer nations. Not the Iroquois Confederacy, the Council of Three Fires, or the Three Fires Confederacy, but separate tribes, separate families. We were strangers to ourselves. Yes, I blame Walter Plecker.

If I ever found it, I would spit on his grave.

12

About the Land

ABOUT TWENTY MINUTES outside of Kalamazoo County proper was the Country.

The old farm house in Mattawan sat at the end of a long gravel driveway. The front yard was encased on all sides by cattails, skinny willow, birch and maple trees. Two full-trunk weeping willows languished in the front yard, seeming to guard the front door and the house's secrets.

Directly in front of those weeping willows, a deep marshy pond was filled with crawdads, and minnows, and humongous pop-eyed bullfrogs (two slimy critters the size of puppies that were my dear friends), and slippery toads. Those and other spiny creatures my grandfather, on occasion, ate with great relish.

To the left of the back door, there was the small plot of land that my grandfather planted his corn, beans, and tomatoes in, whatever the season allowed. I believe at one point he'd worked the entire land, roaming through his five acres on his archaic John Deere tractor in a set of Mr. Green Jeans pants and jacket. Just on the outskirts of the yard, the house was surrounded by a small woods that ran the length of the farm to another road and a house. For some reason, we didn't speak to those neighbors.

The farm was surrounded by water on all sides. Underneath was the Artesian spring, which my grandfather harnessed by plugging a pipe in the base of a willow tree and creating a pond that water plopped right into. He built himself a one-room bait house made of thick bricks, painted an ugly dark green. The bait house held Grandpa Stafford's things: a smattering of fishing poles, hooks, and

knives, mason jars, tool boxes and plows, shovels and axes. Everything to make a life was left to him on that farm for his family.

The land was a gift and was supposed to define him, give him
a place to build us back up. Instead, he lost it all. Unaware of
the farm's history, or simply not willing to share it, my grandfather, Clifford Gaylord Stafford, sold the land he inherited from
his mother, and the rest he bought from his brother's widow,
partly in desperation over the unpaid property taxes and partly
in a drunken stupor. A towering giant of a man, he was born on
December 31, 1911, the last child of thirteen. His birth certificate says he was born in Almena Township, Van Buren County,
but his death certificate says he was born in Oklahoma. When
he died, his race was listed as "Black" and his occupation was
a "heavy equipment operator" at Western Michigan University.
He'd given up farming; that was too much damn hard work for
a drunk.

Despite what any certificate said, or what the boxes marked,
Clifford Stafford was an illusive trickster who claimed whatever
was convenient at the time. Many Mixed bloods did. The question
wasn't how did you get to be Black Indian, or Mulatto, or Mixed,
but rather, "Who yo' people?" And from the last name, and where
you lived, someone with the family memory could trace you back to
your Black, Red, and white kin. Not everything got written down;
not everything had a "record" then.

He was a Black Indian without an African or American Indian
tribe. No history of his family's migration from North Carolina to
Tennessee, Kentucky, then Indiana, and lastly Michigan. For all he
and the rest of us knew, we grew like those cattails and weeping
willows right in that black earth of Mattawan. As far as I know,
he had never been to North Carolina. But when I visited as an
adult, something pulled at me; Sampson and Clinton Counties
felt familiar: North Carolina was a waterlogged state. When the

Staffords and my mother's mother's people, the Manuels, high-tailed it out for whatever reason, they probably had no idea that they would end up right where they started: clearing swamps.

His mother, Caledonia Roberts Stafford, my ornery great-grandmother, was probably related to Enoch Harris, supposedly the original Johnny Appleseed who planted the first apple orchard in Oshtemo. Harris was born in Virginia, raised in Pennsylvania, and did some "pioneering" in Ohio before moving to Kalamazoo. If my grandfather knew that, he kept it cinched in the waistband of his cotton long johns. Clifford Stafford, careless and thoughtless as to the value of legacy, drank the one-hundred-acre inheritance down to a fifty-cent piece. There were only five acres left in 1978.

"Anybody ever done a goddamn thing for me?" he probably slobbered into a Budweiser can. Clifford drank to forget his childhood. When he was little, Clifford's father regularly laced his son's backside with a horse whip any time he stepped out of line. Clifford walked with that memory like glass in his shoe. *Who done something for me? Not one of you muthafuckers.*

About fifty-some years earlier, in the 1930s, there had been a bigger, more elegant house on the property, but one of the kids helped the woodstove catch fire and burned the whole place down. They built another house, but as the story goes, involving another set of knuckle-headed youngsters and matches, including my aunts Mildred and Frieda, who were around five and six at the time, and their Uncle George, that house burned down too.

More bad luck.

The third and last house was much smaller, and maybe it should have burned down.

It started out as a four-room house. My mother's father built things like he drank—haphazardly, without hope, and forgetful of the damage he'd caused. The house was cramped, awkwardly angled, and without any sense of front, center, or back. The front door was a sliver of an entrance that no one entered. Eventually, a burlap couch was shoved against that door from the inside. Everyone entered through the back-side door and into the mudroom that was constantly littered with firewood, empty beer cans, ice skates, and worn shoes. The minuscule kitchen was as big as two outhouses, with a white stove and sink that leaned on the slanting, creaky floor. A black woodstove was cramped next to the living room wall until the oil stove was put in, but both failed to heat the entire house every winter. That wall, when my grandfather deemed it time, was knocked out in 1967 and became a newly constructed bathroom. He'd recently gotten remarried and his new wife wanted all the amenities of decent country living, which, to her thinking, included indoor running water.

"We need an indoors bathing area," I can hear her saying, holding out on the marital duties until water flowed from a new silver faucet in her new porcelain sink.

"I couldn't believe Daddy done that," Aunt Lily said. "All those years we used that outhouse. Mama too."

My mother and her sisters spent their girlhoods lugging buckets of water inside for baths and running to a frighteningly dark outhouse their father had built to do their business, except at night, when they used a slop jar. Aunt Lily later told me that her father still wanted her, her sisters, and their kids to use the outhouse when they came to visit, as if they would somehow taint his handiwork by using the bathroom. What a bastard.

The girls never had running water in that house when they lived there. They slept on narrow beds in the perpetually frigid attic with the scurrying mice. They lived as country as country could get. Barefooted, barnyard straw in their hair, hungry and full of longing for the fairy tale that would never come. That house was story-less. Seems like every step the family took since arriving in Michigan, without moccasins or buckskin, without tribal enrollment cards, was unblessed. Unkissed.

Ghosts lingered in the embers, sparks behind the walls.

ON ONE VISIT home, I combed through text after text in the Kalamazoo Public Library, determined that something about this land, the migration of the Staffords, Manuels, and all the other Black families who came, lived, sweated, and died there, must exist. And they couldn't all have been only Black because we weren't only Black—we were proof of our Mixed blood.

"You look for any mention of Staffords and Manuels," I marshaled Afiya, who shifted from foot to foot with an I'm-so-bored sigh. I turned to my nephew, Christopher, equally bored but an eleven-year-old know-it-all who wouldn't miss this for the world. "You look for Mattawan information."

Lo and behold, what we found was that the first real home built in Kalamazoo, a cabin, a shack really, but a livable structure nonetheless, was built by Enoch Harris, aka Johnny Appleseed, a "Negro," in 1828. This before Titus Bronson, Kalamazoo's supposed "founder," built his shack in 1829. In fact, in many historical accounts, Bronson isn't credited with building a cabin until 1831. One account by Willis F. Dunbar affords this: "Actually, Bronson probably had no house here when Harris built his cabin, and the Harris house may be considered the first family dwelling in the town."

This is what they didn't tell us in school, because that would mean a Black man founded one of the most industrial Midwestern cities in the nation's early history. How could Blacks do that if they were slaves and shiftless lowlifes? First called "Bronson," locals decided Kalamazoo, the local American Indian name, had more of a zing to it. People would want to visit a thriving acropolis in the middle of Detroit and Chicago with a name like that. Bing Crosby even anointed us with the song "I Got a Girl in Kalamazoo." (Years later, so did L. L. Cool J.)

For me, and for my sanity, I needed to know if the musings, whispers, and alcoholic confessions I'd heard in my childhood were even a little true. I needed to know if She was right. She. Our Queen Indian bee: Aunt K. My notorious Great-Aunt Katheryn Manuel. Always as sharply (and ridiculously) dressed as a mannequin, Aunt Katheryn was an intensely private diva who kept to herself, not telling anyone she was one of us, part Black, and related by marriage to the Staffords of Mattawan.

When I was growing up, getting into my aunt's house was like getting into Fort Knox. If we happened to be near her house on the Northside, my poor mother had to damn near prove that we were dying of thirst, or wounded, to get Aunt Katheryn to let us inside. Katheryn was my Grandma Stafford's elder sister, her only sister. Never married, Aunt Katheryn would always carry her father's surname. The neighborhood kids used to circle Aunt Katheryn's front porch and throw rocks at her white picket fence and house, accusing her of being a white witch in a Black neighborhood.

"That's my aunt," I'd chase them off. "She ain't white, and she ain't no witch."

She just didn't like what she considered "little nappy-headed Black kids"—that I knew for sure, because I was one hundred percent positive she didn't like me. Every time her eye landed on my spongy black cotton hair, long like a hand whip when it was pressed, she'd crack a slight smile, because I had that "good hair," but when her eyes kept going to my lightly toasted skin, she squinted like the sight of it stung her eyes.

She would never forgive my mother for marrying a "black ass nigger" and procreating with him. Aunt Katheryn's racism and blatant colorism was like venom; my almond-hued father, a Mississippi mud man on the Black Choctaw side, couldn't even take out her trash. She tried to ignore him until she ended up looking daggers at me. I'd squirm under her scrutiny until we left. I've always felt a slight, guilty resentment that my mother, lost in her own trauma of salvaging her life after breaking up with another man, never defended me against Aunt Katheryn's accusing gaze that screamed I was less-than because I was the darker Indian, not as light as the rest of my siblings, except Popeye.

Aunt Katheryn did look white, I begrudgingly admitted when the kids scuttled home. Her then auburn hair was as soft and wavy as any white person's hair, but she was more golden than white, like a natural tan. Pulsing green veins in her face, neck, and hands showed clearly as if I'd drawn them on with my favorite crayon. Yet, in my youth, and for hugely important self-identification purposes, I'd rationalized that if my mother was as Black as she talked and my father was Black as he looked, then my aunt had to be a "light-skinned" Black, no matter how much I could see through her. Not until I realized that kids in school only wanted to be my friend when my hair was pressed did I confer with my mother.

"Mama, we got Indian in us?" I had to be about six or seven years old.

I was scratching her head for a quarter, one of my Saturday morning chores, while the rest of the kids who'd finished their chores watched white Tarzan find white Jane in Hollywood's blaxploitation Africa. My brother launched himself from the orange shag carpet and tried out his Tarzan scream, making my mother's shoulders hunch up.

"Tyrone, *shut* the *hell* up," she snapped, then relaxed more deeply into her La-Z-Boy to the tickle of my fingers in her hair. "Yeah. I think it's Blackfoot. No, maybe Cherokee." Everybody said Cherokee, I learned later.

"We got some white in us?" I had never seen proof of the Indian blood or white ancestors, except pictures that showed a range of colors from off-white Great-Grandma Manuel. Grabbing my wrist, Mama moved my hand to a spot I'd missed.

"Yup. You got some French, some German, some Indian, some white, and a little, itty bit of Black."

Uh-oh. What did I tell my friends?

According to her, though my daddy was darker than the misrepresented Africans on *Tarzan*, I was a mutt, the least portion of which was Black. I kept quiet but I was confused. Did Black people not want to be Black? Did Blacks hate themselves as much as it seemed my Great-Aunt Katheryn hated them? I didn't know at the time that Katheryn's father, George Thomas Manuel, had been disowned by his white family because he listed his race as white, and his father had married a *Mulatto* woman, my great-grandma, Helen Curtis Manuel. Oddly though, George Thomas Manuel's father and uncle, Peter and Daniel Manuel, fought with the Colored troops in the Civil War. It only took two generations to leave Blackness and Indianness behind.

Is that why Black was last on Mama's list, while I was consistently ordered to mark "Black" on all the forms and boxes I filled out at school and the doctor's office? I certainly wasn't told to check "white," and there were no slots for "half-white" or "half-Indian." And my birth certificate? Race: *Black.* My family culture: *Good Times* Black, not *Brady Bunch*, and definitely not John Wayne's Indians. We didn't have one eagle feather between us. After I loosened that bit of family history from my mother's scalp, I was able to boast to my classmates that my Aunt Katheryn and my whole family was Indian *and* Black. I kept the French-German-white part to myself because I did not know what to do with it. Really, I thought, how much did that matter if they couldn't see it on me? If *I* couldn't see it in me. Instinctively, with a kid's reasoning, I knew I had to choose something to form my identity. White wasn't my identity. I was nowhere near white. But people said my hair was that "good Indian hair." I saw myself in my mother and aunts who looked Indian. That was enough for me.

I was supposed to be the Tragic Mulatto, but no one told me that.

I don't know why it was so important to me to claim both the Indian and Black, but the knowledge of my white, European heritage seemed to somehow blaspheme against the legacy of slavery. And what was a Mulatto anyway? When I was young I could barely pronounce the word, much less know that it was a term created and molded into an identity that set Black folk mixed with Native American and white *apart* from Black African folk not mixed with anything. Cajun was a spice to us, not a race. Not lines drawn in the census sand.

I wasn't trying to expand the notion of Blackness.

Shit, I was in the first grade.

However, my long, kinky curly hair never failed to remind my great-aunt of that "itty bit of Black." As a child, I didn't know why it was so important for her and my mother to claim their white blood. Much later, I realized that social conditioning, jealousy, and self-hatred were stashed and hidden like a secret code in many Black people's psyches. Not our DNA, but our minds. Then later, for some American Indian tribes, that coveted tribal enrollment card functioned as their ticket to Indianness, whether they were full-blood or not.

To Americans in the early 1800s and into the mid-1900s, everything white was right. If you were Black, get back. If you were Indian, don't tell *nobody* because they'd be sure you had some land to take. If you were both, well damn, cousin, you were shit out of luck. We, society, perpetuated that lie until it became a part of our cultural truth. For the older Black folks, tracing bloodlines was associated with tracing your roots in slavery.

They wanted to forget. They *needed* to forget.

THE STAFFORDS MIGRATED from Hertford and Halifax, North Carolina.

My great-grandfather Jason Stafford, born in 1886, was the last son of fifteen children between Jeremiah Stafford Sr. and Anny Sophia Milum. In 1836, while living in Randolph County, Indiana, Jeremiah Sr. married Anny, labeled a "Mulatto." When they married, Jeremiah was twenty-four years old; Anny, as the times permitted, was a twelve-year-old waif. For more than twenty-nine years in nine-month increments, Anny was swollen with child. She had her first at thirteen years old and her last when she was forty-two. Born in western Virginia in 1824, thirty-seven years before the region broke away and formed the new state of West Virginia, Anny is my oldest known female ancestor on the Stafford side. In a black-and-white photograph in which she has been identified, a stern, translucent-skinned woman stares back at the lens, unsmiling. Anny was classified as a free African American, Free Person of Color, and "Mulatto" intermittently in census documents up to 1870. Afterward, she was listed as a "Black" housekeeper for her son, the term "Black" erasing any connections to her Mulatto status and to the Native American tribes of Virginia and West Virginia that the Milum name carried.

Jeremiah Sr. and his family finally settled in Almena, Michigan. He was allotted forty acres by the township but soon purchased eighty acres of farmland in Clyde Township from the state government, which made him well-to-do enough to warrant a profile in a Kalamazoo-area "Who's Who" book of early settlers during the 1870s. A cooper by trade but a farmer out of necessity, Jeremiah also made house shingles. Mysteriously, years later, he was shot and killed on his front porch—the reason and circumstances are unknown. KKK didn't like him owning all that land?

One of Jeremiah Sr. and Anny's sons, Jeremiah Jr., first volunteered for the army at the age of thirteen. After four rejections, he was finally admitted at sixteen and fought in the Civil War as a member of the 102nd United States Colored Troops. He received an honorable discharge in 1865. Later, enamored with the forest, rivers, and lakes, Jeremiah became "unsociable"—a recluse they called him—and instead of living with his wife and children, he took one of his sons with him to live in the "wilds" and scrape bark off trees and pull up herbs to make healing poultices with Ottawa or Ta-Wa Indians. He became known as a skilled medicine man and earned the name "Indian Doctor." Colored people from miles around called Dr. Jeremiah to help deliver babies and cure all their sicknesses because no white doctor would come. The tribe later adopted him and his son.

Pulling these strings together into some cohesive tapestry, I always wondered about "them," my tribe. Did they go to a Christian church or have some old vestiges of North Carolina Indian religion hanging around their necks? Did they wear medicine pouches or dance at powwow like me? Was there any connection to the African ancestry that we had never heard tell of or seen?

The hiding, the Underground Railroad, these bits of history about the Black and Indigenous communities of this region were rarely highlighted in my history books, and when I found them, I sifted them like brown and white sugar cubes in a bowl, comparing them to the photo of the very first house built on the farm in Mattawan; to the records; and to the yellow, red, black faces of my family.

In a proud moment of vindication for our ancestors, a 2010 *Kalamazoo Gazette* newspaper article celebrated the heritage of the Staffords as among the first "non-White" settlers and the state's earliest pioneers of "Indian, non-Black descent" during the 1800s in Almena Township. According to Gwen Tulk, the eldest-living Stafford relative at the time, the family was "a combination of all different nationalities and ethnicities."

I showed my family this article when we were all sitting in my mom's living room, and Tyrone hollered, "Kids! Come here! Right now! Where y'all at? Look." My beautiful albino niece, Ashli, and the other honey-toned children rolled their eyes at how country their dad sounded. My daughter always rolls her eyes when my accent slips out. "Look at what your Auntie Shonda has. I told you we *is* Indian."

Not only is we Indian, but we were among the first "non-white" settlers of southwest Michigan. Proof is proof.

When the Robertses, Staffords, and Manuels got to Decatur, Dowagiac, Ypsilanti, and Mattawan, these were all mostly underdeveloped strips of marshy earth, where white-tailed deer, jack rabbits, and cottonmouths reigned. The tribes in those areas had learned to set up their camps more deeply into the forests until they couldn't anymore. (In Almena, Van Buren County, the Native Americans of this area were first to be "engaged" and then pinched off their lands by the French, then the British.) Over the years, small sharecropper houses, moonshine stills, and mud shacks cropped up on the edges of swamps; then the Fish Hatchery a half a mile away was established and Wolf Lake, the local water hole, received a name. The Robertses would be fine because farming was in their blood, but the Staffords and Manuels weren't farmers; they were river dwellers, fishermen and women who lived on the banks of the Neuse River of North Carolina. Coharie but also Eastern Cherokee, we were Turtle Clan from one or more of these North Carolina tribes, the Tuscarawas, Waccamaw Sioux, Haliwa-Saponi, Occaneechi Band, Meherrin, or the Lumbee. Not knowing who they were or where they came from meant they had to do something to earn their keep.

In Indiana and Michigan, we tilled.

Our family planted roots in the middle of three directions. Surely that was bad luck, as we lacked a fourth direction to go in. Every Indian, full-blood or half-pint, knows you need four directions to win. Four directions represent every nation of this earth; the four directions—north, south, east, west—give us our spirit, our RedBlack heart, our balance. Clarity. Protection. Without a fourth direction, and your place in the center of it, you were doomed, cousin.

A spider without a web.

A dream catcher that couldn't catch dreams.

PART II

Stomp Dance

Stafford sisters: Mildred with Frieda (*left*) and Velma (*right*).

Stafford family portrait, 1920s. My great-grandparents Jason and Caledonia with Linford (*bottom, left to right*); Mildred, Clifford, and Raymond (*top, left to right*).

13

Vision Quest

IT WAS THE fall of 1952.

Standing in front of a classic black Cadillac, the Staffords waited for the camera's click. Velma Jean, eleven, stood behind her little sister, Lily Lee, with a grim smile. She pursed her lips in a much-too-adult smirk, a look her father constantly tried to whip off her face. Seven-year-old Lily Lee grinned at the camera with all the lithe charm and innocence of a Mattawan backwoods fairy. Pixie stick Lily—eyes slit to shield the sun, face tilted—seemed to drink the day's cold heat, while my mother looked steamed and pressed in her black wool coat and head scarf.

"Lily," her mother warned, "be still. Stop messing with your sisters."

"Yeah," Phyllis smirked. "Always messing."

Despite her angular face, beautiful, high cheekbones for days, Phyllis Gayle, the middle sister, was only handsome with a toothy downturned grin on her light-bright face and wide black almond eyes that swallowed her nose and forehead. Mildred, the eldest at sixteen or seventeen, was absent, out in South Haven working on her first baby with her dumb, no-count husband, John A. Cloud.

Frieda Ann, standing next to Velma Jean, was the one with the angelic hair. The second oldest, Frieda Ann had soft hands and catch-a-ghost eyes. She had kindness enough for everyone, even her loud-mouthed, philandering, alcoholic father who didn't deserve it. That day, Frieda looked sideways at the camera, shy and unsure of her place in the world. On that farm.

Almost overnight each Stafford girl had grown into a beautiful quixotic creature, each in her own right a honey-skinned, long-haired, smoldering-eyed young woman. Each gorgeous as all get out, elegant despite their gangly limbs, smart and alert; they grew from knock-kneed giggle-monsters into cautious swans. Although each girl possessed an adult face on a little person's body, each also exuded something a bit netherworldly, neither here nor there, bone structure hinting of those as yet uncovered Indian-French-German roots. Yet they were simultaneously womanly, ripening as if their feet were roots in the black earth, filling out their skin like blueberries on a kind vine.

Phyllis Gayle got her breasts first, curved in places where she used to be straight as an ironing board. Velma Jean would be next. Then Lily Lee, last but not least. In contrast, Frieda had inexplicably started losing weight, her hip bones sticking out against her dress coat. She was a sad sack of bones next to the fleshy legs and arms of her sisters, but there was no jealousy, only caretaking and concern at the others' frustrated tears that boys and grown men had started looking at them differently and brushing up against them in dark corners. Especially the men in their family.

When they came of age, everyone told Clifford he needed five guns. One for each daughter.

"You gon' have a time with those girls."

He would, too. There would always be little nappy-headed boys sneaking around, someone else would joke. There would be lots of nappy-headed boys.

"Dem girls know how to shoot," he'd reply. They didn't. Lily wouldn't learn how to shoot until she was ten or eleven. Her cousin, Bill Stafford, taught her. Velma hunted deer and fished with her daddy but while she carried a shotgun, she never killed a deer. She could never bring herself to do it. Cliff never taught them how to shoot his double-barrel shotgun that rested on the gun rack above his bed.

Their father, unsmiling in the photograph, stood like an iron rod behind Velma Jean, as if he were pinching the back of her coat. With his hawk nose, broad forehead, and sharp cheeks, he could have been an Indian chief if he had on a war bonnet or his powwow bustle. Instead, he wore a white Stetson pushed almost too perfectly down to the right and a nylon jacket trimmed in black faux fur. Next to him was his wife and enemy, Dorothy Lucille Ruth Agnes Manuel Stafford. She looked tired, but still beamed with a too forgiving, too quiet, too soft smile.

Thick cotton scarves shielded all four girls' heads. They were bundled into wool coats against the driest brittle wind the land could brew up that the sun couldn't burn away. They were little versions of their bulky mother. The farm, the skinny leafless trees, and the Cadillac they stood in front of, pulsing with a hard black shine, seemed almost like props behind them.

Back inside the house, nothing stirred; the wood stove sat silent and cold, bare of birch or kindling or flame. Daddy Long Legs had already begun spiraling across the rooms in wide arcs, spewing sticky webs to catch lazy winter flies. The attic had already begun gathering dust that wouldn't move for two years. They were leaving that day, moving to Lansing for a job would bring in more money, Clifford said. "It's a new start. This construction job with Miller-Davis, building a new wing on to the Capitol, is going to bring in some good money." He always had some dumb fool cockamamie scheme that would make money, rather than steady, consistent employment.

"Don't you say nunya about nothing," he said to his girls. "If anybody ask you, we Mulatto. Don't tell anybody where we from. We ain't white. We ain't no goddamn Injun. And we ain't Black."

But they were everything.

Clifford's first chance at city living beckoned to him. Trying to raise five girls and be a farmer was harder than he thought. They were always hungry and he was always drunk. Maybe Lansing, the capital of Michigan, was it. The opportunities, the public transportation. No more driving his John Deere tractor, ripping the skin from the black earth. No more farm work, but honest city work instead. No more nosy neighbors on either side of him asking for some water, or a cup of sugar, but really spying on him and his failure.

They left the farm empty. Even though the water seeping from the weeping willow beckoned them to stay, the waiting seeds in the soil sprouted halfway, the deer in the forest stepped closer and barn owls gave warning hoots. Any Indian worth his salt would have listened. Would have heeded all the signs. Clifford had his mind made up; he wasn't into listening to the wind for shit, or watching for signs. He wasn't raised Indian or African; none of them were. Everyone would have to find their own way.

That was the last family photo they would ever take.

KATHERYN AND GEORGE Manuel, Dorothy's younger sister and brother, were somewhere behind the camera that frosty day in Mattawan. Katheryn's lips, in perfectly applied coral lipstick, were tight with disapproval. George's neck was tense but there was nothing he could do. Neither one had a lick of faith in the unfaithful Clifford or his beer-slurred promises. Both siblings shared a knowing look that life in Lansing would be no different from the miserable life their sister lived on that desolate farm. Clifford would drink most of what he earned.

Katheryn, wrapped in her sable, hands warm in her fur-lined gloves, the family's self-acclaimed Mulatto, probably sucked her teeth when the shutter finally snapped. Probably thinking, "They'll be up shit creek without a paddle soon enough and I will have to be the one to go get them." A hardworking woman who would never have a husband, she knew Clifford was just running away from his responsibilities. He didn't know how to farm. He didn't know how to take care of his family. He'd lost all his money gambling. He and Dorothy fought almost every night. They loved each other like bulls in heat. Katheryn was the only one brave enough to call him on his bullshit. Lansing had better streets, not the dirt roads of Mattawan, and excellent shopping—and yes, Katheryn loved to shop—but it would still be a bust for Clifford.

"For God's sake," she would advise Velma Jean and her sisters for years, "don't tell anyone you're a Stafford."

Katheryn didn't know anything about the well-to-do Staffords that once helped build and run Kalamazoo. She didn't know that the Staffords were probably related to the famed Enoch Harris, the man acclaimed for bringing apple seeds to the region. To her, Clifford was the capital A in jackass and an expert failure at everything he dipped his wick in, everything except for fathering girls. (And that probably pissed him off royally to no end—he couldn't even produce a proper boy.) *You are nothing but a mean drunk and a no-count womanizer*, Katheryn's eyes spat at him every time she got the chance.

Katheryn was the scorekeeper. She knew how he treated Dorothy and even suspected physical violence, though she never had proof. She was awakened every weekend by the pounding on the door at midnight. Clifford picked his girls up from their parents' house on the Northside; they'd waited like four hard sacks of potatoes on the Manuel floor. After Clifford left, Dorothy went to work to clean some white person's bed sheets and bed pans, or would sleep there to clean their house in the morning.

If drinking, he would make haste to disappear inside of the nearest bar in downtown Kalamazoo.

"That just ain't no way for the girls to live," Grandma Manuel would mutter under her breath, fussing in the small kitchen, opening and closing cabinets in search of food for the hungry girls.

One night when Clifford bumbled up the front porch to the girls, their limbs strewn across each other, mouths open, bodies sprawled under the dining room table near the heater, Dorothy's father, a frail, pale-skinned man, said, "Clifford, those girls need to be at home in their own bed."

Eyes bloodshot and cross, Clifford snarled and charged him. Grandpa Manuel skittered up the stairs to his bedroom. Clifford sputtered drunken words up the narrow hallway: "You don't tell me what to do with these girls. I know what I'm doing." He scooped the girls up and did the devil's speed home.

Another night Dorothy had decided to make Cliff take her and the girls with him to one of his haunts. What she thought she could accomplish from that trick was never revealed.

"We'll wait in the car," Dorothy told him. They waited and waited. The night air curled around their cold sleeping breath as the noise rose and fell when the bar's door swung open, then closed. And they waited.

"Why don't you go get him, Mama," little Lily whined. Finally Clifford exited, the orange glow of a cigarette splitting the night as he walked over and climbed in the truck, the smell of menthol Kools, booze, and the vibration of a jukebox on him. Dorothy yelled at him all the way home as he smoked the two a.m. road. Lily remembered glancing at the speedometer and seeing it reach one hundred and twenty. But maybe she was seeing things.

Velma didn't care. She needed to sleep.

SOMETIMES THE BEATINGS happened after school, or before breakfast. Cliff would already have his leather belt wrapped tightly around his knuckles when Velma walked through the door. "Did you do what your mother said?" Velma thought she had. She looked over at her pitiful, spiteful mother.

Velma nodded.

"Everything?" he repeated. Velma knew it didn't matter what she said and prepared herself for the blow. The belt fell on her sometimes before she could respond, sometimes after. Her shoulders, her back, her legs. She smelled the whiskey on her father's breath. Her mother's accusing, satisfied eye sat on her like a toad on her tongue, sometimes watching, sometimes walking away as Clifford raised and dropped the leather down on his daughter like she was a slave who'd tried to run. Out of all her sisters, Velma got the worst of it: Dorothy never protected her, ever. Not once. Velma's mother elaborated, lied, forged ahead with a scheme to keep her husband around the house and not nosing up another woman's skirt.

Velma was hard-headed today.

Velma wouldn't help me hang clothes. She needs a belt to her.

Velma cussed out the teacher today.

Dorothy sacrificed Velma in a sorry attempt to save her marriage before they left for Lansing, to make Cliff feel useful, like they were a mule team, but it was futile.

The other girls, Frieda, Mildred, Lily, and Phyllis, stood by or listened from the attic while the flogging took place. Mildred was gone. Phyllis would gloat until she heard tired whimpering. Lily would cry softly for her sister. And poor Velma was often left to crawl up the attic stairs, bruised, with welts the size of a grown man's fist.

Maybe her father was thinking of his own childhood, back to his father, who had a handlebar moustache and lacerated Clifford within an inch of his life almost nightly. Clifford's mother, Caledonia, threw herself like a bear rug over her son's body to save him time and time again. Because his father called him "weak" and a "runt," Clifford learned to hate any signs of weakness and punished you for it.

Velma wasn't weak, she was just a sweet girl, innocent.

Clifford was simply continuing the cycle he'd learned.

And because it was what she knew, when my mother had her own kids, she dug out the extension cord, a utility rope, a belt, a broom, a hanger, a shoe, and taught us our lesson. She was her father's daughter after all, and knew those kinds of whippings, skin-left-to-blister beatings, were what it took to make a child act right. Discipline was what a child needed and you couldn't convince her any differently.

"My childhood was shit," Mama would snap when I first started questioning her about life on that farm.

That's when I realized my mother had been grieving her entire life.

14

Frieda's Dream

"What is the use of a book, without pictures or conversations?"
—Alice in Wonderland

LANSING TURNED OUT to be hell.

They lived in an apartment. Instead of the wide open space, the woods and cornfields, they played in a concrete backyard. Instead of the natural spring, they drank water out of a faucet. They heard cars and people at night rather than the crickets and bullfrogs. Everything was new and strange and citified.

The apartment they moved into was in a shoddy boarding house; they shared one bathroom with the other tenants. The girls were crowded like eggs in a basket in one small room with walls so thin their octogenarian housemates would bang on them when they giggled or farted too loudly.

"Girls, shut up that damn noise," Clifford whispered loudly.

And then one month later, Frieda started running into walls.

A few months before they'd moved, Frieda had an accident on the playground outside Moore School in Mattawan. It happened under the jumbled songs of the children running and playing. The wind had pelted Lily's face as she clung to the merry-go-round despite the knot of fear that sat on her chest like a boot.

"Frieda, look, I'm doing it! I'm not afraid."

Little Lily's teeth gleamed as she grinned and turned to find her big sister, Frieda, who would smile when she saw how brave Lily was, playing with the big kids without being afraid of getting dizzy and tumbling off into the autumn leaves. Frieda was more than Lily's favorite sister, she was her caretaker and mother. It was Frieda, not their mother, who braided Lily's hair in the mornings before school. Frieda made sure skinny Lily had had enough to eat at breakfast, lunch, and dinner. Frieda gave her baths and put her to bed. Frieda was the one who told her "Good job."

That day on the playground, Lily knew she'd get a wave and a smile from Frieda that would make her all warm and buttery sweet like cinnamon toast. But Frieda's eyebrows were concentrating on the hopscotch game. Graceful and poised on one foot, she looked like one of those gazelles in the picture books about nature that their mean teacher let Lily look at but not hold (and even then, only quickly). The merry-go-round was slowing. Proud of herself, Lily slipped off, pausing to see what she should do next, but then it happened. Lily glanced over just as Frieda tossed her chalk into the next box and jumped. Somehow the next step sent Frieda flying, her cream-colored bobby socks up over her head. Frieda was falling.

"Frieda," Lily yelled. Her sister's waif back and then her head connected with the concrete, banging solidly down like a hammer trying to meet a nail, clean and swift. Later that night, Frieda made Lily pull a stool up to her backside and touch peroxide on the fleshy spot in the back of her head with a cotton ball. Lily wanted to cry because it was gushy. She wanted to run and tell her mother. It didn't feel right that there was a hole in her sister's head. "Don't bother Mama and Daddy with this," Frieda shushed her. Mother was being spiteful again to Daddy on account of he'd been out drinking all night. They fought all the time.

"Let's tell Mama, Frieda," Lily whined.

"It'll be alright," Frieda said. "It'll be fine. Everything's going to be okay."

Lily had kept her sister's secret.

In Lansing, the girls thought it was a game when Frieda started colliding into doors. They teased her when her pretty head lolled to one side as she walked, and one of her eyes started rolling back and up in her head to show the whites. Unknown to them, her vision had begun to blur. "Ahh, here comes the monster," they screamed and squealed. They thought it was a game. Frieda played along. Their neighbors would bang on the walls for quiet.

A few weeks later, Frieda, thirteen, was admitted to the University of Michigan Hospital in Ann Arbor, one of the best cancer hospitals in the country.

She never came home.

To the girls, one day Frieda was there. The next day she was just gone. The land had called her home. It was probably the fall that caused it; the untreated concussion had turned cancerous. Frieda had developed a brain tumor, and like that, she was laid in the earth. What happened next was the surreal ending to the fable of the Black Indian Mattawan fairies.

"It's all your fault," Dorothy blamed Cliff at the hospital. "We should never have left Mattawan."

In truth, the unfolding was already happening. No one could have stopped it. Dorothy blamed Clifford for everything anyway, but especially for Frieda's death.

There were five sisters in the attic, then four, and when Mildred eloped, three.

Dorothy and Clifford argued, pans thrown, doors slammed, cold silence, until one day they weren't human anymore. They woke up and went to bed exhausted, eaten up with bitter hurt. They woke up worn out, beaten up, skin loose against their bones like balloons that had been blown up and emptied, blown up and emptied, used over and over again until they popped.

Frieda had been Katheryn's favorite niece, her first niece: Katheryn was devastated by her death and never forgave Clifford.

Every chance she'd get, Katheryn would remind him of it; so would Dorothy. Clifford responded by staying away as much as he could. He stalked the inside of a bottle faithfully. He crawled to club after club apparently hunting for and finding acceptance and redemption in the arms of every other woman, both citified ones as well as the country bumpkins.

After a string of failed bright ideas and attempts to take care of their family, Dorothy had lost faith in Clifford; but really, Cliff had lost faith in himself. My grandfather had one last Frankenstein idea, though. He wanted to donate Frieda's brain and her organs to science so this mysterious tumor that had developed could be detected in other kids. That was the last straw for Dorothy.

"Are you out of your cotton-picking mind?" Dorothy yelled in the hospital lounge. "Is this just another one of your stupid schemes to get some drinking money?"

Katheryn drove to Ann Arbor from Kalamazoo to give him more hell: "You ruined my sister's life and now you want to let them do this to her child?"

Maybe he had suddenly developed a kind bone in his body, but Dorothy wouldn't listen to him anymore. It was over long before the words were said. One night when they were visiting Mildred in South Haven, and the adults went out to drink, Cliff's woman showed up at the bar. Cliff and Dorothy came back to the house and woke the girls with their arguing. "Daddy said he was leaving us and couldn't stay. And he left us," my Aunt Lily said later.

He probably didn't remove his hat. He didn't have to point out the ever-expanding roll of fat around Dorothy's stomach, making her look like a juicy pear. He didn't have to insult her cooking or anything. He just left.

Later, Dorothy, Lily, Phyllis, and Velma moved in with Mildred for a time, arriving in South Haven like marooned sailors.

"How long are y'all staying, Mama?" Mildred asked slowly. A year after her marriage, with one kid and pregnant, she talked as if she were measuring the words as they came out of her mouth; her prescription pills for postpartum depression mixed with Miller beer she gulped down every few hours to slow the entire world down. Mildred was only twenty-three or twenty-four.

"Where do we put our stuff?" Dorothy ignored her step-daughter's question.

Mildred, the daughter from Clifford's first failed marriage, knew her father was a drunk and womanizer; she also knew Dorothy still loved him. Her wounded face said it. The way she kept her clothes folded neatly in the brown suitcase for weeks said she expected Clifford to come get her, if not the girls, at any moment.

"Did Daddy drink up all your grocery money?" Mildred asked as she tucked Velma and Lily in the narrow cot in little Timmy's room. Her son's room was small but big enough for the three of them. "I can't feed everybody."

Dorothy climbed heavily in the boy's bed, which creaked under her weight. She was always so tired lately.

"We got money." Dorothy closed her eyes and went to sleep.

Did Dorothy dream of Don Harris? He was the neighbor who lived down the street from the farm and he loved Dorothy for years, his heart howling for her like she was the swamp moon. He was Grandpa Stafford's old drinking buddy, but over the years he grew angry with how Clifford treated his wife: a woman deserved better, Don thought. He might have told her as much when he gave her rides to her housekeeping jobs in Kalamazoo. Sometimes, like a good man, he'd wait and bring her home. Clifford made Dorothy take the bus. Don's was a patient, undeclared love that came out like night blossoms and folded up in the daylight. He loved Dorothy's fleshy thighs, her forearms that jiggled with too much skin when she pointed at something. He loved her wide calves and breasts that sank to her stomach.

But even after he left her, she let Clifford back in for midnight sex whenever he wanted, like she was one of his side women and not his estranged wife. Sometimes, in Lansing and South Haven, when the girls were sleeping, he'd slip in and out before the dew disappeared on the grass.

Dorothy either didn't see or didn't care about the damage she was inflicting on the girls by letting them be witnesses to their horrible warbling, the fights, and their dad's cheating. Why put the girls through it, sucking in the ether of their battles and taunts and the fumes of angry, whiskey-tinged breath? Don't women know abuse when they see it? Feel it? Don't we? Do we? It's the old story of love, isn't it? No matter what age or generation, that heart, the strongest muscle in our body, ruins our capacity to run, to fill our air with lungs and just lunge out of the way of a coming train, of a failing marriage, of an absurd life, of self-destruction.

Cliff's presence pulled my mother and her sisters down, inside out, molding them into women who would survive every winter of their mounted lives. Exactly what was it that held them there, in warped relationships, on the back roads of Mattawan, in the smaller townships like Covert, in Ypsilanti, in Pullman, and in those cities, Kalamazoo, Three Rivers, Battle Creek—the land or themselves, the choices they made or the men they loved? Their father or their mother?

My mother and my aunts' relationships with men began with their father. Listening to their stories, I knew they were daughters of a thunderstorm man. When he came home bleary-eyed after nights of drinking, his rage shook them like tipis in a storm as they slept. Feminine limbs entrenched in the black earth, heads ducked under, the Stafford girls grew like the weeping willows. When their father fought with their docile mother, lifted his fists, hollered and stomped on the plywood floors, they bent into the storm's path instead of turning away. They were children. What choice did they have?

After everything that had happened to them, to her, my grandmother turned around and treated my mother like shit for sale.

There were no stars in the Mattawan sky then.

15

Broken Treaties

WHEN SHE WOKE up nearly every morning, before she could wipe the crusty sleep out of her eyes, John A. seemed to be waiting, conspicuously passing her in the hallway on her way to the bathroom.

"Hey, Velma," John A. said with a creepy wink and a crooked, knowing smirk. He was no longer a skinny boy. He'd filled out within the year of marrying Mildred.

"Hi," my mother said, without smiling back.

"Lily, let's go play," Velma would call cautiously.

"K." Lily screamed from somewhere in the house, unknowingly the protector of her sister.

"Finish your chores before you go running off," Mildred said. Velma, who had grown to distrust her eldest sister, kicked a chair.

"I ain't got to do nothing but stay Black and die," Velma said under her breath.

"What?" Dorothy called from her bedroom. "Velma, you sassin'?"

"No ma'am." Velma went to the kitchen, ate cold eggs and toast, then started washing dishes.

After Frieda's funeral, her tiny grave a slender hole in Alameda Cemetery next to the larger graves, Velma's life went the way of a Brothers Grimm tale. That summer after Lily finished third grade, South Haven, a sleepy resort town on Lake Michigan, became their home. As much as Lansing ended their childhood, South Haven was the beginning of the end of everything else.

John A. had turned into a mean, secretive drunk who slapped and punched Mildred on the regular. Both alcoholics, they argued all the time. Unhappily, Mildred was having babies back to back.

She rarely left her dim bedroom because she was always sick with something, pregnant or drunk. Mildred's once alabaster complexion was now washed out and sallow as a dead rainbow trout. The house was in shambles. No food in the cupboards. The kitchen sink was always piled high with dirty dishes and the floors were junky with clothes and trash and scuffed with black boot marks.

"Ugh," the girls said when they first got there.

Mildred's badass babies ran roughshod over everyone, wild as billy goats. Mildred, fragile as a newborn in her mind, grinned: "Sorry the house is so messy." Timid like her mother, but a drunk like her father, Mildred didn't have a clue about how to be a mother or a wife. Apparently, Mildred had always had Problems.

At fourteen, Mildred had disappeared from the farm. One day she'd been there, the next day she and a few changes of clothing were gone. She'd eloped to escape her father, her passive-aggressive mother, and that sinking farm by running away with an older man who, as the story goes, tricked her and tried to prostitute her on the streets of some unknown town in Florida. When Mildred realized what he had in mind, she'd gathered the courage to call home. No one ever knew if she'd actually gone through with any of it. Or what he'd done to her.

"I want to come home," she'd said into the payphone she'd finally been able to sneak and use.

"She made her way there, goddamnit," Clifford said, probably letting loose a cheek full of watery black snuff against a rock. "She could make her own way back."

Dorothy, Mildred's mother, and Grandma Helen Manuel determinedly scraped their floor-washing and sewing money together and bought Mildred a one-way Greyhound bus ticket back to Mattawan. Mildred said her thanks but didn't stay long. This time her suitor, young John A. Cloud, showed up one afternoon. He was lanky, brown-skinned, and a fool, but he wanted Mildred.

That day, Mildred's second fiancé-to-be walked nervously down the gravel driveway toward where Cliff was chopping wood by the side of the house. He was supposed to be a grown man, but he was still a kid.

"Sir," John A. said after a fidgety pause. "I come to ask for Mildred's hand in marriage."

Wrangling his hat between his hands, the insides pigeon-tongue pink, the outsides smooth-haystack tan, John A. waited. The axe rose and fell two, maybe three more times. Lily and Velma were looking out the window, their eyes glued to their father's wiry, stained back, the work drenching his backside.

Cliff put another log on the chopping block. The axe wrestled the wind from its sides and landed, splitting dead center at the heart of the wood, cutting the tie that bound him to a daughter who was sullied and wise in more conjugal ways than he could live with. He couldn't stand to be in the same room with Mildred, spat every time he saw her.

Finally, Cliff rose and let loose a wad of black juice near John A.'s feet.

"Well, somebody's got to marry the bitch. Fuck if I care."

"Thank you, sir." John A. turned and walked away quickly, blessing in hand.

"I don't want you going nowhere near that damn heifer, you hear me?" he ordered Dorothy.

Dorothy snuck over to see Mildred every chance she could. Clifford Stafford remained a passive totem pole, not blinking when Mildred frantically honked the horn on her marriage day. He refused to attend her shotgun wedding. For almost a year, she honked her horn every time she passed the farm on her way to and from her little house in South Haven, only thirty-five or so miles down the road near Lake Michigan. It wasn't until Mildred birthed a son and named him after her daddy that Clifford thawed and directed his old green truck toward her house. As if none of the rest had ever happened. As if this was how forgiveness looked.

"WHERE'S PHYLLIS AND Lily?" their mama was always saying in South Haven.

"They prolly at the beach," Velma said. "Mama, can I go?"

"No, you got chores."

"Why I got more chores than everybody?"

Nobody could answer that. That summer they lived there, while Velma always got stuck watching Mildred's kids all day (somehow her life had become about taking care of people, though no one, she always said bitterly years later, ever took care of her), it was the happiest of times for Lily.

She could be a kid with no one really paying attention to her. Her mother was depressed and rarely left the house if she wasn't cleaning someone's home in Kalamazoo. The heavy, musky scent of Lake Michigan's pendulous body was always in the air. Lily was free. *Free.* No drunken daddy to hide from, to gauge if he was too drunk to kiss good morning. No arguments thumping up and down the attic stairs when Lily waited for him to come home nights, listening for his car to drive up and compress the gravel beneath its weight, no waiting for her mother to pounce. The only thing that made Lily sad was thinking about Frieda; she didn't have her Frieda, her keeper, her sister to brush and braid her hair or watch over her anymore. Frieda was more of a mother to Lily than her real mother ever pretended to be. In contrast to how neglect transformed Lily's life, Velma was an indentured servant, imprisoned in Mildred's constantly filthy house.

"Velma, wash the dishes," someone would call from their room.

"Velma, change the baby's diaper."

"Velma, go to the store and get me some milk."

At dawn, Velma began her day's chores. It was like she'd never left the farm. Only here, she was the solo worker bee. *This isn't fair*, she thought, but what choice did she have? She did want to be helpful, but she never got to play. She slammed the dishes around like a war was happening in the small dingy kitchen. Meanwhile, Lily finished her chores quickly and left the house before anyone could make her do something else. She explored South Haven's beaches on the northeast end of Lake Michigan, and beat a regular path around their neighborhood, searching for pop bottles to cash in and loose change in the streets, so she could eat during the day and never go home.

Even though Dorothy was her blood mother and Mildred was her half sister, they both treated Velma like a Black Indian Cinderella. At thirteen in 1954, pre–Civil Rights, Velma was a live-in slave-in-training for her own miserable slave life. Under the firm orders of her mother, who'd never had a lick of mothering skills to pass on, Velma became a surrogate mother to Mildred's pack of kids: Timmy, Clifford, Walt, and Vivianne. Where was Mildred? Sleeping, drugged up, or drunk. Where was their father? Working or out with his friends.

While Velma became the house drudge, and Lily the escape artist, Phyllis discovered boys. Phyllis decided she was as beautiful as the boys in the neighborhood told her and began to provide retribution in the form of all sorts of sexual favors. She was a horse chomping at the bit. Fourteen, shiny as a dew drop, and free from her evil father. She was a Mixed blood, redbone, high yellow, whatever any man called her out of his car window. She and her sisters were rare oddities, American Indian princesses in a sea of white foam. Few dark-skinned Black kids went to their school. She and her sisters' and cousins' faces stuck out of classroom pictures like soft yellow dots. Called half-breeds in a fight, they were permanently kissed by the sun. The other children, white and black kids of South Haven and Paw Paw, tortured Phyllis because she was beautiful, but she didn't care. Her confidence soared each time she finally found someone to love her, and then, after each boy disappointed her, her self-worth crashed. Then she'd find another boy, give him what he wanted, and he was gone. Already angry and depressed, Phyllis started running with the rowdy South Haven kids, disappearing from school and never coming home for supper. Dorothy had no control over her.

Sometimes at night, Dorothy walked up and down the streets of their neighborhood, looking for Phyllis, and saying to her other daughters, "What did I do to deserve this kind of daughter?"

The girls would look at each other.

"Phyllis," Dorothy pleaded at the top of her lungs as she roamed the quiet, darkened streets. "Phyllis, come home, please. Come home."

Velma and Lily hated being dragged along. Embarrassed, they cringed with each call of her sister's name, a beckoning for what was already lost.

Phyllis wasn't thinking about her Mama. Or going back to Mildred's house, to those squalling kids and lecherous drunk John A. No sir. Phyllis's daddy, the once all-powerful warden in her life who had prevented her from experiencing anything good, was gone. Like Lily, Phyllis had found a kind of freedom, but it killed something in her to be the town's strawberry, easy pickings.

"I'm home," Phyllis said, exasperated. Hands on hip. Sassy, smeared lipstick on her beautiful face. No longer a virgin. No one was going to treat her like she was worthless. "I'm here, now what?" she sneered. Her mother cried quietly and threatened to tell her father. Phyllis laughed. She refused to be like her weak, pitiful mother, a loser wife. Dorothy couldn't even keep an abusive drunk like her father. What made her mother think she could control her, her defiant posture said; her newly developed voluptuous body screamed, "touch me."

Phyllis got pregnant at fifteen, married, and moved to South Haven and into her own legally sanctioned abusive relationship: her own personal hell.

ONE DAY, VELMA found her mother, Mildred, and John A. whispering in the living room. Dorothy, who'd gained even more weight after the separation and her daughter's death, was depressed, listless. Her hair was falling out. In all fairness, Dorothy was probably a little crazy and suffering from acute emotional duress and clinical depression, but Black women had no recourse for mental health back then.

When she saw Velma, Dorothy heaved herself up from the couch.

"Well," Dorothy said. "We're moving back to the farm. Just me and Lily. Velma, you're going to stay here and help Mildred with these kids."

"What, Mama? I don't have to, right?" Velma thought she hadn't heard correctly. "Not me. I don't want to stay here."

The look on Velma's pixie sweet face, panic, horror, and disbelief, squared her jaw more firmly, becoming hatred. How could her mother just leave, after Velma had been working so hard, after everything they had all been through? Her eyes narrowed in a white line of rage at Mildred, who she knew had just been harassing Dorothy to leave her there to help clean and babysit. No one had asked Velma. Children didn't get to have opinions in that family: they got orders like any soldier and were expected to obey.

"Mama, I ain't staying here."

"Don't you sass me, girl," her mother huffed, tired.

"You don't want to stay with me," Mildred smiled. "It will be fun."

"Shut up!" Velma screamed. "No. No."

Mildred had turned into a lazy, sloppy drunk like her father and was allowing life to pass her by in one glossy flicker. She had gotten married much too young and had no role model to orchestrate a happy married life; she had no tools to work it out. John A. was kicking her ass on the regular.

But Velma couldn't articulate any of this.

"I hate it here," Velma yelled. "I hate it."

Velma had never told anyone about John A. staring at her and rubbing up against her when he thought no one was looking. He leered at her all summer long, sometimes groping her in the kitchen when she unpacked the groceries. Was always sneaking peeks when she was undressing or using the bathroom.

"Mama, I'll be good. I promise," Velma begged. Any child who loved their mother would have begged.

"Mildred just need a little help. Velma, don't be so selfish."

It was decided. Velma would watch the kids when needed; Mildred would go to work during the day, and sleep and drink all night.

"Ain't no nese for you to get all riled," Dorothy said. "You just gone stay and help your sister for a little while. Don't look at me like that or I'ma snatch a knot in yo' ass."

The first week after Dorothy left, John A. watched Velma like a dog in heat. She knew she was going to be Mildred's slave. She didn't know what John A. and all his leering meant.

The terror crept up Velma Jean's throat like a horde of yellow jackets, their wings and black bodies suffocating her, cutting off her ability to breathe, to talk, to tell someone. He started fondling her every chance he got. Velma tried hard to stay out of the house unless Mildred was sober.

What could Velma do; what could she say. In 1953, there were no laws against a stepbrother groping a girl. She didn't have anywhere to go or anyone to run to. This was her own flesh and blood, her mother, enslaving her. What was left of her faith in her mother evaporated as neatly as if it had never been.

Velma's mother did not want her. That was a fact.

Velma always felt that everyone was against her anyway. When my grandmother gave my mother to Mildred's sorry, alcoholic ass with four rock-headed babies and a husband who touched her, pinched her breasts, brushed against her every chance he got, it felt like a furious tornado had swallowed her up and deposited her on the shores at the end of the world.

When I was a child with the worst kind of chronic bronchitis, my mother would rub Vicks on my skinny chest and back, easing away the wheeze that almost killed me at least three times. As I hacked like a horse, she sang in a low, soft, trembling voice:

"Swing low, sweet chariot, coming for to carry me home,
swing low, sweet chariot, coming for to carry me home."

I was so grateful, never stopping to wonder how she came to this tune. A slave song turned plantation prayer, signifying escape to those slaves who wanted to go. Those who could go.

My mother took care of me like that, healing me with her hands, with this song, and I lived. Who had ever healed her? And the song, did it save her from killing herself to escape her misery? Was it an echo from the Trail her Black and red ancestors might have been on? Content to be alive and in her lap, I squeezed air out of my lungs. The skin on my nose was fire; I'd blown it too much. Still, she hummed and hummed. I drifted off to a disquieted sleep.

This is the first song of my memory. This is the first memory of my mother's love. It is a kind of heirloom I keep tucked away deep in me, under my blouse: a memory of our survival.

16

Bloodletting

A FEW DAYS after Dorothy, Lily, and Phyllis left, Velma stole a pack of razors.

When she was alone in the room she used to share with her mother and Lily, Velma started cutting herself. The knife felt good against her skin. And when the other thing happened, when she cut her forearms and stomach and legs, and watched the juicy red of herself leak out, she could forget that other thing too.

At school, an eighth grader, she slouched in her chair and stared out the window, listless. Her hair was never combed anymore. She smelled bad: she didn't take showers anymore. Her boyfriend, John Cloud, a nice boy the color of a good cup of coffee with a dollop of milk, tried to hold her hand after school and kiss her like they used to do. Not knowing their puppy love was an anchor on the ocean floor, he adored his buttercup-skinned Mattawan fairy, even if her eyes held the sound of weeping willows. She pushed him back.

"What's the matter, Velma?" John said, hurt. He fingered their initials carved on a maple tree: VJS + JC encased in a crooked heart.

"I hate this place, those dumbass teachers," she said, hardening before his eyes. Mouth clamped up tight like a knot on her face, she spat on the ground like her father. "Shit, I hate everything."

She didn't feel shy and buttery on the inside anymore with him. John was, after all, a cousin of John A.'s, and she hated the elder John deeply.

The next week, Velma started letting Junior Bynum, a brass-colored handsome boy, a luckless bully, a nearly illiterate loud-mouth and a known cheat, walk her home.

John was crushed but he stopped bothering Velma. He faded into the background.

"Y'all together?" one of her friends asked that week.

"Why you want to know?" Velma balled up her fist, ready to fight. Every other day she started fights with other girls over her new boyfriend. She fought with her former friends, classmates, enemies, anyone she suspected of attempting to take Junior Bynum from her. She was always ready to fight now.

Junior Bynum fed the self-hate in her, and the small knife she kept under the bed helped her release it. Sometimes she'd cut once, quickly, before going to school, or at night just before she slept, but depending on what had happened that day at school or at home, she might slice three or four lines into her skin. The relief was immediate: it was something she could control.

When her suspensions ended, she'd be right back at school, because it was better than staying home. She always hated school, she told me years later. But she hated John A.'s hands on her body more.

Velma was twelve going on thirteen when John A. Cloud and his friend raped her in her sister's house. In the house where her mother had discarded her like an old shoe. She'd been a virgin. My mother, a young girl, on the cusp of her womanhood, knowing her mother didn't want her. No one wanted her. And then after John A. raped her, she knew it for certain.

"You bet not tell nobody neither," John A. had spit at her. And then she was no longer twelve, but a two-hundred-and-fifty-thousand-year-old wound.

Her body was a scar.

Maybe when the ringing stopped in her ears, she rose from the bed or floor or couch. She closed her blouse, smoothed her skirt or buttoned shorts. When she walked out of Mildred's house, letting the screen door slam, and turned down the busy street, the sounds of the cars shutting out the memory of the creaking door opening, which had woken her from sleep. Maybe she'd only planned to walk to the corner, the movement of her skinny, wet legs jolting out the memory of the dim room or the rough, salty hand, then a dirty sock gagging her. Hands pinning her.

I want to go home, she'd thought she'd said through the vomit and the pain and the strange, sour smell emitting from between her legs. Where was her sister? Where was Mildred?

She didn't know she'd continued past the corner store, but she kept walking, and found herself curving along a sidewalk toward M-43, ignoring the memory of nervous male laughter, hands choking, maybe massaging her underdeveloped chest. She kept down this road, which was a straight shot to the farm. It was the only road she knew like the back of her hand.

Placing one patent-leather shoe in front of the other, maybe Velma thought her mother had changed her mind and would let her come back home. If she told what had happened, then her mother would have to change her mind. Right? The setting sun's rays smoked in and out of the shadows of clouds. Smell of cows standing in their manure made her wretch several times. John A.'s face, and then a stranger's, his friend, pressed close to hers. She wouldn't cry; she wouldn't cry. She didn't know she was already crying.

How could she be still a little girl yet as old as the ground beneath her feet?

She'd be good, Velma thought, walking faster toward home. She would. She'd promise to her mother. Velma heard the night owls sailing over her and pushed on, thirsty, but not tired. She'd never sleep again. The bareness of her legs embarrassed her now, since John A. had pried her open like a vise there, and maybe the passing cars couldn't see so much in the dusk, that her neck and shoulders were bruised purple (because she'd bruised easily all her life), but Velma would rather be beaten by her father or blamed for everything by her mother than live one more day in Mildred's house, in reach of those hands that had pinned her to the bed.

And like her ancestors, she walked. Her steps away from that house reopened the cracks in the earth from North Carolina to Mattawan. Every trail that had been walked on, carrying every Indian, every African, every triracial woman who had been raped because they could be raped. By kin or stranger or master.

She kept walking, unaware if it was night or day, cold or wet. What month it was. What did she have on: a dress, shorts, her favorite pair of ankle-high pants? It might have been just after dusk, cool, windy even, by the time she started off, not a lot of cars on the road, and her dry patches, their fluids, streaking down her leg even though she'd tried to clean herself when they left her in the room alone. The sky, if it was fall, would have burned a fresh cotton blue folding into dark swamp blue, and if the snow was just melting, the sky would be the color of wet ash, and she, unknowingly, was probably witnessing the same changing of seasons that the Potawatomi or the Taw-wa had seen when they migrated to Mattawan from Wisconsin in the 1740s.

And because her body was a scar, because she'd been ripped open like a pig hanging from a spit on a tree, fresh off the chopping block, Velma could smell everything; how rivers formed and flowed, where the mud met the bank and chilled. The hay in the spring fields. Like the very first inhabitants of Michi-gama, the first Indian mound dwellers, she felt the trees sway as if they were inside her, yet watching her, allowing her safe passage. Finally she could smell the natural spring of her father's farm, pure and clean.

Pure and clean.

It had been miles and miles, maybe ten or fifteen, but Velma saw the giant weeping willows from far off down the street. Their branches swayed, applauding her courage. They would hold her; they'd welcome her home. Sweaty and out of breath, she walked directly to the artesian pond next to the bait house. She grabbed the blue camper cup that hung on a rusty nail on the willow bark, above the cold pipe, and drank deeply, wiping the hair out of her eyes.

Velma kept going. She walked all the way to the small apartment where her mother now lived in Kalamazoo. Dorothy was so angry she called Cliff. When Cliff showed up he went off, accusing Velma of running away.

"What in tarnation are you doing here, gal?" her father yelled when he saw her. He spit snuff he'd had lodged in his jaw and pulled on his suspenders over his long johns.

"What the hell is wrong with you, Velma," her mother yelled.

What the hell is wrong with me, Velma thought: hate, confusion, hot tears in her fourteen-year-old eyes. *You left me to die in that house, with that man.*

This was the mother who had raised her in church, had oiled and combed her hair to be presentable. Didn't her mother love her? Didn't her mother see the pain Velma was in?

"Velma, get yo' narrow ass in the car," her mother swatted her bottom. "Everybody was worried sick when you ran away."

Ran away? Escaped. Her mother could not see her daughter's body was a scar.

"You scared your sisters and your mother," her father said.

Although Clifford didn't live with them anymore, he often came around at odd hours of the night like a dog sniffing out old territory.

Then John A. showed up. Who called him, Velma never knew, but with a nod from Cliff, John A. beat Velma in front of everybody.

"*Get* yo' ass in this car," John A. said.

They dragged Velma to the car, tossed her in, and drove her right back to Mildred. Right back to John A.

A few weeks later, Dorothy moved Lily and Phyllis back to the farm in Mattawan. When Velma was allowed to come back, she was strangely quiet. The day started out fine, a nice visit with food and catching up.

"Let's go watch TV at the Harrises' house, Mama," Velma said out of the blue. "That would be fun, wouldn't it Lily?"

Lily jumped up and down, clapping her hands. Watching TV was always fun, especially since they didn't have one. Velma, Dorothy, and Lily walked slowly along the side of the road, smelling the black earth and water flowing beneath it. They made it to Don Harris's without mishap. It was dark outside, but Dorothy and Don had feelings for each other, so getting her to take that trip hadn't been hard. While everyone was engrossed in some program, probably *The Ed Sullivan Show*, Velma jumped up.

"Oh, I forgot something at the house. I'll be right back." She stepped outside in the cool summer's dark, making the crickets pause in their lovemaking or play, only to have Lily slam into her back. "I want to go with you too."

"I'll only be a minute," Velma said. "Just stay here."

"I want to go." Lily sang. "I want to go, I want to go." She'd missed her sister.

"Just take her, Velma," their mother called. "And hurry up."

When they got to the house, Lily went looking for a toy she wanted to take back to show one of Don Patterson's sons, but when she returned, she saw Velma striking matches and throwing them in the wood bin of the shed that was connected to the house.

"Velma, what are you doing?" Lily remembered asking.

"Come on." Velma snatched Lily's arm and started dragging her back down to Don Patterson's house. But Lily skidded into the living room, blurting out, "Mama, Velma done put the house on fire." They all ran back to put out the fire, which hadn't quite caught yet, but Velma's message got out.

She was going to burn down something.

Her mother's house, her safety net, something. Why not? No one cared about her anyway. Velma meant to destroy something. That week, Velma was taken to see a child psychologist and subsequently put on antidepressants. The doctor discovered the scars on Velma's arm in his examination Lily remembered seeing a deep gash on her sister's stomach, ugly and red, that made her cry. They thought Velma was hurting herself for attention. But she was trying to make herself ugly, unattractive to John A. and the other boys who approached her, made suggestive remarks, caught her alone and touched her without her permission. Maybe, instinctively, she was attempting to get away from Junior Bynum.

"Lily," Dorothy warned, "don't bother Velma because she wasn't feeling well." Stupidly, Dorothy refused to see what Velma really needed was help. She needed to be back home with her mother. Velma needed to feel wanted by her family. Why did Phyllis and Lily get to live at home, but she had to be the live-in slave?

But Velma endured. She stayed on antidepressants for a year until she got pregnant and married at fifteen, having her first baby at sixteen.

She had learned that there were no good monsters.

There were only monsters.

17

Indian Holocaust

"I'M GETTING MARRIED." Velma told Lily before she told her mother. Then Lily ran and told her mother. They started planning, but a wedding never took place.

Velma escaped her drudge's life with Mildred another way. A few years later, having barely turned fifteen in 1959, she got pregnant and married Junior Bynum (Loren Robert Henry). Everyone called him either Junior or Junior Bynum to distinguish him from his father, whom we called Big Daddy, because he was nearly as big as two men in his farmer's blue jean overalls. In contrast, Junior Bynum was so skinny you could see his Adam's apple before you saw him. Velma's second child, Loren, was a spitting image of his father, and she would make little Loren pay for that unavoidable biological slight.

Just married, Velma didn't know if she would be happy; in fact, she didn't know what happy looked like anymore. She just wanted to get the hell up out of South Haven and away from John A., those damn kids, and her beer-guzzling sister. But marrying Junior Bynum was one of the worst mistakes of Velma's life.

Junior Bynum was for my mother what Hitler had been for Europe.

They moved with his family to Oshtemo, a small township a few miles away from South Haven, located down a barely visible backroad on the way to Alameda, near where the family cemetery waited for her. Called to her. All her ancestors' bones said no, not yet. But still, Velma wondered, would it be peaceful? When would she and her sisters be at peace?

Velma now lived about fifteen minutes from my grandfather's farm, but he rarely came to see any of the children. Grandpa Stafford especially hated Velma's new husband: "That cocky bastard grin too much," he said, but really Junior Bynum reminded my grandfather of a more terrible version of himself.

"We know how to handle our women, yes sir," Big Daddy gave his son a hard smack on the back of his bony head. A love tap. Junior Bynum nodded. He came from a family of men who "handled" their women. Big Daddy and Junior Bynum's uncles thrashed their girlfriends, wives, and kids like slaves. The Bynum family had a reputation for having packs of children who worked their land like sharecroppers and who were always collectively dirt poor. Beating women was all Junior Bynum knew. It was a social and cultural disease, an inheritance of domestic abuse. At that time, no one knew what to call it, so "handled" would have to do.

Junior Bynum wasn't only an escape for my mother, he was her revenge on her parents. *Look, Daddy, I'm having sex,* her life screamed. Besides, if she married, someone would take care of her, she reasoned, someone would treat her better than her father had treated her. She was pregnant with his child anyway; he had to love her.

Junior didn't have to do anything for her but stay Black and die.

He drank and fought indiscriminately, at the drop of a hat. He was cruel at times, insulting her about her clothes or her cooking abilities or lack thereof, but there was something tender about him in the beginning, something charming and seductive about his yellow skin, thick lips, and slow eyes. Something kept her there besides his threats to kill her if she ever left him.

I have never asked my mother about the first time she remembered Junior Bynum hitting her and what that felt like. Were they still in middle school or was it just after the marriage? Was it before or after the first child, Bobbie Ann, was born? What exactly made her feel worthless enough to ignore that first or second swack? Also, I always wondered what made a man one day decide to hit his woman, and if wasn't a decision but just an impulse, what made him do it again and again like it was a game, until her blood leaked out of her like bug juice?

Once when Bobbie Ann was five, she heard someone cry out. She crept to her mother and father's bedroom and pushed the door open to catch him slapping Mama repeatedly in her face, shaking her like a rag doll. The TV was on, loud and fuzzy, exuding an ethereal sixties blue, and for a moment Bobbie Ann didn't know what was real and what wasn't.

"Daddy?" Bobbie saw his hand rising and falling. Her mother was somewhere in that dark room.

Junior Bynum turned when he saw her little fingers and eyes curled around the door casing, and he yelled at her, "Get out of here, Bobbie Ann." Junior Bynum's mother, hiding somewhere in the house, must have heard them tussling, but she didn't interfere with her son's business, just like no one interfered with the whippings she herself had suffered at the hands of Big Daddy.

Grandma Bynum knew better than to get between a man disciplining his woman.

After a while, Junior Bynum moved his family to Covert, to a white house on a hill. Maybe my mother thought things would get better. After letting them settle in, Lily dropped by my mother's house unexpectedly. The moment she walked in, Lily could feel the tension, causing an uneasiness in her own chest.

"Hey, Velma," she said. My mother nodded a response.

The anger seemed to ripple through the air as Junior Bynum, a scrawny but strong six-feet-something, prowled throughout the house, chest puffed up, steps hoary as a grizzly bear's. Since my mother couldn't cook worth a lick, and gracefully burned water, the smell of overdone rice in the kitchen curled around the palpable anxiety and their Goodwill furniture. Wanting to take some of the burden off Mama, who was pregnant again, with my eldest brother Loren, Aunt Lily decided to pitch in. She took the baby food from Velma. "I'll feed Bobbie Ann. You have a sit down."

Bobbie Ann was almost two at the time. Lily approached the toddler with a spoon topped with hastily mashed vegetables. The toddler bunched up her face and started crying. Though Aunt Lily got the spoonful in, Bobbie Ann spit out a colorful goo, swinging her legs with angry glee in the highchair, like any child her age would, testing the limits of her newfound motor skills. Junior Bynum snapped. "You better swallow that," he yelled, picking up the two by four and raising it over his head, aiming for Bobbie Ann's soft, furry afro. Maybe he was just trying to scare her. Maybe he'd just tap her with it, faking his wild man look. Maybe he was just stupid enough to believe none of his actions mattered. Disbelief cottoned Aunt Lily's mouth. She jumped up and wedged her slender thirteen-year-old frame between Bobbie Ann and Junior Bynum.

"You gon' hit this girl over my dead body," Lily told him through clenched teeth. Eyes bubbled, Bobbie Ann shook quietly and uncontrollably in her skin. That's when Lily realized that both her sisters were getting their asses beat by their no-count husbands.

As Bobbie grew up, she begged to spend the summers with either Big Daddy, Grandma Stafford, or Auntie Louise, her grandmother's sister. She didn't want to be at home with her rabid-dog father.

Mama was just learning how to work, Bobbie Ann remembered, so she sent the children to places where babysitting was free. "I told her I didn't care," Bobbie told me later. She just wanted to get away from her father. "Daddy was mean. He used to whip our butts, even if he just had a bad day. We'd get it."

Once in Covert, before I was born, Bobbie Ann said Loren kept messing with her, so she picked up a rock, cocked her left hand back, took aim, and clocked Loren dead in his head and laid the skin open. Loren was rushed to the hospital for a possible concussion and stitches.

Junior Bynum spanked Bobbie Ann so hard she had blisters for three weeks. Yet she knew that it wasn't just her unruly act that made her father hit her like that. Junior Bynum whipped Bobbie equally as bad when she fell off a horse because he had to chase it around the field afterward.

"I never fell off a horse again," she said quietly. "I have so many scarred memories because of Daddy. That's why I didn't want to be with no men. A lot of that had to do with me not wanting to be around no men. I'll just be myself. That's fine by me."

This, I know now, was the beginning of my eldest sister's terror and hatred of men, her relentless pummeling of neighborhood boys and our two brothers when she was in her teens, and her love of women. She'd perfected her rabbit-jab left hook, dropping her opponent in seconds. She turned to women because they couldn't hurt her like her daddy. Men didn't treat women right. All her life, she'd seen men beat her women kin, treating them worse than livestock.

Over the years, my mother often gave me the impression that living with Junior Bynum was like living in a recurring horror movie. Only every time my mother tripped and fell when the killer was chasing her, she just got the shit beat out of her and tossed back down like a rag doll until the next take.

My mother was always the reluctant antagonist.

Junior Bynum, the eager protagonist in which every plot point was a fist in my mother's face or gut.

The life she led with that man was not what she had envisioned when she'd freed herself, her sixteen-year-old dreams, her pulsing amber skin, her horse-tail mane, from South Haven and memories of the farm. From her father. It was a much nastier, despicable shade of love. A rotten, bug-infested, waterlogged love. Many times, I'm sure, Velma wished the ground would just have mercy on her, open up and swallow her, smother her with cool, impalpable hands. But she had to think of the children, my two brothers and three sisters, almost stair-step arrivals. She was always watermelon round and sickly, almost seven years straight, and Junior Bynum lacerated her body with love taps that turned her every color in a kaleidoscope.

Bobbie Ann was seven when the news came. Uncle Aaron, Junior Bynum's brother, was the first to hear it. They sat Velma down.

"Junior Bynum dead, Velma," Aaron told her. "He was runned over by a chicken truck."

The company that owned the truck, a regional chicken franchise called Farmer's Fresh, took full blame and set up a trust fund for each of my mother's children. The kids were six, five, three, and two. Bobbie Ann didn't remember crying. Over the years, the stories about the day Junior Bynum died remained hazy. As a child, I always heard he'd fallen asleep while he was driving and assumed the "he" was Junior Bynum. Now I realize they meant the driver of the truck had fallen asleep. But I wonder whether it really was an accident. Is it possible that someone who saw the pincushion he made of Velma's beautiful face pushed him out in the street? It was just too good to be true. It was for my mother, I'm sure, like Kate Chopin's "Story of an Hour": the relief she must have felt when she realized he was really dead.

At first, Velma didn't believe Aaron, thought he was playing a cruel joke on her. Then she waited and waited by the door, her gaggle of runny-nosed children watching her as she started to unthaw. I bet she didn't even shower until the door never opened. Didn't breathe until the silence stayed silent. Whatever happened, it was a gift for my mother.

Then maybe, cautiously, she smiled her first free smile for the first time in almost eight years. Junior Bynum was permanently not coming back, not waiting around the corner to smack or impregnate her. For the first time in a long while, Velma didn't fear going to sleep and waking up with an angry drunk in her bed; she didn't fear for her life anymore, because surely he would have eventually killed her had he remained alive. These kinds of stories were in the paper every day, and still are. But this nightmare ended on a happy note; not only had he disappeared from her life, she was receiving money for his blood. It was repayment for all of her blood that he had spilled.

Seven years and five children later, she was released, not dead. Money was coming to her and the children, money that she would end up mismanaging and squandering, but at least it was there. She hightailed it out of those Covert backwoods and bought a decent house on North Edwards in Kalamazoo, where she met my father.

I never once heard her say she hated Junior Bynum for what he did to her. I don't know if it was because of the children, or if she possibly still felt somehow connected to him, or maybe even beholden to him for rescuing her from South Haven and her daddy's temper and John A.'s maniac gaze. Perhaps she even missed Junior Bynum, a concept weirder than flying basset hounds to me.

Everybody knew Junior Bynum was whipping my mother's ass. Why didn't they stop it? Everyone knew; why didn't anyone help her?

They say an addict or an abused woman can't be helped until they admit they need it. I think my mother, and other Black and American Indian women, and all abused women who stay—unable to devise a way out—are caught between denial and desperation. No rainy-day pocket change, no support from family or friends. Maybe they don't see themselves as a slowly bending tree, neck about to break. They must, of course, at some point in the madness, fear for their children's lives. But when they eventually look in the mirror, maybe they don't see a swollen-faced monster; they might see, for a time, however long it takes for the blurry vision to clear, just a woman in love.

18

Pullman Bloodsport

MY EARLIEST MEMORY is of running.

Like lifting a rock to find the underside a sparkling prism, I uncovered my smallest self, arms and elbows flaying, the taste of black Michigan soil gliding into my mouth, slapping my cheeks and embedding itself in my hair, as I skidded around the house, across the backyard, and toward the gaping barn. I was always grimy and smelly. My mother made me wash my feet every night before I went to bed, smelling like a wildflower, rank with wind and all of the day's heat. I didn't care. At five, when I ran, the black ground seemed to rush up to meet me, then disappear. My knees folded into my body like waterfowl feathers, and I almost felt as though I was lifting up, barely letting my feet touch what I knew was there but never looked down to see.

No one had died yet. No one had to be buried. It was just my family: my mother, our dogs, cats, chickens, and horses on a small farm in Pullman.

And if Kalamazoo was our urban oasis, a metropolis where the Kalamazoo Railroad was still one of the top transporters of the nation's goods, and Upjohn Pharmaceuticals produced leading drugs, and Ford Motor Co. churned out vehicles that kept the locals gainfully employed, well then, Pullman was our sticks. The boondocks. Dirt roads, gravel walkways, and trenches for rain. Whereas Mattawan was marshy and wet, Pullman, two minutes big, was flat and mostly dry. It was a place where few Black families passed through or lived. I don't know what my mother was thinking, moving us out there, with all those white kids raised by KKK parents, except maybe to escape my father's love.

It was 1973.

It seemed like my mother worked around the clock as a nurse's aide and left us like field mice to raise ourselves that summer. The small township was a few miles from where my mother grew up on the marshes of Mattawan and about twenty miles outside Kalamazoo. The house she bought in Pullman, a single-level white structure with wide, daunting hallways, came with a real farm whose grass blades murmured susurrus possibilities, fingering the humid air. We had acres and acres of land, a big barn, and a chicken coop.

While the outside seemed open to us, plush as a newborn's first crop of hair, inside there was always the uneasy smell of a house not quite ready for us. Mothballs and old shoe polish. Soaking teeth and forgotten onions shriveled in the bottom kitchen drawers. The carpet was never quite rid of the first owners' scent; perhaps some shriveled Polish couple had died there and left the mumbled stories of their own escaping, the journey from a European ghetto to a Midwestern backwoods waterhole, creaking in the floorboards.

Although Mama was a small-time gambler, addicted to potentially harmless sports like bingo and the Michigan Lottery (she regularly spent my new school clothes money on her bad streak of luck), she was attempting to both spoil and quiet us, both entreating and ordering our cooperation while she tried to take care of her tribe the best way she knew how. The country was what she knew. This was her people's land, her father's land. The swampland, where the Staffords had planted roots close to a hundred years ago, and since then, no one could ever quite pull them up. My mother was familiar with the terrain, recognized the erasing solitude, the cornfield quiet humming beneath her own feet. She needed the space, needed to remove herself from Kalamazoo; she had just separated from my father.

This land, pleated by wheat and barley fields, layered with tomato and watermelon patches in the summer, fondled by John Deere tractors from dawn until the day's stifling end, would heal her. And in the winter, ravaged by snow plow trucks, she needed the silt of her childhood while she nursed her wounds, and maybe, so did we.

Velma Jean Stafford and John Al Buchanan had been lovers as well as friends, before and after their divorce. But somehow, his ambition to be a preacher had infiltrated what she wanted and needed—his attention, his utter devotion. In Kalamazoo, they attended church after church, mostly before I was born. Right after my birth in 1968, they divorced. From what I've been able to recover, one minute they were happy and carefree, a gorgeous, sun-kissed couple roving the church circuit: Baptist, Pentecostal, Episcopal, anywhere Daddy got a chance to deliver the word of God, like all the other wannabe preachers. And the next minute, my mother and father were just done. Finished. No explanation to the big kids. They were whisked off to backwoods Pullman without notice.

God did not follow them there.

The land was withered, harsh, yet rocked us for a brief period, lulled us, like my father's now absent hands had. Velma Jean was hiding from something all right, but we had time to figure it out. We had about three acres' worth of long gazes running into the flat horizon and the distant birch trees beyond the mowed front lawn and overgrown backyard. The barnyard was always drowning in slivers of hay that caked the soles of my feet. (I constantly hid my shoes; being barefoot was akin to religion for me.) Black cotton dirt clods pushed between my toes while the frantic air in my chest bulged and burned, spinning up my nose and head as I floated across a field, the front yard, the living room.

I was a "nerve-wrecking" child who couldn't keep still and was always jumping off something, running somewhere, crashing into who-knew-what and limping back, soggy, whiny, and pissed. I ran in dizzying circles like a lab rat. I think I was simply born with an ebullience tingling through my blood. I loved to move, to push myself against the wind. I didn't know I had wolf medicine then. I was always a traveler. A runner. An escape artist. It felt good to leave everything, something, anything, like a tree or a bed, a room or a person, behind. To escape a confrontation, a nagging voice, a man. Rochelle watched me from a distance. She always chose to stay and fight.

Both my mother and I, I found out later, liked to run.

At the time, that farm in Pullman held all I needed within the perimeter that my skinny legs could carry me through. The night sky held bleached-bone stars that cut a jagged path across the liquid black. I was fed, bathed, and clothed, and enamored with the horses.

"Shonda, come inside here," my mother called.

"The big kids coming too?" I asked, jealous that they got to stay out a few minutes more than I did.

"Get your little narrow ass in here for I make you bring me a switch off that bush with you. Don't make me snatch a knot in your ass."

"Okay, Mama." Reluctantly, I'd drag my feet across the ground, mashing my toes in the dirt extra good. The fenced-in corral led to a worn horse path enclosed by a rectangle of thick gray planks. These buildings were already on the property when we moved in. The stable, really just a drafty plywood lean-to, connected to a barn and housed our horses. The puny stalls must have seemed like shoeboxes to them; I came up to the horses' rusty chins, and they looked enormous to me. The color of the barn hovers just under my memory, maybe distressed red, but the inner cavern was suffused with the immutable odor of horse manure and body heat. One steamy summer afternoon, I glided to a halt inside the barn and was rendered catatonic by the spectacle of dust particles floating across the amber-lit stalls, and how the horses' sensitive hides shivered involuntarily each time a fly landed.

One day, a baby black stallion named Flicka, obsessed with bucking, reared back wide brown lips to snap at Bobbie Ann, trying to catch her skin between his stained, strong teeth.

"Mama," Bobbie called, scared. She waited a few more days to try to ride Flicka again. The horse was supposed to belong to Bobbie Ann and me, but I was too little to saddle him. Sonny, a sweet-tempered, honey-hued thoroughbred, was Rochelle's and Tina's. A massive black and white painted horse named Matches was supposed to belong to Loren and Tyrone, but Loren rarely tended him; he'd discovered girls and thought they had much nicer legs. Tyrone's diligent attention to Matches, feeding and brushing him down in the cool evenings, made everyone know that the horse was his.

At first, though I kept it to myself, I was afraid of the horses: their hard, heaving bellies, their baleful glares at me as a short, two-legged human.

"Don't let Shonda be out there with them horses by herself," my mother told Loren. She knew I coveted them but could potentially get the shit kicked out of me walking too close behind them. I was fascinated watching them graze and move, muscles rolling like water under thin hides, their muzzles silkworm-moist. Those horses were the bribes in the treaty to keep us pacified about having dashed so abruptly from the city, from all our friends and from my father.

One day I looked up, stopping mid-gait, and saw that the white shed behind the house had an upside down horseshoe tacked above its shadowy doorway. I remember asking somebody why it was up there in the first place and, furthermore, why it was upside down. "It's up there for luck and upside down so the luck won't run out," a disembodied voice answered. That struck me as incredibly idiotic.

I still can feel my little head clocking the answer every which way, trying to make sense of it. Luck. What did we need luck for? We had horses.

THAT DAY THE air was so hot and soggy my thighs rubbed together in my cut-off shorts every time I moved, leaving painful rashes. An incision had developed on the thin pearl skin behind my baby toes. I was in constant pain. But it was summer. The landscape seemed to melt when I looked far off down the road; the edges where the horizon met the sky shimmered like a pool of fire water, and I knew if I stayed in one spot on that road, it would catch up with me. Defeated, I hobbled to the house, trying not to let my thighs meet, and snaked my worn tennis shoes from under the bed, someone's hand-me-downs that had finally given up and flapped when I walked. Perfect for the mucky pond's outskirts and dirt road.

"Watch out for bloodsuckers," I heard Mama's voice come from the open door. I dashed off before she could tell me I was too young to go. At the pond, two slimy leeches attached themselves to Loren's calf. Then on the way home, six buck-toothed white boys—bloodsuckers—appeared, who must have followed us on that lone dusty road. They were jealous of Tyrone's Olympics-worthy acrobatic moves swinging on the rope that hung from the oak tree above Blocker's Pond: they were jealous of Tyrone's bravado and confidence.

"Hey, yellow niggers," one of the white boys called.

"Y'all sho is uglier than hell," another one said, hitting the ground with a stick.

Tyrone and Loren pushed us girls behind them, fists up.

"Come on, honky," Tyrone snarled. "You bad."

We looked every bit our redbone Mulatto blood, with hair that curled like Cocker Spaniels when wet, and these boys were the sons and grandsons of cross burners that lurked in the backwoods, setting snares for raccoons and the like. Suddenly, like ghosts, Theresa, our German Shepard, streaked out of the woods, followed by Justine, our Alaskan Malamute, fangs bared at the white boys.

"You white honkeys is lucky cuz if I'da sicked my dog on you, you'd be dead," Tyrone yelled.

Theresa and Justice formed a front and back guard, protecting us as we walked the rest of the way home. I can't remember if we ever went back to that swim hole. Possibly Mama had had a premonition—"watch out for bloodsuckers"—but she could also have meant beware bad decisions and bad men.

Because that day when we got back to the house, a man was living there.

I'm sure that's not how it happened, so suddenly, but that's what it felt like. One minute it was Mama and us, and the next Robert Gene was buying Wonder Bread and fixing hinges on doors. I can't quite remember his face, but his presence hovers over that piece of the past like a silent watchdog: the mean, stealthy kind that waits for you to get close enough to bite. That's how he lingers in the periphery of my mind. I didn't know what to make of him then so I avoided him, but my brothers skulked and rebelled. A stranger had replaced them as the men in the house. A man other than my father and their deceased father lived in our house and slept in our mother's bed. I never asked them, but I imagine their own father's freak death had left them as bereft as any orphans. Probably, they'd rather have had him than this interloper—no matter how much Junior Bynum used to wear them and Mama out.

All the men my Mama chose seemed to be stand-ins for her father.

I didn't know then that Robert Gene was my daddy's uncle.

A long, dark winter came. The cold fingers of the season's comforting darkness laid themselves into every corner of the house:

the kitchen and bedrooms, the living room and service porch. The falling snow seemed to muffle our words and gestures as if we were silent movie characters and our parts were already written, rehearsed, ready for the take. I woke one night, blurry-eyed and disconnected, the sound of television static scratching the night. I must have fallen asleep on the couch after some program, and my mother, who'd come in late, had cushioned my head in her lap for a brief time before going to bed. Now I was alone.

I inched off the couch, my heart thumping like a baby rabbit's heart in my chest. My feet sank into the shaggy yellow Funkadelic carpet. Out of the corner of my eyes, I saw something move. When I looked, it was my mother's three-foot-high lacquer statue, a small black figure in repose, and I broke into a run, scared shitless, thinking the statue was chasing me. The light in the kitchen flicked on.

"What are you doing?" Robert Gene's long shadow tilted over me, and maybe it had been him I'd seen after all, but if so, what was he doing? Where had he come from? Really, how had he gotten to that spot where he was standing, but also in our house? I never trusted his gaze, his presence. Now his devilish laughter trailed me when I took off down the hallway, and the memory of what happened next collapsed, but I knew his presence had something to do with all my childhood fears.

Maybe it wasn't the statue at all but Robert Gene's shadow infiltrating my space. The next day, with a sideways gaze at Robert Gene's back, I gathered enough courage, to poke at the statue's unblinking eyes. Warily, I tested its observation skills by walking back and forth out of its view to see if its eyes were moving. I only went to bed every evening that winter after I touched the cold, still eyes of those statues, until something worse replaced my fear.

It was one of the coldest winter nights I can remember. A blizzard had been pounding our house like a giant flyswatter the entire week. I was jarred awake by the sound of heavy walking and a door slamming. "Somebody help! Matches is dying! Help me!"

A harsh cough that sounded like bricks swirled in a bucket echoed from the barn. A door slammed. I crept out to the kitchen to see my brother Tyrone sobbing, his face in his hands. "No, Mama, no. Oh, God," Tyrone cried. Then, boots half buckled, he slammed open the back door and flung himself out into the whirl of snow and wind. "Tyrone," Mama yelled. "Get back in here, boy."

Mama had locked up all the horses in the barn because wild dogs had been sighted roaming the fields. But when she tied up Tyrone's horse, Matches, to keep him from getting out, she forgot to remove the steel bit in his mouth, and with the winter storm, no one had ventured outside for a week.

When Tyrone found Matches, the harness had severed his mouth nerves, and his lips were too slack to eat or swallow.

The horse's once robust stomach heaved with a harsh, blood-lined cough, and every time he hacked, his stomach would inflate, contract, and release. Inflate, contract, still. Hoarse dry cough.

Without food and water, Matches caught pneumonia. The other horses stomped their hooves in the stalls, neighing, tossing their heads up, and slapping their tails against the walls. They smelled death on the cold air over the snowfall. The night Matches died, I remember the oil lamp's flame, or a flashlight flickering through the house. Maybe our power had gone out. Maybe it was the living room light being turned on and off when Tyrone rushed outside to the barn and back into the kitchen for water, supplies, blankets, anything he thought of that would help his horse live. The kitchen light sent off a tarnished corn husk glow, making us all look unreal and scared. The light was indifferent. And the winter was not laughing.

Winter stole Matches.

All was quiet in the house, but outside, an unnerving harsh wheezing rumbled from the barn. I knew Tyrone was sobbing again, his face crumpled against his horse's heaving neck, limp straw clinging to the knee patches on his corduroy pants as he rubbed the horse's hollow belly with one hand and scratched under the sweaty, dirt-caked mane with the other. His throat had turned scarlet from the cold and the effort of crying, his tears all bundled up in the already wet part of his neck. I imagined his Adam's apple bobbing up and down in his freckled throat at the senselessness of this night, and boys having to be brave, and loving hard. I might remember this incorrectly, but my mother didn't seem devastated at all. She seemed to accept it easily. She had already been through it all and lost so much. After a while, her sympathy dwindled, and Mama comforted Tyrone with her daddy's toxic love.

"Shut all that goddamn crying up. I said I was sorry. Shit."

She knew ten-year-old Tyrone would have to learn to let go of much more as he grew up. But Tyrone never forgave her for this first act of betrayal, destroying that which he loved most. He bitterly blamed Mama for the death of his horse, and for the death of his father before that. He never forgave her and has since, perhaps unknowingly, continued to look for instances in which Mama would betray him and, even though he loved her, prove to him how horrible she was beneath the skin. He grew up to become a successful businessman, but he couldn't stop faulting her for the deprivations of our childhood. "You remember when Mama gambled all our money on bingo, and bought that house, and spent all our insurance money on Jessie [her boyfriend after Robert Gene, and then her third husband], buying him clothes and jewelry?" The knowing stuck in his craw. Every few years, Tyrone would refer to the money he and the other kids received from their deceased father's death insurance money. From that moment in the barn, he mistrusted my mother, and he came to mistrust almost every other woman he would love because of this night. The night of death.

But living on a farm, every day we witnessed the possibilities that come with things ending in horrible, tragic ways.

Whether it was a coincidence, a parade, or a warning, after Matches, I began to notice death in a way I hadn't before. I found numerous dead birds in the fields, and frogs, skunks, and squirrels flattened by tires or a careless boy's bike. Baby chicks and hamsters disappeared. That spring, when we arrived home from Easter service, we discovered that our dog Justine had eaten our rabbits, Easter presents from Robert Gene. Blood and fur littered the grass like confetti; Justine had stripped the rabbits' bones to parchment, and we also found half-gnawed ears and surprised blue eyes tangled in patches of pink fur. We had only gotten to play with them once. That day, just as the snow was starting to melt and spring was not far off, I thought my heart would fall out of my body I cried so hard. That second lesson in detachment, things leaving you in a mangled leap, not all at once but in pieces, prepared me for the rest to come. Though I resumed my child's life, I realized now that things didn't live forever, and you had to be careful of who and what you trusted.

Whatever you loved might eat you.

ONE SPRING DAY during that year and a half in Pullman, before we returned to Kalamazoo, my mother was inside the corral with the horses, yelling her encouragement at Bobbie Ann on how to manage Flicka without getting bucked off. Bobbie's mouth was set in a grim line, determined to master the horse, while the black stallion looked at her legs out the side of his eyes, waiting for my mother to let go of his rope so he could send Bobbie flying. The rest of us teased her from the splinter-riddled fence, egging her on and pulling slivers from our hands. Suddenly, Mama let out a yelp.

"Holy shit."

"What?" We followed her gaze. "What happened?"

A big country mouse the size of a raccoon had risen up from one of the thousands of tufts of dirt in the field. Of all the things my mother hated, mice were underlined and bolded at the top of the list. Bugs Bunny–like, she leapt and did splits in the air and then took off running, tearing up clods of dirt as well as any horse, while the horses, startled, snorted and broke into a trot beside her. For a brief moment in time that seemed to lean itself across the horizon, my mother was almost neck and neck with the horses. Then the horses pulled away, and a tribe of jackrabbits scampered out of their holes, ears like flags and feet broad as fried chicken thighs, to hop past my mother's windmill legs.

"Run, Mama."

"Look at her go."

"Mama fixina outrun the horses."

My brothers, running beside her, laughed and gawked at the sight. She was *faster* than they were: an amber-skinned candle flame, her thick black tresses flying like snakes, gulping the air as she rode the wind.

Her delirious laughter trailing behind.

OUR MINDS RECOLLECT what they want, and for some reason I only remember the horses, Blocker's Pond, strange Robert Gene, other swimming holes, brothers and sisters who protected me, my mother and myself running. I also remember the nightmares and dreams that started, causing my brothers and sisters to look at me strangely when I tried to explain to them what I dreamed. They said I always talked about things I shouldn't have, told them I could see things or that something was about to happen. I don't remember this. I didn't tell anyone about my dreams with the men and their melting faces, looking at me, their faces sliding off of them like hot wax. My mother's face in the soft darkness of autumn, tender and salamander pink, as blurry and bright as a Christmas tree star, her eyes powdery red. I received rushed kisses on my forehead; hands tucked and folded the odd corners of my body and clothes and hair in the necessary places, but always with a heaviness. I sensed something in the way that children know things.

This time it was Robert Gene, not her father, not Junior Bynum, who was molding her into another shape on the back roads of Pullman. It was Robert Gene chipping away at her with each blow and kiss when we kids weren't around. Each saliva spittle that flew from his mouth; each wince as his hand, fist, or foot landed and sank into my mother's soft flesh. He dealt Velma his monstrous self against the bald General Motors' headlights, against the leather seats of his car, the hard, cold hood; against the tangent scent of oak trees, their hulking trunks bent in shame.

That was her waltz in Pullman.

My mother must have been afraid. She must have wanted to run again (and eventually she did). She must have tried to tell people, but maybe not. Maybe she didn't feel worthy of saving. Her mother and father had both abandoned her time and time again every day of her life except the miserable day she was born. They never came to her rescue. Not once. The only one who seemed to care whether she lived or died was her sister Lily, who was shocked but unable to help because she had just left a husband who'd been fighting with her too. Velma was too scared to leave Robert Gene.

"She didn't let me know for a long time that he was beating her until she came to me with her will." Aunt Lily snorted at the memory. "Gone leave me all your kids. I said, 'Shit, you got to have a will to give me all these kids? I got three of my own, I just left my husband. What I'ma do with all these kids?' But I'd a took them cause they were mine."

THEN VELMA MET Jessie Jackson, the blackest Black man I'd ever seen except in books. Born in Jackson, Mississippi, he was so dark he looked like a yummy fudge brownie with golden casings on his front teeth when he smiled. Aunt Katheryn almost shit a brick. My daddy's beautiful Blackness was about all she could take; Jessie's glowing licorice skin made her tell Velma not to come to her house with him or any of her nappy-headed Black ass kids. Namely me.

Brave enough with Jessie on her arm to protect her, she broke up with Robert Gene then. One day he was there, and the next day, boxes that had been in the living room were gone. I remember the vacancy of the rooms, but I don't remember if a moving truck came and packed us up too. I do know we forgot the horseshoe.

We forgot our luck.

Mama bought us a house in the Real City, in Kalamazoo, with the Bynum kids' daddy's death money. She moved us back a few days before Christmas. Our new three-story house on Southworth Terrace on the Eastside was bare and prone to echoes and ghostly footsteps. The ceilings were high. For some reason we didn't have any furniture, but we had a fireplace in the living room and a huge back, front, and side yard.

Our cousin Jo Ann babysat us that Christmas Eve, even though Rochelle and Tina bitterly complained that they didn't need babysitters at nine and ten. I tried to act grown-up, but we all looked up to Jo Ann for her crazy cool attitude and silky brown skin. She possessed a svelte body, all fluid in blue jean bell-bottoms; her dance moves were always the funkiest, especially when she did the bump, popping one leg up and snapping her fingers loud to the beat. Her full, perpetually glossed lips showed like smooth brown crystals under the ray of her afro. Jo Ann's hair stayed styled, pressed and flipped into wide bouncy curls we called feathered, haloing her face. I worshipped her.

"Go Jo Ann, go Jo Ann," Rochelle yelled as Jo Ann broke down the robot to Michael Jackson's "Dancing Machine," hooking her arm and bending over. Like Michael, she was cool as ice.

When the phone rang we were playing Spades on the living room floor and wrapping gifts with more tape than wrapping paper. Mama was at work, and like all kids when their mother isn't there to cuff them, the bigger girls were using more four-letter words than any sailor, words they'd heard from Mama and Aunt Phyllis. My sisters and cousins were laughing and munching on Christmas cookies as someone called "cheater!"

Jo Ann answered the phone. When she hung up and turned around, her beautiful brown eyes were big and glossy, like she was suddenly hot.

"Robert Gene." She stopped. "Aunt Velma said we gotta put everything in the room right now. *Now*." Like a single-minded bloodhound, like a bad penny, he had followed Mama to the city, to the eastside; the monster knew where we lived.

We scattered at Jo Ann's orders. Pushing everything—the toys, the prickly Christmas tree, the presents, even my dog Sam—into the front room with the lock. *Lock the door. Turn off all the lights. Don't answer the front door. Stay quiet.* The Christmas tree, the gifts, the lights, our blankets, and us under them—all layered in that room. My mother wanted it to appear as if no one was there. It was dark and hot in the room. I could smell the musty heat under my sister Rochelle's arm as she held me tight and I tried to ignore her vice grip. I'd scratched my hand on something, a nail on the as-yet-uncarpeted floor, and fought back tears. The fear in my chest tightened. We crouched beneath our own holiday paraphernalia in a Shakespearean twist of fate, a Midwestern Comedy of Errors, as if we were hiding from the bogeyman. We were.

It only seemed like seconds later when I heard a car pull up outside and the sound of footsteps on the snow, the doorbell ringing against the walls. We whimpered quietly. Then another car pulled up. A door slammed. "Shush, be quiet." My sister squeezed my hand hard.

I don't remember the Christmas tree, whether it was a tall, healthy, tinseled one or a plastic, middle-sized tree, the kind where you had to stick plastic branches into the plastic center pole. I remember my body pressed into my sister's bony hips, and that it started to snow—flakes as big as chicken feathers—and when I peeked out the window, or maybe when someone flung open the door to yell at the car as it sped off, that I could see my frightened breath on cold glass. I remember being concerned about whether I could make an angel in the snow, when there wasn't the kind of fluffy white magic on the ground that there had been in Pullman.

Most vividly, though, I remember seeing the car parked at the curb and Robert Gene punching my mother as they sat in the front, his winter coat-clad arm rising and falling into her, and she cringing back, holding her arms in front of her beautiful broken face. *How could I see it so clearly?* Then, when he pushed her out of the car and she limped in front of his chrome bumper, the street light gleaming a harsh lemon color through the night, he revved the engine and tried to run her down. Fortunately, she'd just stepped out of the street onto the curb and fell in the snow, her descent cushioned by the soft white earth. Her nurse's aide shoes glared like white blocks of cheese as she rocked up from the ground and stumbled up the walkway. His car sped off.

At that time of my life, maybe I was four or five, I didn't even remember my father's face.

But I remembered that night.

19

War Paint

WHILE HER SISTERS floundered in squalor, in trailer parks and makeshift homes, in marriage and make-it-up-as-you-go-along motherhood, with the same daft behavior they'd seen their mother impart, young Lily tried to take care of her mother in Mattawan. Route M-43. Right down the street from Wolf Lake and the Fish Hatchery.

They seemed so utterly alone.

The farm was empty for Lily at first. Lonely long months greeted her infectious grin. The house was quiet except for the field mice that nibbled holes in the walls and scattered when footsteps approached. Because Dorothy rarely chopped firewood, the small rooms were perpetually chilly. The farm had slipped into decay and disarray, from which it never quite recovered. It took Lily a while to replace her sisters with cousins who were a little older and more experienced; they were all she had. Her new crew, Cookie and Darlene and friends, met at Paw Paw High School and began their Saturday night escapades into Covert, a few miles from Mattawan and Paw Paw. They lied to their parents about the car breaking down when they really wanted to go to a house party. They hung tough, clad in white bobby socks and poodle skirts, sporting bouncy ponytails, scarves, and bangs. They danced their black patent leather shoes to dullness, adorned in orange drugstore lipstick. The girls all sang in the choir at Second Baptist Church in Kalamazoo, giggling at the sweaty boys in robes who didn't care nothing about singing to praise God. It was just a way to get away from parents and cockfight around girls.

Her mama thought it was safe. Church. A large crowd.

One night after choir practice, Lily and her cousins caught a ride home with one of the preacher's sons, Chucky Warfield. All night in choir, she had felt male eyes staring at her and behind her. Cookie and Darlene giggled into their sleeves until the choir director hushed them up.

"Y'all gonna sing or laugh?" the preacher's wife said. "Either sing or sit down and shut up."

The blouse Lily had taken to wearing was purposely loose, to hide, or so she thought, her developing breasts. Unfortunately, her nipples always seemed erect no matter how hard she tried to hide this embarrassing body function. Most of her clothes were hand-me-downs since she and her mother were alone and working hard and living on a meager budget, and nothing fit quite right. But that day at choir, for some reason, her nipples were hard. The boys nudged each other. When it came time to ride home, Chucky Warfield volunteered. It wasn't until later that she realized that though he had a long ride back into Kalamazoo, he was taking her home last. The long dark road ahead of her was hungry. Chucky was quiet. The silence was strained. The music in the car low.

He made a turn down a deserted road and slowed to a stop.

"This is not my street," Lily said. Chucky turned and put his hand down her shirt. "Let me just feel them."

She fought Chucky, scratched at his eyes and face, but he was bigger. Twenty-one, a man engaged to be married. She, at thirteen, was soon shoved against the leather and bleeding between her legs. It was quick, faster than the second time when Chucky's nephew, Donald, seventeen, took her home one night after choir practice and raped her too. Word had gotten around. Lily was easy. She was free. She was unprotected.

She was in hell.

Lily refused to go back to choir until both men promised they wouldn't do it again. But they did. Lily always thought Cookie and Darlene knew what was happening, but no one said anything. Maybe it had happened to them too. Maybe they were secretly jealous of Lily's supple beauty, her milky complexion, her long, black, good Indian hair. The attention that all the males, young and old, in every room they entered showed her. Maybe they wanted her broken.

A young girl, still innocent in the head, Lily kept thinking something was wrong with her. *Why are they picking on me?* She thought she'd enticed them or somehow had done something to deserve it. That second time she was raped, her father had come home for a rare visit. When Chucky let her off at the edge of their dirt driveway, she saw Clifford's truck, burst into tears, and walked slowly down the gravel driveway. She'd just finished fighting, kicking and screaming at Chucky. She was embarrassed. Embarrassed to have to walk past her father, to face him, a man, while the semen of another man dried and cracked on the inside of her thigh. Embarrassed that his little Mattawan forest fairy, the imp who made everyone laugh, had been sullied twice.

She was still crying when she entered the house. Clifford was at the kitchen table. Her mother was in the bedroom, angry at her daddy for something. Lily's daddy looked at her.

"What happened gal?" he asked.

Sobbing and shaking, trying to cover her breasts, Lily told her father. She couldn't stop crying. The wind blew outside. Clifford paused and scratched his head. The scent of a long day's work and several beers was on him. His eyes, usually bloodshot and hostile, were closed while he thought. Clifford leaned back, then fixed her with a resigned stare, much softer, more defeated than she had ever seen him. Her father's hands and shoulders looked softer than she remembered. His once brown hair was slowly turning the color of woodstove ash, and before her was an old, disappointed man who seemed conscious of age, of loss, of his terrible weakness. He couldn't even enlist in the war after having sold all his farm equipment and left for Chicago, for the draft. His own eyes betrayed him. Lack of acute vision had prevented him from the glory and adventure he'd desired in the swamps of Vietnam. When he returned home, he had to buy everything back and restock everything. But what did he know anyway. A half-breed, with crushed black hair and a charming, lopsided smile that you couldn't trust. His yellow skin looked more American Indian than Black, but anyone could see plain as day the anger, the bitter self-hate, on his chiseled face, his broad nose. He had the yellow complexion of a white man who'd had too much sun. None of this made any difference to anyone but the ladies. They made him feel like something. And his stark, hateful beauty mattered to Dorothy, who would love the marrow out of his bones till the day she died, no matter how much she hated him.

That night he looked at Lily, violated a second time, bony, just a girl still. A young girl turned woman while he wasn't even around to pat her head, a girlhood stolen while he was out drinking and womanizing. But tonight, Lily represented all of his daughters at that moment, all of his failure as a father. In her eyes, he saw every demon he could never conquer. He had no advice to give her other than the kind he'd given each daughter who'd lost her virginity on some winding back road or by being raped near the South Haven shoreline. Men were bastards, he knew well, and his girls would learn it sooner or later.

She looked at him, waiting.

"Well, you just got your cherry busted," her father said. "We'll just have to go on and make sure it doesn't happen again."

Lily swallowed, her face hot and itching. Her legs hurt; her face ached where Chucky, the rapist, had kissed her and gotten away with it. How many girls had he raped while taking them home after church, she wondered. And here was her father, telling her he wasn't going to kill the boy. He wasn't even going to call the Warfield boy's father and threaten to shoot him. He didn't even reach for his double-barreled shotgun.

"Goodnight."

She went to bed that night knowing she had only herself. No sisters, no brothers. She had those crazy Stafford cousins, but she was too embarrassed to tell them that she'd been stupid enough to let it happen twice.

And her father wouldn't protect her.

That night she couldn't sleep. She thought back to when she was nine. She had been baptized at the church of God in Kalamazoo, where her father would take them when they were all together, a family. She'd felt so light, so different after the water washed over her face; there was a peace on her, and she knew things were different, she was different. She had always loved going to church. She never thought that peace would be shattered in connection with a place that she trusted, a place that had brought her so much joy. After that, she turned against the church and its ways.

Lily sank.

Then one summer night, she met Donnie "Bull" Wilson at a party. Bull, Aunt Lily knew, got his nickname on account of his stocky frame, his snout nose that looked mashed on his face like a bulldog's, and his demeanor when he drank and fought—he put a hold on his opponent to the death. She could almost smell the perspiration stained in his arms. When the lights went down, The Marvelettes blared on a record player by the screen door. Everybody's faces disappeared into the warm hollow of their partner's shoulders as they necked in the dim space. Bull pulled her in a corner, pasting her neck with slug-like kisses. He was nineteen and she was fourteen.

"I never really liked him," she said later. "He even called me a stuck-up bitch sometimes, but I didn't want to be left out."

They became an item. About a year later, when Vietnam draft papers started showing up like Christmas cards in mailboxes, there was a knock on her door. Out of breath from the run down the road, Bull burst in with his square-collared shirt half tucked into his pants, shoved the draft papers in her face, and said, "Look here, we got to get married."

"I thought I was saving him from the war," she said, "so I said okay."

It never dawned on Lily that both of her rapists and Bull, who would become the father of her sons, were men, much too old for her. Not until Mildred took her for her first doctor's visit when Lily discovered she was pregnant with Bull's child did she realize that she could have him put in jail. She was ashamed that she'd gotten pregnant in the first place instead of going to college like she'd planned. She wanted to do what none of the sisters, what no one in her entire family, had done. But she lost her way. She was sixteen. She didn't know nothing about being a mother.

Lily knew she'd made a mistake on her wedding night. Though she wasn't a virgin, the first kiss turned into a tussle and then brute rape. The next day during the wedding reception, Bull snuck off with another girl. But the damage was done, Aunt Lily's freedom irretrievable. She was caught like a spider in warm honey. She started drinking too. Back then, no one accused their husbands of rape. You just simply didn't say, "This man, my husband, raped me," and you certainly weren't listened to if you did report it. Poor and in Mattawan's hick country, if you were a woman, belly swollen, ankles bare and cold, you didn't have much say-so in your own life.

Months squeaked by for Aunt Lily and the first boy, Donnie Jr., was born. The day of her firstborn's first Easter was the first time Bull hit her. She'd bought Donnie Jr. an outfit for the special day out of her husband's paycheck. When she told Bull, she was dutifully surprised to feel the sting of his palm rattle her teeth. She thought she'd left that behind with her father.

"You ain't have no right to buy that outfit without my permission," Bull crowed, drunk. His other piece of ass was somewhere near, she was sure.

I have a photo of that day, with Grandma Dorothy, her mother Grandma Manuel, and Aunt Lily holding Donnie Jr. I'd always wondered why they all looked so caught off guard, like they didn't want the camera to hold onto that moment; they looked like they smelled something rotten. And I wondered if she'd had an inkling, before that photo was taken, that she would gently lay her firstborn down on a white filmy blanket (a gift from the christening) and calmly walk into her mother's kitchen for the butcher knife. When Bull turned around, Lily was charging him with a war cry she'd learned from her father. Bull grabbed a chair and brandished it against the swift jabs of his young, beautiful, infuriated wife, as she laced the bottom of the chair with deep, expert strokes. In fear of disembowelment, Bull threw the chair down and fled out the back door.

"Lily done gone crazy," he yelled on his way out.

"I didn't get beat up," she told me later. "I tried to kill a nigga. And I didn't wear no shades either. I went around bare-faced so everyone could see he'd hit me."

Lily had turned feral, tired of being used as a sparring partner. Bartenders perked up when she came through the door because she had inherited not only her daddy's chin but his whiplash temper when she was drunk. One night at her favorite watering hole, some unknowing guy brushed up against her, fondling her breasts, laughing, looking into her eyes to share the joke. He was six-foot-three. She was five-foot-four. She stood toe to toe with him: her pumps to his construction worker boots, her finger in his face, her neck arching up to see the edge of his chin. She was a wolverine, ready to rip him in the places she knew she could get to before he squashed her like a roach. Lily cursed him five different ways before she was thrown out. Eventually, she was put out of bars all around Covert, told never to return. When she was finally strong enough, she threw Bull out. She was tired. One night, drunk, he called her and told her he was coming over to kill her: "Here I come right now, Goddamnit."

"Not if I kill you first, you sonofabitch," she said. "You come on then." She hung up the phone. Lily loaded her daddy's shotgun, almost as big as she was, and went outside to climb the roof of her car. It was raining. She kept having to slick back the water out of her eyes, but when she saw Bull riding a bike from far off down the road, she aimed to the best of her ability and cracked a shot off.

"Come on, you stupid muthafucker," she yelled, liberated and deliriously elated. She cracked out another.

"You crazy ass bitch," she heard Bull yell as he fell, but he quickly climbed back on his bike and sped away.

Aunt Lily remembered that night with salty glee but spent the next fifteen years of her life trying to pull herself out of a personal hell, moving out of Michigan in 1988 and then returning to visit maybe five times in twelve years. It took her until she was forty and in therapy to realize that she had been raped and violated, because at that time, no one told her she was not to blame, and no one, most especially not her father, had come to her rescue.

20

Reservation Dreamer

As I GREW up, stories of subjugation, violence, and violation rocked me to sleep. These were the lullabies that my mother later told me and my siblings to get over, especially when I start asking questions she didn't want to answer in 2001. "You can't blame me for everything that happened to y'all, grow the fuck up," she said. I don't blame my mother; I blame history. I blame what we inherited. A legacy of addiction and abuse. The migration trail, miscegenation blues. I have tried to explain this to every man who said he loved me, but somehow I never find right the words.

"I come from a family of fighters, of dreamers," I tell them, expecting the men to understand that my chest is nothing but a cavity full of the stories my people carry in their blood. But I also come from women who learned, no, were taught, never ever to trust a man.

Over the years, I tried to understand how a woman could stay in a relationship with a man who swelled her eyes and busted her lip like she was an enemy. Sometimes, I tried to envision myself as a man: flat-chested, with wide muscular arms and a penis. Say I've got a construction job, a wife at the house, children, drinking buddies. Sturdy boots. A favorite bush by the side of the road to piss on when I'm too drunk to wait until I get home. I married the woman I loved when I was seventeen, my Adam's apple still not set right in my neck. What would make me turn around and stomp a mud hole in my woman, regular as lunchtime? Maybe she lied or cheated on me. Perhaps I was angry about something that happened at work, the foreman's racist remarks, and wanted to hit something. I could even conceive that my wife was just nagging me because I wasn't romantic enough or watched too much TV. Maybe she smiled too much at the milkman. Trying to fit those scenarios into my mother's relationship with Junior Bynum was like trying to slide triangle blocks into square holes. None of it—the excuses, the what-ifs, the maybes—impressed me enough. I could never see the honor in it.

In my bony seven-year-old chest that night we hid with our Christmas tree on top of us, I felt both shame and fear for the women in my family, and that continued into adulthood, until I felt like I was choking on the rancid air of memory. After I'd heard about or seen a fight my mother, aunt, or sisters were in, I was angry that they stayed. They *stayed*. Like it was a testament of faith, like sleeping in a snake pit and praying the snakes had already eaten. It was a crazy war dance of ardor that my sisters and I could tap out in hopscotch. I remember that confused anger, held it on my heart like a pinpoint of white light. My sisters saw all the violence too, and those little five-minute horror movies, the beatings, the abuse, came out in our own lives in different ways: Bobbie Ann was our lesbian; Tina our biter; Rochelle our heroin and alcohol addict; me the tattletale, the escape artist. But I wanted to be a teller. I wanted men to know I wasn't going to be quiet if they hurt me.

Older now, I recognize that my mother and her sisters had so few options, especially when they'd married so young. They had no work skills. No real means to support themselves. Their mother, Dorothy, was just like every other domestic worker in those days: most Black and Mulatto women from the countryside were scrubbing floors of wealthy whites while their husbands dug ditches, worked construction, laid tracks, and tilled the ground for their keep. What did most poor, uneducated Black women know how to do in the early forties and fifties but cook, clean, and spit out babies like well-oiled machines? But they weren't machines. Maybe they weren't all fragile, like I romanticize them to be, but they were soft; they were women.

I wonder about Dorothy and the lessons she taught her daughters, though she might not have planned to teach them these things—to stay and tolerate it all to the very last taste of spit in their mouths. The one thing they did have, from their father's home training, was the power of words; they could curl one sharp word from their mouths like a sword in the air and slice a man's balls clean off. They could make a man check himself to be sure he was still packing. But words weren't nothing against balled fists. Against sturdy boots in your ribs and alcohol and a dark night.

When I attempt to find the reasons for the men's behavior, hard-pressed, I look at our history in this country, and the more educated part of me understands that they were afflicted, too. Imbalanced. My mother's childhood and first marriage were about something arcane and deviant, about control and power. Dominion over the home front, and my grandfather's split identity: his role as a Black man, a man with some Indian and some white in him. He could never find his place. This was also about a woman's place. No one questioned the man who hit his wife while he provided, because provisions were gifts. The women and men of that era in Michigan were barely one or two generations removed from slavery. Sons and daughters of ex-masters, ex-slaves, Free People of Color and freed-man. White sheets and burning crosses that no one talked about. The stories I heard of the caterwaul fights, the ones I saw, felt like enactments of the desire to erase the past of bondage. To control at least one aspect of a man's life, something in his immediate vicinity, anything, and get paid fair and treated fair, and *that goddamn woman*. A strike, in the wrong direction, for manhood.

And then there was the re-memory of prejudice and discrimination, of fear that if you said anything, the government could come and get you, like in the olden days, take your wife and impregnate her, take your children away from you and drop them in a boarding school, take your livestock and eat them, take your land and farm it and turn around and sharecrop it back to you. That was how it was for the Indians back in the day, in the not so far removed past.

American Indians had no claim to nothing.

Black slaves in the 1700s and 1800s ran away to Indian tribal lands and began marrying into tribes, and Black Indian babies were born, and there were repercussions. A kind of pogrom began against the Indians, full-blood and Mixed. There was, in earnest, an organized attack on lives and/or property of anything Black Indian, and on Indian institutions that contained or educated Indians with Black blood.

This was the social legacy of erasure. This was the shaping of the Domestic Abuse Crisis Hotline. This could have been why my men were so hogtied angry; why my women kept goddamn quiet. Come hell or high water, we stuck together.

Still, after all these years, I find it hard to be sympathetic to the men who hurt my women. On so many levels, I realize I have my Aunt Lily's spirit. If a man who says he loved me hit me once, I would tell on his ass, and I would walk away. If he happened to get the chance to hit me again, I imagine I would try to end his life. I know I have it in me, something rock hard and ancient as Pompeii. My aunts must have sung this lullaby to me like warriors' songs when I swam in my mother's womb, one they forgot to sing to my sisters and their own daughters, because each one of my cousins tangoed with their men. My mother must have been tired of it. Tired of the yawning fear, the perseverance that forged them together like used car parts. They wanted someone to survive. Unhandled.

They must have circled my crib one night and wove a spell out of willow reeds and swamp mud and crawdad pinchers. Must have danced and toasted their work with well water and whiskey. And they waited. And they wept and they prayed.

Sometimes, especially in my dreams, I feel like I am all of them. From the first Mildred, my great-aunt (my grandfather's sister), who drowned herself, rumors purport, to my sister Rochelle, to my daughter. But I am still waiting for that man—a friend, a husband, a lover—to be tender, to be constant and solid as Noah's Ark with his love. Though I have loved men, I have never been able to get it quite right. Something stops me from trusting them all the way, as if that man who says he loves me will lose what I give him, this satchel of prayers whispered into me since my first breath, since before I could breathe, when I was only a star in my mother's womb. Crooned to me through membrane and memory. The sound of my mother's voice over my head—craggy, off-key—as I drifted to sleep: "Swing low, sweet chariot, coming for to carry me home."

Despite everything, I recognize, and to an extent even admire, the steadfastness next to the misery, knowing that, for my mother and her sisters, there had to be love somewhere in the beginning. Something shared and good before the bad times. But theirs was not the intimate love of seasons changing but the obligatory love of soldiers, an acceptance of the pallor of war. I know I could never be that brave.

That strong, weak, and in love, all at the same time.

21

Blanket Dance

IN ANOTHER TIME, another place, a Midwestern light flittering through, and a steady Lake Michigan current propelling her, my mother had been cherished by at least one man—my father, John Al Buchanan. They met in 1966 on North Edwards Street, a few weeks after she'd purchased a house there. She met him, she was fond of saying, despite the fact that Emma Gamble, Daddy's on-off girlfriend, "tried to keep him hidden behind her own house every time I came home from work or grocery shopping."

My father's sister, Lil' Bit, lived across the street from Velma, and next door to Ms. Gamble. One day, by chance, Lil' Bit saw my mother climbing her front steps into her house and called Mama over to meet her brother, John. My mother crossed the curbless street, where the thin, soft layer of pavement seemed a last-minute idea, and nodded her head during the introductions. My mother rarely shook hands. Maybe John said something funny and she looked down her nose at him with that long look meant to keep men at a distance.

"I *beg* your pardon," she'd have said.

My mother says it wasn't love at first sight, but I don't believe her. My father was a strikingly handsome man. And Daddy—I imagine him pretending it wasn't a watershed moment either, with a slight shrug, so slick-daddy Chicago cool, but I'm sure he broke out in a sweat under his arms. In spite of the five grubby hangers-on she was rearing, my mother was still unbearably beautiful. A queen on that Northside Kalamazoo street. Sparkling walnut eyes, coffee-black brows, arched in a lavishly creamy face.

He'd probably stepped coolly out of his car, a '57 Chevy, or one of those box cars that rode smooth and close to the ground. Sporting freshly pressed black slacks, he was dressed sharp as a catfish gill. He wore the spit-polished shoes he'd traveled all the way to Detroit to buy with his last paycheck from Buck's Tools. Maybe he wore a jacket, but he was definitely armed with that Buchanan smile, a sultry half grin that tugs at the corners of our mouths when we're excited or nervous or both. Almost always both. My mother probably tossed out a flippant joke about his car or shoes or the hot day. And she laughed. And he loved her at once when he heard the sound. Her abandoned laughter, a gorgeous, reckless meter telling of her survival, but he didn't know any of that yet. He was entranced by the sound, got lost in her peach-pit dimples. Smelled her soft, baby doll hair, busy with the summer morning shampoo scent.

The trouble started right then and there for poor Emma, who, my mother delighted in recounting as a testament to her own fierce Stafford prowess, would just throw a hissy fit all up and down the street.

"All over the Northside," Mama said, "rolling out in the street and screaming, just screaming for your daddy to come over to her house because she *needed* him." Eyes wide, my mother blinked innocently, as if to say, *I thought she knew.*

I often wonder if maybe Emma fell out because both women were pregnant at the same time with Daddy's offspring. My half brother, John Jr., was born about a month before my December arrival. Possibly Emma's famous "hissy fits" were prompted by the fact that they already had a little girl, a year or so old. She most absolutely had a mental breakdown when John married my mother and not her.

My mother and Ms. Gamble were second cousins. They looked like they could be sisters, both light-skinned with sable hair and slender, vulnerable mouths, but my mother had those bold, come-get-me eyes. Ms. Gamble's nose and cheeks were flecked with a light sprinkle of cinnamon freckles, as if a giant's mighty sneeze had scattered them carelessly there. When I was younger, my brothers and sisters would poke me in the shoulder, teasing me whenever the Staple Singers' song rasped out on the radio, "Poppa was a Rolling Stone." They sang the word "Yo" before Poppa. I'd laugh awkwardly, not really knowing what they meant with their derisive sneers. I tried to imagine my father contorted into a rock, mowing down everything in his path, but then the confusing words "wherever he laid his hat was his home" would follow. My daddy wore a black Fedora that he always took off as soon as he stepped inside anyone's house. But why would he lay his hat down whenever he stopped rolling? Though I giggled with my siblings, inside my frail body, some small part of my heart deflated, because I was almost sure I was betraying my father, but I didn't know how.

That my father loved him some women was not even a question, I realized when I was older, but he didn't beat his women, and that made my mother love him like a timber wolf for the rest of her life. I think my mother fell in love with my father's scent. In life and in my dreams, my father always smelled like tweed in the winter air and nearly gone peppermint candy, the red stripes faded and sucked down to white. If it was spring, his T-shirts and button-downs held the cinnamon tinge of Old Spice and perspiration. In high summer, he had a hint of red clay and honeysuckle behind his ears, an aroma that had followed him from the Deep South, the Bible Belt, where he was born and raised. With a wide forehead, strangely light brown eyes, broad nose, and high cheekbones (from the Choctaw in us, he'd say), he was a ladies' man to the quick and a country all to himself. An Okolona, Mississippi, mud man. A black earth man. I sometimes pictured him as a cornbread-fed golem with no other purpose than to get the hell out of Mississippi, which, in those days, was nothing but a bone yard for Black men. He was smart and eager to learn, even though he only had an eighth-grade education. Daddy came from a family of fourteen kids. Needless to say, they were chitlin-eatin' poor, like most Black people who sharecropped, but they were a tight-knit family. Where he grew up, they didn't have sidewalks or parks, just rickety houses, with skeleton filament fences and oak trees, whose leaves always managed to cast an ominous shade.

The one summer visit I took with him, a tense road trip from Kalamazoo to Okolona, was harrowing. While in the car and at rest stops, when he wasn't looking, Daddy's roly-poly wife, who hated me, either slapped, pinched, or yanked on my arm or hair every chance she got. When we arrived, I was grateful to have more adult eyes, which gave me a brief respite from her. And when night fell, I discovered a place where the flying cockroaches were so big to my eight-year-old eyes, I just knew they could carry me on their backs. "They have their own little cities, complete with stoplights," my father said. I woke up that Fourth of July morning breathing like I'd slept on coals and my bones were simmering like embers in the furnace my body had become. The humidity was brutal. That's why he was always smoldering with thick sweet scents and burning heat and I'ma-catch-you love. He *was* Mississippi. Every chewed slip of barnyard hay, every red rock, every tomahawk.

In the photos of my father before he married my mother, he is broad-shouldered, dapper and cocky. He cared about his appearance. Taken in 1960, when he was a skinny twenty-two, one photo catches him squinting uncertainly in the bright spring light, his hair lightly conked into a lump in the front like a real doo-wop singer. He dons a white jacket with deep, wide pockets, an equally brilliant white shirt underneath, and a cigarette dangles between his fore and middle fingers. His right leg is out, knee bent, and his head is cocked coolly to one side. On the back of the photo, a small notation says, "taken on Sunday while we were at rehearsal over to Aaron's on Edwards Street. March 20." The handwriting is elegant and flowing; it is not his or my mother's, because they both wrote in a sort of chicken scratch code (which I am, to this day, damned to possess). Daddy must have given my mother the photo as a keepsake when they became an item years later.

My father was a messiah for my mother—even if he drank like a fish, his breath faithfully tainted with a hint of whiskey under Listerine. He was like the sterling shadow of the moon pulling her tides into better, less tumultuous waters; he wasn't an angel, but he never hit her. John Buchanan effused country boy genteel manners, but more importantly, he was black enough to piss off her high yellow father. My mother fell hard for my father.

Another photo shows them on one of their first dates at a Masonic lodge—the group had tried to get him to join, but he refused. He'd found God by then. It was New Year's Eve. In the picture, they wear matching turquoise V-neck sweaters. Fingers hooked around a cigarette, my mother sports a white blouse beneath her sweater, while my daddy unfashionably dons a brown-collared shirt under his. By the red and white Winston packs and the four glasses on the table, with various levels of sudsy golden liquid surrounding a pitcher, I can tell that other people were sitting with them.

My father's face is plastered with a Chessy cat grin, one arm curled behind my mother's malleable back.

His grin says he'd struck gold.

Their love is palpable in the photo, so loud I feel as if I were in the room, overhearing their moist words tumbling into the corners of each other's hair and cool, vacant parts.

"You sho' is the finest woman in this room, Velma," my daddy'd say.

My mother would cock her head: "You damn right and don't forget it either."

The others at the table, unaware of their nesting, wait for the waitress to bring the next round. The music is blaring out of a jukebox, or maybe there's a band, and they are having a good time. It would be 1968 in a few minutes. My father is about to ask my mother to marry him. You can't see me, but I'm there, a ghost hurrying them up. My mother would be pregnant with me in three or four months.

On December fifth, I would enter a world steeped in charcoal and smoke-tinged sorrow, a world, from Mississippi to Sri Lanka, wallowing in an unfathomable mourning. Black America's prophet, their savior, Martin Luther King, Jr., had been shot on April fourth, eight months before my birth. My mother and father would break up a few months after my birth.

Maybe because of all this loss, this losing of kings and fathers, maybe that's why I like to know about the sad parts first.

Like most from my generation, I read about the fight to end desegregation in history books, yet I never knew marches had taken place on the same streets where I caught the city bus downtown. Times were tense but electric a few short years before I was born, change clinging to the horizon like the scent of burnt cane fields. Hot, thick, and sugary sweet. Suffocating to some. Comforting and timely to others. From the photos, I could see in the strained faces that retribution for cotton field labor was in the air. But there was also fear, lakes and lakes of fear. Where would this fight lead? I could see the hard question above the heads of kneeling Christians in the South: to freedom or the end of the world?

On other faces, confused and infuriated whites *and* Blacks wanted a return to normalcy. But their lives were about to shift forever. Wasn't nothing coming nice and soft to nobody anymore. Although billed as a peace movement with Gandhian aspirations, the Civil Rights Movement had piranha molars. The words "we shall overcome" and "Black Power, baby" were the passwords into the deep blue sea of the fight against segregation. Its time had come. The white sheets knew it; the old folks whose hands cramped picking cotton knew it; and poor white trailer-dwellers knew it. Politicians knew it. Only the South, the ugliest Faulknerian, honeysuckle-scented belle at the dance, kept her shawl on. But segregation had to end.

In Kalamazoo, there were marches downtown and pickets on the Northside against store owners who refused to hire Negroes. The tension had been building since Dr. King's visit to Kalamazoo and speech in 1963. King's appearance not so coincidentally intersected with that of Mississippi governor Ross Barnett. He was famous for his quiet handling of SNCC youth leader John Lewis (later Congressman Lewis) and other Freedom Riders in Mississippi, by jailing them during their dangerous bus crusade across the South that would end in the beating of a busload of Civil Rights protesters, Black and white. Ross wanted to make an example of them. Kalamazoo police officers were equally as brutal to their Black marchers and didn't want "their Negroes" getting too uppity.

My mother doesn't remember where she was when the '63 and '65 riots happened. "Maybe watching them on TV," she says. She didn't know that Dr. King, fearing for his life and the safety of his family, shortly before his assassination, had bought a handgun. She was busy with her own survival. But I believe I felt the anger of the world in my mother's womb. Myself and the other 1960s babies were heralds of the unrest that peppered Kalamazoo, and the country. We were bearers of Malcolm X's inestimable strength, as well as his "suspect death," as Kalamazooans called it. And in the Midwest, when the summer of 1967 came round, and one of the worst urban riots in history bucked Motor City like a barebacked tornado ride, it must have seemed like everything would be swallowed up in its wake.

Two hours from Kalamazoo, the Detroit riots raged: looting, destruction, the burning of both Black- and white-owned businesses, likely started by arrests made at a bar in a Black neighborhood. Frustrated with racism, lack of jobs, and the effects of inequality, the arrests incited militants, innocent bystanders, uncles, and cousins to push and move, and push and move, and they pushed and moved until over forty-three Blacks were killed and hundreds were jailed. Entire neighborhoods were left in smoking shards.

I remember images from this time, and specifically the *Eyes on the Prize* special that took me years to watch all the way through. The screams started, without fail, and my skin began to crawl and tingle, and I wanted to shed it. When news of King's death spread, the cameras caught it all; it was as if the world was going in slow motion, the black-and-white footage granular as the tears fell on stunned faces, and when time sped back up, America was left naked, segregation a souvenir of the past.

But the marchers didn't know that they'd won then. At the moment when the bullet pierced King's soft flesh, they were simply devastated. The walking wounded. I heard the rustling of starched pants moving against each other under the singing and clapping, heard hearts pitter-thump, pitter-thump under T-shirts and borrowed calico dresses. I heard their breath beneath the taunts and jeers of the white onlookers. I smelled the tear gas. Saw Sunday best hats in the wind and felt tired feet in good shoes. Every time, after the first fifteen minutes of watching the scenes, I was only conscious of a penetrating anguish in my chest, cleanly peeled to my core by those tides of bodies who all felt the same thing—not being equal, knowing they could die, knowing they were fighting domination. They meant to be free. It was a revolution good enough for Goya's haunted eyes.

In many ways, I know that helpless waiting and watching stance. When I finally saw all the footage of *Eyes on the Prize*, I wondered how the white people who sneered and yelled, "Get them *Niggers*," felt years later when they saw themselves on television or in photos.

When a white child recognizes their mother or father taunting Black marchers—men, women, and children—or sees their white fireman daddy has turned on the fire hoses to rip the skin off another human just because it was Black skin, what do those kids feel? Are they as angry, embarrassed, and ashamed as I am for them? But how can I have sympathy for that brutality, those kids, most who would grow up to be like their racist fathers? How could I empathize with those human monsters and not my mother's attackers?

The men who abused my mother were also practicing their craft of domination. Both the racist and the batterer have to be in control over someone or something in order to feel "big." One form of this abuse was wreaked on an entire race across the country; in my mother's home, on a smaller scale, a similar thing was happening. Only she couldn't quite call it what it was. Power. The sheer need to bend something.

To break it like a spirit.

And though I couldn't articulate my feelings about it as a child, I was enveloped with the same helpless fury when I watched Black people clubbed on TV or saw them being jailed. The connection was there, deep and plundering, invading and heady. My mother suffered. The protestors suffered. It was inhumane.

That same month King died, I was conceived. Eight months later, my winter baby screams pierced Borgess Hospital corridors. My mother never taught me resistance, but I was born with the ethos of struggle and a century of transformation in my blood, impressed by the furious sounds I heard through the thin membrane walls. I was a child of the movement. A fighter. But what kind? Which fight was my fight, the revolution or the home front? Where was my place in this family, this generation, where women and kids were pummeled? Where no one talked about it. Did I make war with the "establishment" or with my mate? I had no idea. Yet, growing up, I continued to listen to the sounds in the streets for clues. Leaned out windows into the day's business, catalogued my siblings' terrible fights with each other. I was always listening closely to what adults were saying. They hated that.

Through this all, my mother took no stand for or against the struggle. I think, for the most part, it was because she was caught in her own battles. As far as she knew and cared, she was French, German, Indian, white, and a "little bit" of Black. Her father was Mulatto, born of a Mixed father with Indian blood. Her great-grandfather on her mother's side, Thomas G. Manuel, was a white man—according to Aunt Katheryn and his Social Security application. But he was passing anyway. My mother wasn't taking sides. She wasn't getting in the middle of any race conflict. She had her own war.

Growing up, my mother never overtly taught me Black pride or talked about my African heritage, maybe because she didn't think it applied to her or her kids. We never owned a Martin Luther King, Jr., album. Pregnant for nine months of the year for ten years, she needed freedom from her bed, from the kitchen. She could only focus on what was in front of her. Dodging smacks upside her head. She focused on staying alive.

When it was over, when she met my father, she rejoiced, though hesitantly. She had just survived Junior Bynum. She was trying to feed and raise her kids while the bruises were just blending back in with her normal skin tone. Velma was also exhausted, and still angry. Her mother had moved in with her to have fat removal surgery and ended up dying of cancer only months later. Did my mother mourn that loss?

When my father entered her life, she was healing from many things. In the 1967 photo that New Year's Eve, the one of her and Daddy curling into each other like church mice, both smiling, she looks so young, so relieved, vulnerable. She's almost translucent with happiness. And maybe a bit guilty that happiness, despite the world's best attempt to explode it, had finally come.

22

Daddy's War

MY FATHER SERVED in the Vietnam War before he met my mother, sometime between 1962 and 1966. While he didn't necessarily distinguish himself, or as far as I know kill anyone, I nonetheless believe he was both scarred and scared during those times in a foreign land. Freedom and equality had been non-issues for him and other Black southerners all his life; it just simply didn't exist. The North, the Midwest, was supposed to be different. It wasn't. Daddy's kinfolk, like so many other sharecropping Black families, had ducked out of the South to escape Jim Crow and the fight against discrimination. Nearly 3,500 Black men were lynched in the good old boy states between 1882 and 1968, so the Midwest and the North were supposed to be havens for Black people. But with the race riots, bus boycotts, and general unrest, it seemed no matter where they migrated, they couldn't escape volatile change and all that came with it. No Black person in America, no Mulatto or Mixed blood, would be able *not* to take a side.

African American men were dutifully drafted to fight in a war for a country that refused to fight for them. That maimed them. Castrated them. Enslaved them. Spit on them. Raped their women. Indiscriminately murdered them. Yet on pain of incarceration, they *had* to fight in someone else's country, despite that two-tiered existence (For Whites Only), despite the hypocritical social strata of their own country (No Coloreds or Dogs allowed). Equal enough to die in a white man's war, but not equal enough to drink from a white man's water fountain or use his bathroom. When my father was drafted, I wonder what was going through his head. When he finally got to boot camp, to a barrack, or handled a gun under the hawk eye of a white commanding officer, what was he thinking? I can't pretend to know what it was like for a Black man to go to war for America in the '60s. For a country that was still lynching their uncles and cousins back home in Mississippi and Alabama, bodies dredging up on riverbanks like driftwood. Their eyes and mouths open like bleached and bloated trout.

"Don't get killed, nigger," a pasty-faced sergeant might have said. "Then I'll have to be out there in front and catch the next bullet. We don't want that, now do we?"

"Yes, sir!"

"What? Which is it? No, sir or Yes, sir?"

"No, sir!"

"Whatcha doing here, brother man? You don't belong here," another might have said. "You wanna kill somebody? You think you can kill somebody?"

Pause: "Yes, sir. I think I can."

I will never be able to understand the small, hard knots John Buchanan's balls became when he was posted next to a white man with a gun in the trenches, or walking point before him. I'm sure when you walked the line, you had to at some point develop trust in the man in front of you and behind you, no matter their color, because your life depended on that mutual respect, but when they came back home, nothing had changed. My father came back inebriated, not looking for redemption but to forget it all: his luckless upbringing as a sharecropper's son; the relentless war; the insults and constant anxiety; the unforgiving South; his fear of being a Black man in America, sometimes touching his dick out of habit to make sure it was still there. Daddy never talked about Mississippi, but whatever he'd come across, noose or jungle, he drowned those memories in a bottle. When he finally stopped, he kept a tall, corked bottle of whiskey on his fireplace mantel, so he would never forget what he was and how far he'd come.

When I was eleven, Daddy made a surprise visit to our home on M-43, where we lived on Grandpa Stafford's farm for three years after his death. My father kept on his raincoat and slickers while motioning for me and Rochelle to sit down on the scratchy brown couch. "One day," he said, looking at me, but side-eyeing Rochelle, who he knew had started drinking, "I got so drunk I could feel myself drowning to death in my own body and I went to Hell."

"Whaaat?" we said in unison. He was a pastor by then. Mama had told him Rochelle was coming home smelling of weed and getting into trouble in school, skipping classes. But Rochelle sat at attention as much as me, keeping a straight face.

"I'd gone to a bar," he said, probably his old Northside haunt, the Seven Seas. "I downed five, six, maybe seven shots of whiskey. When I leaned back, I fell off the barstool, but I kept falling through the floor and down a hot tunnel, down and down to hell."

He died on that bar floor, he said, and when he got to Hell, one of the devil's minions took him around like a real estate agent, pointing out the different-sized boxes elegantly carved into the crumbling walls, already holding sinners like Daddy.

Daddy pulled out his handkerchief to mop up the sweat sliding down his face, despite the chill in our house. He was still afraid. "I knew that box was mine. When I came to, I still had the black soot of the furnace that burned down there stuck inside my nose. It was a whole year before that soot was gone. I just kept wiping and wiping, but it reminded me that I was doing wrong. I quit drinking and turned my whole life around."

When he awoke, my father was a changed man. He zealously cut out old, sinful friends, stopped drinking, and started attending church. He stopped all his womanizing, and since he already had a beautiful wife, Velma, with the light-skinned, long, crow black hair swinging down her narrow back, he was ready. He had everything he needed to start his new life. When he heard the calling (got scared shitless is another way to say it), he turned his life over to God. He became a preacher.

For some reason, my mother was furious.

Mama could have been Arabian or an Indian princess, but for Daddy coming from the South, she was two shakes from white; touching that taboo was like riding a mad bull. Being his trophy she didn't mind, but she didn't marry no *righteous* man. While she did attend church with him, and oiled the first five siblings up with Johnson's Baby Oil every Sunday, she secretly fumed. She wasn't going to be no *preacher's* wife. What the hell did he think he was doing? Messing with her life, smearing her image of him. At least that was one version of the story. The other version is that they were both unfaithful, and the entire church community knew, and Velma and John Al Buchanan broke up. Poor Daddy. It's possible that my father thought by making Velma a preacher's wife, he could somehow make her demons go away, maybe save her. Save her from herself and the past. Make her admit to feeling safe—something she would laugh at in his face if he whispered it to her in the middle of a swamp-black night.

Poor Mama. She was a go-go dancer for a few years because she had to feed her kids, but then she started working in a nursing home for the worst pay. She was trying to do right, but she simply couldn't see herself in the role of a preacher's wife. I've always suspected that she divorced him for fear of the expectations she'd face, but also, my mother was desperately threatened by the prospect of being this kind of safe. To her, it meant being noticed, in the limelight, giving herself over to a status and a position she didn't have the self-esteem to hold up. She'd rather set her hair on fire. Most importantly, she could hardly see giving herself over to a God who had never answered her pleas when she was getting her face smashed in. When she was being raped by her sister's husband. When she wanted to die in her own body.

"What has God done for me?" I remember her yelling when I was sixteen and full of born-again (I'ma-convert-you-whether-you-like-it-or-not) Jesus love. "Not a *God*damn thang," she said vehemently. Like *hell*, she'd be a preacher's wife. She wouldn't do shit for a God like that because he hadn't done shit for her, not once in her miserable life. She could be my Daddy's wife so long as he was drinking and womanizing. That's what she was used to from her daddy and her first husband, and all her sisters' husbands, but she refused to oversee Daddy's flock. That was a crock of shit, in Velma's humble opinion, and it was more than she could handle. She had kids to take care of; her mama had just died.

But secretly, before his drastic change, she *had felt* safe with my father; that was something she'd never had. He made sure she knew he loved her. Whereas Grandpa Stafford exuded the devil's charm, my daddy was dark and charismatic in a kind way. Grandpa Stafford would seduce you into his cave and then let you know afterward that you'd crossed the boundary line; then he'd snap your neck. Grandpa Stafford would love to have snapped my father's neck.

At their wedding, my mother was beautiful, donning a rich, long-sleeved, mint-green brocade dress, her hair coiffed elegantly on top of her head like a crown. The wedding was at the old Second Baptist Church on the Northside. It was a beautiful wedding. A big church wedding. A fairy tale wedding.

When Grandpa Stafford gave her away, his face was shriveled up so tight his lips disappeared, munching his whiskers into a tense blond caterpillar on his face. "We were scared he was going say something," Aunt Lily remembered. "Especially when he kept snapping his fingers in loud, hard thwacks because he was mad." He walked on down the aisle in a suit, though not in his trademark green plumber jacket, tall and stiff. He didn't chew snuff and spit. When the preacher said, "Who gives this woman," Grandpa Stafford said, "Me." An audible, collective sigh released from every chest in the room. Reportedly, he didn't want my mother to get married so soon after Junior Bynum's death. But I believe Grandpa Stafford was lonely after his wife's recent death, even though they weren't together, and he'd remarried too quickly. I think he really wanted one of his daughters to care for him like Dorothy had. When Mama refused to be his bed nurse, I could almost hear him say in his Skoal-shattered voice: *Damn ungrateful women. That's what they was born fer, wadn't it? To take care-a me. After all I did for them ungrateful sons-a-bitches. Goddamn ungrateful heifers.*

After my mother and father separated, Daddy made the circuit of churches, trying them on like new shoes. My father worked his way up from runner to deacon to Pastor Buchanan and eventually founded his own church on Douglas Street in 1978, dubbing it St. Mark's Baptist Church. But he was never truly happy. His second wife was a scheming plump tortoise, a bitch who pinched my arm white if I fell asleep in church, a prop in his box of tricks that preachers had to own. Nothing but paraphernalia. He always loved my mother almost as much as he loved God. He'd given up his first family for her, jeopardized his reputation by being with Emma Gamble's cousin, and still, my mother rejected him. Yet years after their breakup, she opened the door every time he knocked, to talk or touch, their aged bodies making love like papyrus reeds, their hot breath blowing on that flame that stood unwavering between them. Mama didn't love his elected vocation after they had already taken wedding vows. She only loved him.

But she also thought he was cheating on her. Her young, vengeful self said if he was doing it to her, she was going to give it back, harder. And she crushed my father when she started dating Daddy's uncle, Robert Gene. Daddy nearly lost his mind. Several times, my father drove all the way out to Covert to bemoan his fate to Lily, sitting at her Formica white table in the dinky kitchen of her rented house. "What am I going to do?" he asked Aunt Lily, crying into his coffee, black, two sugars.

My mother knew exactly what she was going to do. Punish him.

She sold the house on North Edwards and hightailed us back out to the sticks, to Oshtemo. Because my mother had grown up, learned to fight back in her way at last, my father could never control her. After a near death experience that made him become a preacher, after surviving the South, Daddy still couldn't have or handle my mother. She'd been places he would never know, done things he would never do. Lived a life before him, and he would never really know all of what happened. She'd learned to keep her stiff-lipped silence. She would never be a preacher's wife. Even though Daddy had stopped drinking, stopped whipping my brother Tyrone for stealing sugar cubes out of the cabinet. Drunk, sober, cursed or blessed, a cross or a brown paper bag in his hands, he could never keep her. Never spin the dangerous magic that she liked. That she was used to.

But she loved my daddy, the middle of her four husbands, best. Nights she spent perched on the front porch of our Southworth Terrace house on the Eastside, cigarette embers painting the darkness, her heart howled silently for him like he was the moon. When I approached the topic of their breakup with my father, I was sixteen. He was driving his old Monte Carlo through the south side, an oak tree–minted summer breeze stole through the windows, and before I lost my nerve, I shot out, "Why'd you and Mama break up? She said you cheated."

That silence was the loudest gulf of hush I've ever heard.

He had to be about forty-three, forty-four at the time. He needed a haircut. His short afro was graying slightly at the temples; a trademark toothpick roamed his mouth. Through his day-job

scent, the sweat earned from mopping school hallways and empty-
ing trash cans, I smelled the hurt, the misunderstanding, his judgment of how much he should tell me against how much I thought
I knew, in all my newfound sixteen-year-old wisdom.

"She actually cheated on me," he said slowly. "You know fella,
when two people are together, even though they love each other,
somehow they still end up hurting each other."

My mother hadn't said anything so wise or forgiving when I'd
asked her.

"Mind your own business," she'd said, and I sensed the mas-
querade of her words. She probably didn't know how to tell me
how bad it hurt. What it meant to be a woman in love. What it
meant to be a woman. She and my father were gorgeous in their
pretentious Great Gatsby youth, full of the abandonment, minus
the wealth. They were swingers. They'd survived a country's war.
The assassination of a king. They loved hard. They had survived.

But I also sensed that my mother quit trying mainly because
Daddy's new career had challenged her to change again. To trust
again. To move over. She hadn't dreamed this. The years she spent
in her father's house and then her husband's weighed on her like a
rain-heavy sky, one she'd finally found shelter from. Change again?
She wouldn't. She couldn't. But she missed my daddy for the rest
of her life. They longed for each other. If their love was a season on
trial, it was the cusp of summer.

Their love, misrepresented by spring.

23

Leaving Mattawan

WHEN I WAS very young, we used to have family reunions. Grandpa Stafford's farm was what we considered the Country, but really it was just twenty or thirty miles outside of Kalamazoo. (All of the Midwest was actually all country.) Brady Bunch–style, we'd pack chicken and coleslaw, blankets, board games, and toy cars. Mama would fold us all in a station wagon and spread her hand over our heads every few minutes so she could see out of the rearview mirror. As we drove, our city skin peeled off and shed by the roadside in the dust. We were different, freer children when we reached the gravel driveway of my grandfather's farm, pulling up on the lawn next to two massive weeping willows. When we heard the spring water running, smelled the hay-dipped air, we were nascent beings.

In the summer, Mattawan was a melting land. Grandpa Stafford's small hairless dog, Lady, barked herself hoarse as she chased each car that pulled up in the driveway, no matter if she knew the car and it had been pulling up in the same spot for the last twenty years. She was a mean cuss, just like Clifford Stafford, and treated us all with the same derisive lack of respect, snipping at your fingers even if she liked you.

"Shut up all that got-damn noise," Grandpa Stafford yelled at her without affect. Lady would glare balefully at him and slink away until the next car drove up, then she'd get to snapping and snarling all over again. Everybody was afraid of that yellow hairless hussy because she'd bitten us all at least once.

"What the hell y'all doing?" he'd yell at the boys. "Don't just stand looking like dummies, come and get to work. Goddamn lazy, shiftless niggers."

My brothers would pile out of the car, long and skinny as yellow wax beans. Reggie, Donnie, and Rodney were Aunt Lily's boys. My Aunt Mildred's boys—Walt, Timmy, and Cliff—seemed taller than corn stalks to me, even in their teens, their heads almost touching the cotton clouds. With glossy black hair and teeth crisp and white as chalk, each one of them could have donned a headdress and a couple of stereotypical stripes of face paint on their broad cheekbones and been the most authentic-looking extras in any John Wayne flick.

Horse flies buzzed lazily, weighed down by the blood in their bellies gleaned from a Palomino's twitching flank. The scent of the scorched topsoil, depleted of moisture by the sun, and a listless breeze rolled over our laughter, the clink of bottles and Miller beer cans. There was always a cooler filled with beer next to every other lawn chair. Behind the house, my brothers and cousins, in tight corduroy cutoffs and T-shirts, taunted each other into manhood, playing the dozens.

"Yo Mama so fat . . . She so drunk . . ."

"Well, yo Mama so ugly . . ."

They would bust up laughing, taking each insult dead in their bony chests until someone got mad and swung for real.

"I'ma kill you," the war cry went out and all hell broke loose. Two of the boys would try to strangle each other quietly in headlocks until their faces turned cherry red. Grandpa Stafford, always sneaking around, would appear out of nowhere, snagging the fighting boys around their rib cages and tossing them in the pond. Clothing, argument, all. "Oh, Daddy, don't!" the women yelled.

"Don't 'Daddy don't' me. Them little fuckers needed to be taught a lesson."

No one ever knew what that lesson was.

Grandpa Stafford pretended to farm, but mostly, besides drinking, he sold live bait: robust worms, spiny crawdads, anything that fish in the surrounding lakes would swallow. On breezy days, the scent of the bait, sometimes reeking like three-day-old roadkill, would hover over the farm. He kept his supplies in the bait house and earth-filled, broken-down refrigerators at the edge of the woods. The bait house was also stocked with mason jars, plows, drill bits, and jagged tools hanging from the ceiling. As a scaredy-cat girl, leering dark corners spooked me. I only went in on a dare.

I never saw my grandfather have a gentle moment in his life, and soused, he was a red-eyed bull, prone to jumping, yelling, and spitting, especially when prodded by female voices. Drunk or sober, he'd let nothing pass him by, man, woman, or child, without a hawk-eyed look and a comment that severed body parts.

During the reunions, I stayed far away from him and scampered in the field like a jackrabbit, splitting the cornstalks when I ran. The black dirt, soft as pound cake beneath my feet, spread between my toes. Showers landed in my plaits and the folds of my hand-me-down cut-offs.

"*Shonda*," my sister Rochelle hollered, angry because she'd be the one responsible for later washing my hair. "Get back here."

Ignoring her, I raced my shadow down each cornrow, my soles caking blacker and blacker. I loved to run. Later, while the grown-ups ate barbecue and piled up empty beer bottles in a bucket by the house, I made thick, chewy, fist-sized mud pies out of the Grade-A choice dirt from the sides of the pond. I've eaten soil all my life. I would always slice my make-believe friends the smallest piece, my pet bullfrog the second smallest, and save the rest for myself. To this day, I don't mind the taste of a good pinch of earth.

Faint whispers of music came out of someone's car, old honky-tonk or backroads blues, probably B. B. King. I imagine my mother dancing. I have a picture of her, maybe at twenty-five, in go-go boots, laced from ankles to calves in cream satin. When the music stopped, she posed her right thigh out for the camera, her entire wholesome leg bare and sleek up to the edge of the matching satin shorts that flirted with exposing everything. I secretly coveted that photo, enamored with her defiant face. I envied her daring, visualized how she tossed her head up and back, and with her mouth like a sailor—a proud family trait—if anyone told her she looked anything other than foxy, she'd snap out a few scathing phrases that'd make a rhino blush.

I wasn't even a thought when that photo was taken, but from stories I've heard growing up, I could guess how the afternoon ended. After the hickory smoke from the grill died down and everyone's stomachs were filled with potato salad, corn on the cob, and hamburgers, beer bottles went crashing against a plywood wall. An old argument that sat in someone's eye like a grain of sand would start. The argument scattered around the yard like wet, wounded rats. A fist in a hard wall or soft flesh. Things that happened in the past coming back to haunt them.

And my mother, no longer dancing.

24

The Eastside, Ray Charles, and the Supremes

SATURDAY MORNINGS FOUND the sounds of Ray Charles's "Born to Lose" suffusing the house from my mother's gigantic record player the size of a couch. If anyone was passing by, they'd get a whiff of Lysol, Pine Sol, Ajax, and Pledge coming through every screen door and open window, as we soldiers scoured the three-story house on Southworth Terrace so we could go play or watch *Creature Feature* with Vincent Price.

The houses on our street held Armenian and Russian retiree immigrants and second-generation Polish families with no children and lots of dogs. I never thought about the absence of children, about the atrocities that my septuagenarian neighbor and friend, Fred, might have experienced. With gnarled hands, Fred pulled open a drawer full of yellow rock candy from another country. When his sleeve slid up, I saw a green tattoo on his forearm, but never realized that he, or the old lady with diabetes down the street, may have suffered his own ethnic-cleansing war.

Mine was the only Black family on Southworth Terrace for years. By moving into this mostly immigrant neighborhood after Pullman, Mama had both changed our class status and shaken up the landscape and direction of the community. Besides our token faces, my mother and her boyfriend at the time, Jessie, weren't married. We were the only family with a single mother of six, and two sets of cousins on the next street over, who would pop up or call at all hours of the day and night.

Most Saturdays on Southworth found Ray Charles's scratchy voice easing through our house, followed by Aretha Franklin, then Stevie Wonder. One by one, the forty-fives Mama had stacked on the spindle clapped down, the needle swung over vinyl, and the music floated upstairs into my room. I was enjoying the small pleasure of not waking up with someone's foot crushed against my face or a toe in my mouth, and being able to stretch my skinny legs as far as I wanted on the cool sheets. The luxury of space was a delicious slice of paradise for me. I crunched my eyelids tighter together.

"Shon-*da*!" Mama called from the bottom of the stairs. "It's time for you to get up. Get up, right now!"

Usually the first signs of stirring from anybody in our house were an indication to Mama that every room should be filled with the rumble of young limbs and old arguments. That day, everyone else must have already been given their Saturday morning chores, because I heard the vacuum cleaner being pushed frantically across the rug, water running, toilets flushing, broom and mop handles banging against walls and occasionally someone's head. What was left for me? I prayed not the dishes. I hated washing the dishes.

Tyrone and Loren were in charge of giving the dogs baths and then cleaning the bathroom they'd soaked to high heaven. They also cleaned the garage and did most of the yard work, mowing the lawn and trimming bushes. All the other work was assigned in rotation; Rochelle's job was to dust every surface in the house and clean the kitchen, while Tina cleaned the upstairs and downstairs bathrooms. Bobbie Ann got the basement, which included sweeping and de-cobwebbing corners behind the furnace. I was scared of the basement. The baby girl, I couldn't really clean well yet without breaking something; someone was always supervising me. I did like to sweep, though. Only the broom was too tall, and the dirt never quite acted the way my mind willed it to and kept sliding under the dustpan or to the side of it, rather than inside. In frustration, Rochelle would push me out of the way.

"Here, let me do it." She blew her breath hard to let me know how useless I was to everybody and especially her, a serious pain-in-the-ass obstacle to her first day of summer plans. My army family scoured, mopped, dusted, and swept our three-story house into submission. The one thing I could do well was the china cabinet and the shot glasses, because my hands were small. Mama set a dust rag and furniture polish in front of me, and when I opened the cabinet, a dusky-sweet, pungent scent wafted out and slipped inside me. This was, I know now, my first taste of poetry, as I struggled to describe that scent and the dust that spiraled in and out of the sun beams, stealing through the window above me.

Mama orchestrated our lethargic movements from the couch, a roast pan on the floor between her legs next to a half-peeled of bag of potatoes for the scalloped cheese potatoes and ham she would feed her small army. She chose a cold, plump victim from the back of the bag, relieved it of its outer skin, sliced it long, and placed it in the roast pan filled with water, occasionally smoothing her hand over the pile, their shapes resembling ostrich eggs.

I mulled over the collection of shot and wine glasses, snapping the dust into the sun's rays and stalking the dust particles. Mama poked her head out of the kitchen.

"Shonda, you gonna polish the glasses or snap that rag all day?"

The black butcher knife she clutched paused in the air. She watched me, then shook her head. Around thirty-four or thirty-five then, she was trying to figure me out, her last baby, her girl child. The dreamer.

Already, my active imagination had its own space in the house. I hummed incessantly when I was happy; I talked to myself. I didn't need an imaginary playmate. I had corners to whisper to, and towels, and the blue jays outside our bedroom window. They whispered or warbled back. I hated dolls, ruthlessly pulled their heads off every occasion I got. My favorite place to nap was inside the cool, hard dryer, or on top of the washing machine in the basement, despite the nervous tilts of grayness throughout the service room. Something about the sound of the water pouring in circles and plummeting against the clothes lulled me. I liked to fold myself into small places, the linen closet or under a stairway, and practice slowing my breathing, until even I didn't know I was taking up room in the world. I was my father's daughter as much as I was hers, shy but bold. Certain, but still wary of too much noise, too many people, even if they were my blood. I knew Mama loved me; she just didn't understand my curiosity. The right corner of her mouth tilted up as I observed the universe of dusk particles scurry away from my open hand and the dust cloth I'd shaken.

I took everything off the three shelves, dusted them, and set them next to me. Between smoothing and slicing, Mama hummed a little, sang the wrong words along with the songs, mostly off-key, but she didn't care. She loved to hear her own voice, and even though it often sounded like trucks grinding into gear, her voice was a comfort to me too.

"Be careful with my glasses," she murmured, wiping the sweat from her forehead with the back of her hand, expertly wielding the knife.

Finally satiated with my game, I'd dust the shelves, and with lips puckered like a diamond, I'd put each glass carefully back in its place. The bustle of activity slowed to a lull around eleven and my siblings disappeared, slipping out the doors before Mama could inspect. My nose was still stuck in the China cabinet, inhaling the secret heartwood aroma until I grew dizzy. The house was empty. At least for a few hours, I had Mama, Diana Ross, and the Supremes—and the scent of the summer—all to myself.

ONCE, TELEVISION BLARING over the buzz of conversation in the living room, my brother Tyrone nudged Tina as she lay on the floor watching TV, crossing and uncrossing her legs. "Stop doing that." We were watching some program that the bigger kids had decided on, as usual. Mama was at work. Tina ignored him, clicking her feet behind her, catching and then releasing her ankles. "Stop, Tina," Tyrone ordered again.

SHE LOOKED BACK at him and rolled her eyes with a "this is *my* body" look and turned back around, feet still in the air. XW. XW.

"Tina," Tyrone half-smiled, disbelieving that she'd disobeyed him. "I *said* stop."

It got quiet. Maybe they'd had a previous argument and he was continuing it; she ignored him again and popped her gum in the silence. In a blurred flying leap, Tyrone, impersonating the monsters he'd seen handle our mother and momentarily becoming one himself, landed on her back, snatching Tina's head up. We all screamed his name in unison as his fists ricocheted off her face. A cascade of blood spurted out of her nose as she screamed and looked for a place to lock her teeth in his skin. (Tina's nickname was Cannibal for the chunks of flesh she'd taken.) I'd seen my brothers and sisters fight before, but the ferociousness of this act must have snapped something in my young mind, because I became a screaming siren. Loren grabbed Tyrone, yanking him off Tina.

"Shonda!" Bobbie Ann grabbed me and shook me. "Stop it. Shut up! Damn it, Tyrone! Look what you did!"

Tina palmed her bloody face and stumbled upstairs. We heard the door slam shut. Tyrone shrugged Loren off and shook his head, turning back to the television program with his half-bemused smile intact. "Told her silly ass to stop."

An hour later, the phone rang.

"Tyrone!" Hysterical and angry, my Aunt Mildred screamed through the phone. "I ought to come over there and kick your little narrow yellow ass from here to kingdom come. You little dumb shit."

Tyrone's normally butterscotch hue turned the color of an ice cube.

Stunned, we looked at each other. How'd Aunt Mildred know what had happened? How could Tina have called her with no phone in the room? We ran upstairs to find her bedroom empty.

"She gone," Loren said.

Apparently, when she went upstairs, Tina had flung herself off the roof of our two-story house, and not caring that she'd broken her arm in the fall, ran the twenty-some-odd blocks, roughly two miles, to our aunt's house.

"See," Bobbie yelled at him. "Aunt Mildred done called Mama at work. She on her way. You *is* in *big* trouble."

When my mother got home, she tried to whip the Black Indian off Tyrone's back and thighs. From that moment on, in my little ten-year-old brain, I gained a healthier mistrust of men, especially my brothers. I resented and feared the power men had, the sheer physical advantage, which even our brothers gleefully wielded over us. I began to learn to protect myself with controlled silences, choosing when and what I wanted to let go of or reveal. I learned to smooth things over. To lie when I had to. I knew when to stay quiet. When to tattletale. And when to hide.

For my mother, there were times when she had every right to drown the lot of us. It is remarkable that the six of us, seven, including my mother, made it to the trough every evening we lived together, because surely no family in the world loved or hated each other as much as we did. There was always sabotage, subterfuge, switching of alliances, and constant strategic spying. We were living a dramatic play, each moment of our lives an example of hard-won battles, of the glory and the tragedy of growing up in a large family in the Shakespearean Midwest.

To some mothers, raising children, being the hub of the family structure, is like doing time in prison. The time and work involved in raising one child—a crier, liar, a perpetually sticky human being—is probably the equivalent of lifting a ten-ton 18-wheeler at least once a week.

Imagine lifting seven 18-wheelers.

I'd always been suspicious of the smiling, apron-laced women on TV who always *gave* love without seeming to expect anything in return. It seemed unreal to me. Women were expected to possess something instinctual, some inner mechanism that allows us to cope, to bypass the desire to break down and stay broken until the storm passes, until the child sleeps, until children stop fighting, until the husband goes to work after a quickie, not even kissing you. We were famous for following expectations. But some women would rather pack a heavy lunch, grab the car keys, and cross a state line or two, never looking back. Women stay because, yes, we are nurturing but mostly because *staying* is prescribed onto our little white mouse brains.

My mother did the best she could as a woman raising seven kids virtually alone. The first five my mother bore for a man who brutally dominated her life and spirit. She hated men soundly after that. I, the sixth child, was a reminder of the only man who really loved her. She let that love go and hated herself for it. But the last kid, Popeye, who almost killed her with his birth, made her forget.

My siblings and I fought and tortured each other within an inch of our lives until we graduated high school (or didn't) and moved out of her house. There were broken bones and stitches, natural stomas and bats (both the real, screeching ones and wooden ones meant for baseball); there were ruptured kidneys, broken arms, busted noses, blackened eyes, throats slit, and rabies shots. Sometimes, all in one day.

I was sure my mother loved us, but I knew she wanted to run.

I have several displaced memories of my mother patiently rubbing my back with Vicks, nursing me back to health after a bronchitis attack or a sleepless night haunted by ghosts. It was always a twilight-hour attack. The moisture and heat in my lungs clanked like rusty nails when I coughed. Between midnight and six a.m., in my feverish recollections, she was either on her way in or out the door. I remember the blue nightgown she quickly slipped over her head or, more frequently, her white nurse's shoes, tapping in time to the hum deep in her throat: *Swing low, sweet chariot, coming for to carry me home. I looked over yonder and what did I see, coming for to carry me home, a band of angels coming after me, coming for to carry me home.*

It was only much later, after I had my own daughter and sat up nights with her to ease a cold or sleeplessness, that these memories came rushing back to me like an unexpected breeze on a Michigan shore—and it was only then, after I'd loved and let go, that I knew my mother's humming was the song of her own salvation, voice cracking on notes she tried to carry to a higher lilt. She'd sing the hymn in a hoarse whisper until I fell into a fitful sleep. Those unsteady, bent tones of hers stole into me, seeded survival in my bones.

I was kept alive by plantation prayer and an angel.

25

Tribes and Tragic Mulattoes

"Is Teresa ready? It's Shonda, Miss Aguilar." I hopped impatiently from foot to foot.

We weren't the only half-breeds on the eastside anymore. The Aguilars had moved in around the corner a month or so ago, and I could tell by their dusky taupe complexions that they had some half-breed in them. Teresa Aguilar went to my school and, for a brief time, was in my eighth-grade class. I liked Teresa. I liked saying her name because it rolled off my country tongue like a foreign place I'd never been to. She had a scared, quiet smile. I could see the bones in her neck under her wispy black ponytail. She always wore baggy pants that cinched at her ankles. She never asked me, "Are you Mixed?" like the other kids in my school who glared suspiciously at my thick, wavy hair. Maybe she also got slammed with this question each place she moved and didn't want to make me feel like I had made Nigel feel that day years before, ostracizing him because he was biracial. The most she shyly said to me about my appearance was, "I like your hair."

I see my brief friendship with Teresa through a foggy veil, but I know we were tight, and every day I would stop outside her house before school and wait for her to come out. I remember she had a big family; her dad and mom were a dumpy, smiling couple who didn't speak English. Her house smelled like peppers, and the only time I went halfway in, I could barely get through the front door because they had so much stuff on the floors. Teresa's family had kept more of their country's culture—some Spanish-speaking country, maybe Mexico—than us Black Mulatto kids could handle. The neighborhood kids made fun of them. Their clothes. Their house. Their Spanish, which sounded like popcorn in a pan to us. We were so country bumpkin dumb we didn't know what a Mexican looked like anyway. We all liked saying their names, but somehow their reputation for being dirty and unkempt moved through the neighborhood like locusts. My mother asked me if it was true: "Yeah," I hemmed and hawed. "But it's not *dirty* dirt."

"Don't ever go inside, you hear?" My mother locked toilet paper and bars of Dove and Irish Spring soap in her linen closet so she, we, would never be without.

"Okay Mama."

I only went into Teresa's house that one time. When I was older, I realized how sad it was that we made distinctions between ourselves because of color. If you were too black, you got ragged on because "at night, who could see you except for your teeth?" If you were too light, we just knew you had a white parent somewhere, and that obviously made you think you were better than us. Then you got beat up for that white privilege you never even knew you had.

No one ever said to me, "Are you a Black Indian?" It was always, "You Mixed, right?" And when I nodded my head, or shook it no, they thought they knew me. They put me in the "Mixed box." Defining me that way made them feel comfortable in their own skin, while I withered in mine. And when Mama started dating Jessie, so black he looked like walking licorice, that didn't help my biracial case one bit.

BEFORE JESSIE, WITHOUT an "other" at the bid whist parties my mother played with my aunts and uncles, she must have felt lonely. After, when her boyfriend (later husband), Jessie, entered the picture, he was a decent temporary stand-in. What I didn't know at the time was that though she brought Jessie into the fold, and he courted her and all us kids in proper Southern fashion, she always had something, a little sugar on the side, to compensate for all she'd lacked. "Put about five men together," the saying went in my house when I was growing up, "and you get the one you need." I grew up with the knowledge that a man had to be damn on point for us to go only to him for the things we needed. Because of this, all my life I've been hard on men and shoes.

When my mother said, "Shake that money maker," I did; I didn't know I was supposed to get a few coins for my trouble until much later. A real man, a good man, was supposed to take care of his woman at all costs, and it all cost him something: food, clothes, child support. Jessie didn't know none of that: he was country as the day is long

In the beginning, Jessie was my hero.

Because I was the baby girl, he'd always arrive from work late at night, his dark green janitor jacket pocket bulging with a candy bar or suckers for me. But then James "Popeye" Jackson was born.

"Let James choose first," Jessie said. "He the baby."

I stabbed my little brother with my eyes. *I* was the baby before him.

Jessie wasn't the watered-down, milky black of our tribe but "midnight black," "frying pan black," the bigger kids would snicker behind his back. And my siblings were especially mean, peeking around corners, falling to the floor in fits of muffled laughter as he slept, and they pointed at his corn-riddled feet and "crusty" hands as though he were a domesticated Bigfoot. They figured it wasn't an insult to say the fact of the matter, and the honest-to-God truth is that when Jessie smiled in a dimly lit room, you could see his teeth glowing like lights. I shit you not.

None of that mattered when he handed over his night's find-ings to me, candy and coins, as if I were a princess and he the father trying to please me. If Jessie could afford it, the big kids would sometimes get a couple of snacks to share, which became a mouthful each, but I always had my teeth liberally slicked with caramel and chocolate. My sisters and brothers seethed. "Why he don't bring *us* nothing?" My real daddy was on the other side of town, and he never brought sweets, only handed out peppermints in church while gnawing on his stupid toothpick. I was always told I'd been the spoiled favorite, but I had no memory of Daddy in the house, no memory of him stuffing chocolate in my hands. I had no idea that Jessie was fostering the conquer-and-divide technique in me. Trying to weasel away one of my mother's staunch supporters, to break into the ranks that the Bynum kids and myself, the only Buchanan, had formed. I was already a big crybaby and a tattletale, but now Jessie was trying to put me in an entirely different camp, so when my siblings passed me by, it was always with a quick hard pinch or a shove. Like white slaveholders driving a division between Indians and Blacks, Jessie was dividing us. He was pulling me to his side, had marked me as his source of information and comradeship. I didn't understand power dynamics in that way, the manipulation of a child. I only saw the baubles and sweets he offered me from his upturned hands, palms salmon pink.

As far as I could see at first, Jessie was a good guy. That same horrific Christmas we moved to Southworth, he'd brought me a fuzzy ball of a dog, part Alaskan malamute, part pit bull, the most beautiful mutt I'd ever let kiss me. That act seemed to seal Jessie's good guy status. I knighted the dog Sam, and he fumbled in my loose arms and shivered from nervousness; I did the same, unsure if he'd like me. Despite the jealousy spurred by the candy bars, that summer we were free, young and free. From what we couldn't really articulate or name, but we felt it in our eyeteeth. The sun seemed turned on to its highest volt. Jessie was our mother's guardian, a huge ebony watchdog on Southworth. Gullible and innocent, I was bought off easier than the rest. Later, Jessie coerced the older kids with a few dollars if they helped him with janitorial work, told them some jokes, gave them a few pats on the head. Mama seemed happy.

"She shouldn't have married him though, that's her problem," Aunt Lily ranted years later. "You don't have to marry every damn body who's nice to you."

Marry him she did, and Mama was grateful. Jessie had scared away Robert Gene, one of the worse monsters she'd encountered. That was probably the first time that a man had interfered on her behalf against another man and actually saved her. Her own father hadn't even done that. She didn't have any heroes, human or divine. So, in the beginning, she forgave Jessie a lot. Then later, she went to work with him at his janitorial jobs, even if she had worked an eight-hour shift at the nursing home. She'd go with him at night to the banks and empty trash while he vacuumed. If I was allowed to come, I would eagerly bang the black trash cans into the trash bag we'd brought with us, and joyfully polish countertops.

I had no idea that this was part of Mama's way of keeping track of Jessie, who she had come to suspect was spreading his love around town. My mother was still working off the fumes of having for once been the distressed damsel, but Jessie was taking advantage of it. Hailing from Benton Harbor, about fifty minutes from Kalamazoo, and by way of Jackson, Mississippi, Jessie obviously had no idea what family he'd married into. He mistook Mama's gratitude for weakness and of course, Mama being a Stafford, that simply wouldn't last. Plus Mama's new best friend, Stella, a salty Polish woman with a bulldog glare and a sailor mouth, wouldn't let Jessie get away with mistreating her friend.

Looking back, I realize that the Black friends my mother had were only those she'd kept after breakups. Mostly relatives. Everyone else Mama consorted with were either her light-bright family or white people. Nobody seemed to mind or take note of that fact. Jessie was pleased as punch to have Mama on his arm. For a while, Jessie loomed like a lone waterlogged star over us, cooling everything down, which wasn't so bad, until it wasn't good.

THE FIRST AND last time Jessie ever whipped us was the night we broke the girls' bed. Loren and Tyrone were home rather than out terrorizing the neighborhood. For some reason, we were all grounded. Bobbie Ann had moved out earlier that year and was on her way to California, her first big trip away from Kalamazoo. Overnight, Loren became the new sheriff in town, walking around the house with his skinny chest puffed out and ordering us around:

"Shonda, get me a glass of water."

"Tina, get me a pillow upstairs."

"Rochelle, hand me the phone."

Every day, Tyrone would challenge Loren every inch of the way, and though Loren had to fight him for the crown, at least Bobbie would no longer be using him for a punching bag. Both of them being skinny boys and all, it would be a fairer fight.

But this night equalized us all. We were playing headless horseman. It was suffocating, sticky, and dusty under the bed where I was hiding, waiting in the darkness for the signal from my sisters to poke my head out. If my brother were on top of the bed, waiting to roll his head around as if it had been chopped off, I'd scream. I just knew it. That would get us in even more trouble than our skinny knees and elfish feet banging on the floor. Mama had one of her famous migraines; she feigned a fainting spell and lay on the couch in her pale blue nightgown like the Mulatto Scarlett O'Hara. But she'd get up the energy to come to the stairs and yell at us every once in a while.

"Shut up all that Goddamn noise! Dammit all to hell!" Mama slapped the wall. "Don't make me come up there!"

We hushed each other and hunkered down for a few minutes, then resumed our game as quiet as thunder mice. Jessie came to the foot of the stairs.

"Y'all Mama not feeling well and you need to go to bed like we said, now." Jessie sounded hoarse, like he wasn't used to yelling at five kids all at once. He was probably wondering what he'd gotten himself into. We decided to shift our positions, with the girls on the bed and the boys on the floor. It was Loren's turn to be headless horseman.

"*I'ma coming to get you*," Loren's disembodied voice floated around the room, and when his head popped up, we were so scared that a collective scream pealed involuntarily out of our mouths. I felt a sudden wetness between my legs; I'd really peed on myself. Now I was going to get it, but I kept quiet. I wanted to keep playing.

At that moment, the sounds changed in the room, akin to a redwood falling, and without warning, the bed frame and box squeaked deceitfully off their hinges and crashed to the hardwood floor. The sweaty tension was excruciating as we waited for Mama's heavy gait up the stairs and the expected beatings she would give us, whipping us up one wall and down another. After years of skinnings, she'd made it a kind of art.

"Shush," Tyrone said. He cocked his ear.

"Mama gone kill y'all," I sang, happy that pissing in my pants would be ignored. Besides, as the baby girl, I rarely got real beatings like the older kids.

"Shut up, Shonda." Loren looked doleful. Because he was now the oldest since Bobbie had moved to California, and by what he now realized was simply a stupid inheritance, he would be responsible for what happened in the house: whatever was broken or lost, whatever got smashed or kicked, he would get the worst brunt of it all. Mama would make sure of that.

Our eyes locked in agreement that since we didn't hear Her coming, this was a saving grace and, consequently, the end of the game. Time for bed, for real this time. Solemnly, we opened the door, prepared to file out of the room. Jessie stood in the doorway.

Sinisterly, he smiled. His teeth gleamed white against his greasy dark face. A crack of thunder may have flashed behind him. His grin was almost maniacal, as if he'd been anticipating this moment. We yelped again, startled by his luminescence.

"Uh-huh, I was listening the whole time." He tapped a thick leather horse whip against his left palm, about a foot long. The length included the separated pieces of strap that spread the pain out to the wielder's desired location.

He was not really going to use that on us, I thought. For a moment we were stunned, frozen in incomprehension. Surely, Mama had not granted her approval for this to happen. A stranger, a man who'd only just ingratiated himself a few months earlier, punishing her brood. We looked behind him. Mama was nowhere to be found.

"Line up," he said, still smiling. He was not going to do it.

Like soldiers, we trudged into range of his upraised hand, but we didn't believe it. Not until the blows came. A look of malicious glee lit his eyes. He might have licked his lips, he surely bit them when my brothers tried to lightning streak by, and Jessie grabbed them, locking them closer to him when they tried to fight back.

Years later, thinking on how she could have let this happen, I figured Mama was just tired. So tired, she just couldn't work up the energy to punish us this time. In all honesty, we were a horrible bunch: disrespectful, sullen swamp rats, wild little black-red wolverines, and taken all together, we were probably the closest thing to a tornado with six heads, including Bobbie. *There's a man here,* Mama probably thought, *let him do it.* And possibly, unconsciously, it was her bizarre way of establishing that she trusted her new man, letting him beat us like that. She wanted him to know that she trusted his judgment. Though this smacked of the past—her mother, Dorothy, relying on Clifford to parcel out the beatings—it was all she knew.

Today, some psychiatrists might call what happened to her, and us, post-traumatic stress disorder.

They might even venture to say she was one tired Tragic Mulatto, still waiting to be saved. Still an abused child, an abused woman.

According to a report by Amnesty International, Native American women experience sexual and domestic violence at a rate that is 2.5 times higher than that of non-Native women. The Stafford girls, RedBlack girls, were all raped or molested several times, each one beaten within an inch of their lives, trapped in a mire of physical and emotional suffering. They didn't know any of this. We didn't have any of those words, *post-traumatic stress*, in our mouths.

We caught fireflies at dusk. Wings ripped from our backs.

We ran the sun down and vaulted into the hot dark.

Mama would clock us with any number of objects—extension cords, hangers, house shoes, brooms, and dustpans—because we were hers and no one else's. I like to think she knew nothing about the horse whip Jessie used on us, that he'd kept such an object in his cleaning van and came to our house with it, thinking that maybe, just maybe, he'd go riding the next day and might need it for a horse, not kids.

After that night, that whipping in the hallway, the light a sickly greenish gold on our twisting bruised bodies, a trust we had in Mama broke right then and there. Not our spirits but our pride, and the simple feeling that we'd all been in it together up until that point, that she was there to protect us against any man and we her. If we stuck together, we thought, not Grandpa Stafford, nor any of the other relatives or men she loved with blindingly fast fists and hands, could hurt us. Not all at once. But now, she was with Jessie, and we six little Black Indians were all by ourselves.

26

Ghost Dance

THAT SUMMER, MAMA packed us in her circa 1977 station wag-on and carted us out to Big Daddy's house in Bangor, Michigan. Big Daddy was Junior Bynum's father, my brothers and sisters' wide-girthed grandfather who ran his family like a chain gang. I never remember Big Daddy wearing anything but stained white sleeveless T-shirts that showed off his flabby arms, his fat stomach protruding over a pair of patched blue jean overalls.

When we spilled out of the wagon and scattered, Big Daddy watched us, bug-eyed incredulous, and yelled, "Y'all lazy little niggas gone get to work." My two skinny brothers, fifteen and sixteen, with small hills of muscles barely pushing out of their biceps, reluctantly followed Big Daddy and his four sorrowful-looking sons to the musty, dilapidated barn. At the "pssst" from the other direction, my sisters and aunts hurriedly disappeared through the front door of the massive house (to my young eyes, anyway) to do their chores: clean the house, wash clothes, wash dishes, and cook whatever had been killed for dinner. I was only able to escape Big Daddy's wrathful eye because I was the size of an exclamation point.

"Where dat little one at?" he sometimes called, maybe making sure the pigs hadn't eaten me, but I never answered. He didn't remember my name either because I didn't really count. I was a nine-year-old weakling who couldn't carry anything heavier than a few corn cobs, a small basket of laundry, or a sack of potatoes.

Plus, I was what they called fanciful. *Touched*, my sisters said, meaning touched in the head, not in my right mind. I turned any chore into a search for fairies or magic wolves. I turned sweeping into a scene from *The Wizard of Oz*. When I heard music, I seemed to float into my own wispy cloud of singing and dancing, vibrating with the sound. My siblings laughed but I didn't care.

My young auntie Paula, a year older than me, liked that I was a little weird, but maybe only because, as the youngest of her family, she also "saw" things. Deemed mildly off, and not yet worth her salt either, Paula and I were pretty much left alone to run around barefoot and wild-haired for the next two weeks while Big Daddy stomped back and forth between the barn and house, orchestrating his kids and my siblings as they shoveled poop, plowed the fields, pulled corn ears and shucked the husks, fed buckets of corn to the echoing silo, cleaned the house, mowed the acreage that made up his farm, and did anything else that was commanded.

"I'm feeding y'all, ain't I?" Barely. Pots of greens and hog maw, and mashed potatoes with corn on the cob, fried corn, and corn-bread were prepared by his wife, but Big Daddy always got firsts, seconds, and thirds before anyone else was allowed to eat. The boys fought like baby wolverines when it was their turn, devouring everything on their plates. My brothers even woke up before the sun rose to sneak food out to the barn: they were starving. Often, Big Daddy belt-buckled the boys or kissed them with swift, unexpected head cuffs and chest punches if they looked cross-eyed at him. If the girls turned up their lips or sucked their teeth in anger, they received whoopings from their mother, Mary, a sweet, translucent-skinned white woman, who I always thought was from another country.

Lucky as a three-legged dog, I slipped and slid through my minor chores and out the back door to cozy up with the goats, colts, and pigs as soon as I could. One day, the farm and house were quiet. The kids had all piled into Big Daddy's truck bed for an ice cream run to town. His wife was watching soap operas in a rare moment of reprieve from her husband's fierce gaze.

Lying on my stomach on a small hill overlooking the front yard, I became engrossed in a car parts magazine I'd found on the back porch. For some reason, I was momentarily fascinated with spark plugs and pistons. (I'm pretty sure this was the beginning of my "information for information's sake" attitude that irritated my family.) The Michigan July heat pinched fat drops of sweat from every crevice of my body. The muggy air saturated between my shoulder blades and under my armpits. I'd tied my drenched T-shirt just above my navel and constantly tugged the much too short blue jean shorts out of my crotch.

The sun slanted against the corn stalks as a slow, flat breeze tried diligently to push through the humidity. A small black box radio sat a few feet in front of me. Bangor was in the middle of Hicksville USA, where the only radio stations that reached us were devoted to soft rock revivals or '70s pop—not the gospel, Stevie Wonder and Diana Ross tunes, or B. B. King blues I was used to.

I let the music roll over me, peculiar tunes I had heard my sisters and brothers make fun of as "white music." I turned the magazine pages slowly, tolerating the pukey sounds my auntie Paula said she adored.

She plopped down with her bounty from a secret kitchen raid.

"Oh, I love this song," she clapped. "Turn it up."

"I knew you wasn't really Black," I teased. Her family, shaded pale, creamy yellow to see-through orange, looked white except for their sandy freckles and curly, duck-feathered hair. Paula stuck her tongue out. "I'm Black enough to kick your little Mixed butt." She turned up the volume, and a song that I later learned was Kansas's "Dust in the Wind" blared out: "everything" was "dust in the wind." That meant me. My mother. This world.

The sun suddenly split me in two, sliced right through the top of my scalp, and severed my forehead down to my neck and heart.

Against my will, I could feel something open up. The ground or my soul.

The violins and acoustic guitar solos tapped inside my skull like a curious bird at the window. My body filled with the syllables, the refrain, an almost chant, and I experienced one of those euphoric moments where the world falls away and you're floating. Those weren't my hands or my stomach on the ground. Those weren't my feet attached to the legs that weren't mine. I was rising. I was higher than the ground and Paula was growing smaller next to my own body, existing only on the periphery of the song.

When it ended I felt an almost keen pain. The words of the song wove an entirely new path before my dirt-caked feet. I'd had what was called an out-of-body experience, appropriate for the psychedelic '70s, filled with philosophical, drug-induced discussions around war, but at the time, I had no idea what had happened. The radio announcer talked so fast and low through the static that I missed the name of the group, but later I learned it was Kansas. Then there was silence. Paula left to get something when the next song began. By this time, my teeth were chiming.

A strange sound, skinny sitar chords or maybe an electric guitar, filtered out of the radio box, and with the first drumbeat of the next tune, I was transported to another world. Again. This one dark, inviting, salacious, forbidden: It was "Hotel California." The images of a dark California highway, demons, "cool wind" in the singer's hair, lifted me from the ground. The lyrics combined with the guitar riffs were a door I didn't know existed: unconsciously, I knew I had a different choice at life. I was a Mixed kid, with, according to my mom, "some Indian in us." I grew up with Motown in my house; I didn't know this kind of music existed. Realizing there was so much I didn't know, everything, every question, every sweet possibility flooded through me at once. The images in the song lurked over me like sweet pieces of fruit on a tall tree. And where the hell was California? At nine, I'd been frightened and fist-fed (like any good preacher's kid) conflicting narratives of heaven and hell, but the image of the bottle of wine, first as a spirit, then as pure seductive evil, took me years to unravel. Still, right away, the eerie story instilled in me a sense of decadence and impermanence, a ripping away and an assurance that there was more to life than I knew.

The song folded all the possibilities of youth, imagination, and madness into one moment on that hill where the wind had just begun to move. The heat let up momentarily. The twin guitars serenaded me like the devil's flute, opened me to the alleyways and smoke-filled rooms and marijuana plants in Humboldt County before I knew what any of this looked like. Later, each time I caught the song on the radio, I tried to decipher the metaphors, the plea for help and sanity, for salvation and forgiveness, that the song implied.

"Hotel California" let me know that adulthood was coming like a speeding car, and my life could be that dark desert road that held only me: no family, no mother, no one fighting or arguing. My life could be different: my life could be my own. My sisters had visited California; my cousin Cliff lived in Los Angeles but I could barely find it on a map. The image of the solitary traveler seemed as freeing and full of abandonment as it was spooky. I could be free, from what I couldn't quite articulate, but it had something to do with feeling trapped by my small-town life, by the family that I loved and feared, that shadowed me with their needs.

I had no idea that years later I would live in Los Angeles, and I would become that traveler, roaming the dark streets for something nameless, pushing my car over the concrete labyrinth that was the abyss and the mountains of California, all in search of deliverance: of sanity, angels, hell, and release.

The eighteen years I lived there, traversing communities from Watts to Beverly Hills, I would see everything in both of these songs. I would come in contact with flower children who believed in the verses Kansas sang so truthfully: the past, present, and future apparent all at once. I rode the bus with transvestites and gang-bangers; I met the devil more times than I could count and lived to tell.

That afternoon when I was nine, my mother picked us up too soon, and we spent the bumpy ride home in the back of our stepfather's open-bed truck, lying skin to skin, dusty feet next to rough hands. Work bruises against the intact places. If someone had inspected us, I'm sure they would think us feral; they would see our fur matted from the summer roamings. They would see our hungry, hot eyes and smell the wet behind our ears. While my brothers and sisters recounted our adventures in hoarse whispers, nursing wounds and sharing survival stories, the sun slipped into the western sky and the warm night air kissed our burnt skin, hooking its last rays of summer into the rats' nests our hair had become. I smiled at their whispered relief and recountings of the worst and best of Big Daddy's farm, but I was silent. Something sweet and potent had seeded in my navel.

Somewhere between the leaving of home and the returning, I had grown up.

WE PULLED UP into the driveway close to midnight. It was the twilight hour where the bodies walking in front of your half-open eyes looked like walking mushrooms with feet. We piled out of the car and up the front porch. Mama unlocked the door and flipped the light switch.

"Oh my God."

"Velma, what is it?" Jessie shoved past her.

A dank, acidic scent mixed with sweaty alcohol invaded the living and dining rooms. Through a sleepy, lemony blur, I could see the mess. All of my mother's things—her clothes, pieces of furniture, her shoes, valuable records—had been overturned, pulled out, strewn on the floor, and doused in acid. The china cabinet had been rifled through, her personal papers, pictures, and books lined with acid. Her bedroom was strewn with smoking clothes taken out of the drawers. She found the note.

"That crazy mothafucka." My mother wept against her fist.

Robert Gene had broken into the house. He said he hated her and that he was taking back everything he'd given her or he'd destroy it. He was obsessed with my mother and wanted her dead. I didn't start crying right away, not until I saw my mother's face fold inward like a trampled bud. If the act was meant to frighten her, it had done its job; if it was meant to hurt her, her heart was a bull's-eye.

"I'ma kill him." Jessie grew about ten shades blacker, a slick-road black, blackberry black, solid volcanic rock black. He couldn't protect her, he knew now, nor could he stop her past life from popping in on them. Regardless of his impotence, he tried to take charge.

"Nobody don't touch nothing." Jessie pointed to the cheap '70s chaise lounge Mama had extravagantly bought earlier that year. "Big girls, y'all make the little kids stay there. Velma, call the police. Boys, let's look around. He could still be here."

We'd brought all of Big Daddy's kids back with us, so my brothers had more backup power, felt less afraid. Indignant, skinny-chested boys, their normally tawny faces were chokecherry red that someone wanted to hurt their mother like that. My brothers and uncles fanned out. They followed Jessie's orders and scouted around upstairs and downstairs. Suddenly, there was a rumble from the basement and a yelp. I clung to Paula on the chaise lounge, intensely aware of her mother's smell on her skin, emanating like a talisman against dangers such as this.

"He still here! God-damn crazy bastard," Jessie yelled. "Get 'em!"

Jessie banged up the basement stairs through the kitchen after Robert Gene, chasing him out of the house. I saw only dark streaks and then the screen door slammed shut. Excited by the chase, the boys streamed out of the back door like silverfish. I heard feet pounding on the ground around the house. Then cold silence. We little kids looked at each other. Standing in the middle of the room, Mama was no use to anyone, her face wet from silent tears.

When they came back, the boys collapsed on the front porch.

"We chased him as far as Rockwell Park," Tyrone said, "but we lost him."

The police arrived and Mama poured out the story. A few head-shakes later, after a filed report and snapped pens, the police left. "Breaking and entering, nothing stolen, domestic dispute." I could see how unconcerned the police officers were, as if hot and violent criminals lurked in other corners of Kalamazoo and they couldn't wait to get at them instead. After the police left and every crack of the house was checked, every window locked shut, we kids finally climbed the stairs, fanning out to the three upstairs rooms on floors and beds.

I lay my head down but couldn't sleep. I didn't realize I'd actually nodded off until I heard glass breaking and another scream from Mama. The bigger kids, fueled by adrenaline, hadn't succumbed to the weakness of sleep and had stayed up talking about what they would do to Robert Gene if they saw him. Then we heard the crash and shatter. "Mama, you alright!" Loren yelled. My brothers, cousins, and sisters sounded like a herd of elephants running down the stairs. And again, the boys tumbled out of the house with baseball bats. Robert Gene had waited for the lights to go off and hurled a wine bottle through my mother's bedroom window and ran. He meant to kill her.

Luckily, she was in the living room with Jessie comforting her. If they would have been in bed, they both might have died from the shards of window glass or the bottle. It must have been terrible for my mother, to be loved like that.

Finally, as I slept, breathing three a.m. air, tangled in my auntie Paula's limbs on the bed, I had a nightmare so vivid that the taste stayed on the roof of my mouth into adulthood. I was back at Big Daddy's, on a hot, dusty road that we'd taken in search of an elusive swimming hole. In the dream, I was walking down the dirt road alone. It was so hot I could feel the sweat running down my neck. So hot the sweat flies weren't even bothering me; they were just kind of floating in the dream air. Though I just kept walking and walking, as if I was on an escalator belt, a small structure on my right continued to stay there. When I finally turned to look, it was a dilapidated, one-room shack that I couldn't leave behind. There were three men staring at me from the window. Their waxen, vaudevillian faces began to melt from under their black, box-shaped hats. Melted right off into the windowsill and then into the sand below. Horrified, I ran, but I just kept coming upon that house again and again, with the men waiting for me to look and start their hideous melting. I continued to have this dream until I was in my late twenties. I know what happened that night had something to do with it, but it also felt like a kind of foreshadowing. A few weeks later, a man molested me in a car sitting in our driveway. In the daylight. Monsters are always monsters.

The Bynums' Aunt Lorraine brought her new husband, a Mexican from California, as if she was showing off a prize. He was like a unicorn to us, handsome and unique with his slicked-back hair and black hurricane eyes.

"Call me Uncle Freed," he told us. A new uncle, I thought, excited.

That same day we were all going to the store, and because the car was packed, I had to sit on Uncle Freed's lap in the back seat. As soon as I sat down, he slid his hand under my halter top and started massaging my breasts. I was nine years old. I squirmed and tried to get off his lap, but he held me tighter, trapped. Someone climbed in the back seat, and while he was distracted, I broke free and jumped out of the car. I ran to the basement and hid in the darkest room, not caring about the spiders and other critters I knew lurked there. What had happened? *He'd touched me.* After that, if he came over, I never stayed in the same room with him ever again. If I knew he was on his way to our house, I ran and hid in the upstairs bathroom closet with the sweet-smelling towels, or I folded myself in the washing machine in the basement. I listened until he and Aunt Lorraine were gone.

I never told anyone, not until I was older. As Uncle Freed could see me, was watching me with those hurricane eyes from wherever he was in Kalamazoo, I started wearing long-sleeved shirts with buttons so I could button myself up all the way to the neck. For some odd reason, I stopped washing my neck. Maybe I thought Freed would see me or come into the bathroom. Irrationally, with a child's mind, I thought this even when I knew he'd gone back to California. When my teacher, Mr. Eaton, tried to get me to unbutton my shirt when he saw a button cutting my throat, he saw how dirty my neck was and reported it to the principal. Nothing happened. I still looked like Shonda the innocent girl, but that bastard, Uncle Freed, tore a hole in me. I learned to stuff that moment in the basement of my mind and forget it was there until I was pregnant with my daughter. When it flooded through me, I felt unclean, dirty, and ashamed all over again. It was a physical act to dredge up that memory, as if I was in denial that it had happened. As if normalizing it, I would always think, *I was only touched, not molested, not raped like my mother.* Nothing like my mother. "But you were molested," my friend said. "Anyone touching you like that molested you."

The melting faces in my recurring dream became both my mother's fear and mine rolling into one spiked ball. Though it only happened to me once, that moment broke me: ruined me as a child, haunted me as an adult woman. *He touched me.* I think about being molested at least once a day now. I can't imagine what Mama's breaking looked like, then, and all these years later.

27

Miracle Baby

THE TEACHERS AND principal of Bruckers Elementary, clad in polyester and spandex, patrolled the usually quiet hallway, waving us to keep quiet as we sat Indian-style under bulletin boards and art class projects, our backs mashed against the cold cement walls in the basement for what they told us was a storm drill, but their mouths sat long across their faces, their eyes blank marbles in their heads. Their hands shook, leaf-like.

"Children, heads down," Mrs. Redmond said. My fourth-grade teacher's usually powdery cheeks had slowly lacquered into a familiar cherry red when confronted with unpredictable or unruly kids or uncomfortable parents. With Mrs. Redmond pulsing like a lighthouse, I knew this wasn't just a tornado drill. It was the first time we'd been ushered to the basement. Our bodies lined the floor like rocks along a stream. The fluorescent lights had been extinguished and replaced by an eerie buttery glow outside. Pencils and papers rustled on our laps with an occasional titter slipping out from a bolder, less attuned student, but all else was silent. A low, moaning wail issued from outside.

A tornado was coming.

In what seemed like a sudden scramble, the principal, whose face and name have faded but not the sound of fear in his shaking voice, announced that we were going to be let out early. We cheered. We clapped.

"Quiet down, children," he said. "This is serious."

We gawked at him; was he serious? An early dismissal was like a Barbie Dream House from Santa. Cartoons were waiting. Cap'n

Crunch cereal was waiting. The teachers sternly waved and shushed us as the principal talked on, but we continued to rustle like butterflies in a field. Our papers and books would stay exactly where they were, he said gravely; no one could collect anything from the classrooms. The buses were waiting.

When the school doors swung open, the giddiness in my chest plunged. The wind was tugging the world sideways. The sky was a terrible swirl of grays and white, encompassing all the colors of a heron's wings. My imagination added gnashing teeth as I boarded the rocking school bus, and then, a large, wet, pink tongue as I ran home from the bus stop past the towering empty houses of my neighbors, wincing at the idea of a tongue ready to lick me up as if from an ice cream cone's first melting scoop. Usually, I liked storms. Under the amused gaze of my mother, I'd fling myself into downpours, or jump into puddles, or dive into snowbanks. One winter I flapped my arms and legs for hours, making angels in the snow until I couldn't move. I was frozen, saved only by a friend who lugged me up to the house and dropped me on the back porch to thaw.

Watching thunderstorms was our family sport, and, truth be told, a weird Midwestern pastime. As if we were at an airplane show, we'd all crowd on our porch with chairs, waving to the other families who'd brought out their own chairs. I think my mother even made popcorn once. Whenever the flash struck the peeling hazel-black sky, we cheered, and a shiver of excitement lit through me. The lightning crackled, the thunder rumbled, and for some inane reason we applauded the ferociousness of its power and ability to destroy. Maybe we applauded its life. Its indestructible life.

But as I ran home from school that day, my bones chimed with warning and the wind sliced through me: this storm was different. Just as the tornado alarm began its high-pitched groan across the city, it started to sprinkle, then pour torrents of rain. The wind changed and I was running in slow motion. Tree branches and debris, pop cans and chip bags, were snagged, then whirled past me, and I clamped my teeth together, folding myself over against the tug, the lure of weightlessness, to keep from flying away. I mumbled prayers I learned from Sunday school that had meant nothing until now, praying the sky wouldn't drop on my back.

When I got home, the house was empty except for my dog, Sam, who leaped into my arms as soon as I opened the door. The house echoed. I almost peed in my pants. I expected someone to be there to embrace and protect me from the storm, undo the knot gathering in my chest. But I was alone this time. All our lives, Midwesterners prepared for storms. Tornadoes, blizzards, floods. It was a part of our internal clock. Instinct.

Kalamazoo has the misfortune of being in what meteorologists have termed a bowl or valley. When the tornadoes hit us, they shake up along the sides, knocking the teeth out of fields and parking lots, tossing around cornstalks and husks; strawberry patches and wheat; tractors, cars, and barns indiscriminately, like confetti at a parade.

And tornadoes sometimes killed people too.

I was familiar with every place to hide or tuck myself into during any potential catastrophe that arose, until the waters ebbed, until the snow stopped, or until the heavy licking clouds of a tornado passed over. I knew we were supposed to do any number of things to avoid being sucked up in the unconcerned funnel, but at that moment I couldn't think of what.

I dialed my mother at work. In Galesburg, at Matheson Nursing Home, she was at least thirty miles, three townships, and numerous meandering highways away from me at home. I could see the distance stretching out over the lone darkened roads as the tornado (three, I later learned) gathered grit and speed. The phone line crackled with static. A disembodied voice told me to hold on. My mother picked up quickly, as if she'd been standing next to the phone.

"Take Sam down in the basement," my mother said in a rush. "Get under the stairway or in the bathroom tub but stay away from the windows." I hung up and dashed downstairs, scared but strangely excited, as if I was watching the storm come to me and fold over my house like a hand closing into a fist. First I ran for the bathroom, but though the window was small there, I could see the world tumbling past. I dashed under the stairs that led from the kitchen, not caring about the spiderwebs brushing my face, winding around arms and legs. Suddenly, the house shuddered and moaned violently, as if trying to give birth, and then a quiet that I had never before or since heard descended on our house. That buttery gray light that had saturated the school hallway had found me and crept down the basement stairs like a ghost. I was in the center of the tornado. Sam whimpered and dug at me with his claws. I whimpered and clasped him tighter. I could hear my breath under his, our sounds crystallized, hardening into precious stone. As timeless as that moment was it ended abruptly. The tornado shifted, pounding against the house. I flattened Sam against me and screamed as the windows and doors rattled and a final deafening pound, then a *whack*, signaled the tornado's departure.

I waited for the sounds to subside, then crept upstairs to look out the side door. As if placing an exclamation at the end of a sentence, hail plunged from the sky, shattering the air, raining down upon the house, littering the yard and driveway with white, lollipop-sized balls. *Those little fuckers can kill you*, the gleeful voice of my Grandpa Stafford stole through my head. I later heard that some hail had been so big, car roofs were dented. I don't know if anyone died in that tornado, but the damage was legendary.

When my brother Tyrone came home from school, we inspected the house and yard. "Holy shit," he said, rounding the corner. The oldest, largest maple tree in our yard lay like a marooned ship. It had been ripped up by its roots and flung down, leaving a hole the size of a Volvo gaping in the ground. The spindling white roots, rocks, and dirt dangled from the tree's base. "You're so fucking lucky, Shonda. That could have fallen on the house."

Had I hesitated at the bus stop or allowed myself to gawk at the storm's beauty like I normally did, I might have been under that tree.

That was the second time I almost died, according to family lore. The first time, my father told me, was when I had bronchitis as an infant when we lived on North Edwards Street on the Northside. One day when my mother was working, I was having trouble breathing between the bronchial coughing and spitting up. He'd been dialing my mother's job when the back of his neck started to prick.

He heard my arms moving but no sound coming from me.

"Your color slowly changed," he said, "from brown to red (probably from indignation as much as lack of air) to purple. Then blue." I'd stopped breathing.

Panicking, Daddy heard a voice say, "Lay hands on." That term has followed Black people from the South but also, I'm sure, from Africa, a story narrated by the first African griot, I'm sure. It is how you heal people when nothing else will work. The simple act of touch is sometimes the best medicine. And my father, being the born-again and recently professed preacher that he was, did what the voice told him to do. He touched me softly as I struggled to breathe, placing both his hands on my discolored squirming body, and from his divinely ordered administrations, I vomited up a series of mucous balls that had been lodged in my lungs, choking me.

"That's why you're a miracle baby," he finished humbly. He told me this story when my sister Rochelle and I survived a freak car accident that left both of us unscathed, the car totaled. She'd just gotten her license. Losing control of the car, and destroying my mother's only mode of transportation to and from her job two towns away, devastated Rochelle. She never trusted herself again;

that accident, the possibility of my death at her hands, lingered. But we were alive. For me, that was number three.

Miracles are supposed to come in threes.

MONTHS BEFORE I was born, before my father saved my life, Dorothy scheduled an operation to remove excess fat from her belly. She took medication that promised to shrink her down five sizes. It was experimental liposuction minus the years of trial and error and industry warnings. Dorothy was the perfect guinea pig. Uneducated, Mulatto, divorcée. No lawyer. If anything went wrong, she was on her own.

"I want to be attractive again for yo' daddy," she probably told the girls in a rare conspiratorial moment.

Shortly thereafter, while Dorothy was scrubbing some white woman's floos, she noticed a trickle of blood seeping down her thighs. Blood was soaking through her cotton dress and apron. She was hemorrhaging. Her employers called an ambulance, secretly scared this yellow negra would die in their spotless house, the house she herself had just cleaned.

When the doctors opened Dorothy up, "she was fulla cancer," a phrase I've heard all my life. Her death certificate said "extreme embolism." Blood clots. Yet why did my mother repeat the myth of cancer? Whatever the reason, after Dorothy gave every ounce, including her spit, to Clifford and still trying to please him, Dorothy was actually going to die for him.

When she was released from the hospital, Dorothy moved in with Velma because she didn't have anyone to take care of her; Cliff wouldn't do it. My mother resented this like hell. Mama was the only daughter who didn't drink. It was just assumed that Velma would do the caretaking. No one asked.

In the summer of 1967, Dorothy was forty-six years old when she died.

In my mind, I always combined my grandmother's death with another story, one years before her death when she started taking a different kind of medication to restart her menstrual cycle which had mysteriously stopped. One day, when Dorothy was combing her hair, she suddenly confided to Lily, "If I didn't know any better, I'd think I was pregnant."

What did little Lily think of this comment? That her mother was melodramatic, obese, and wimpy? That her mother was too old to get pregnant? Was this another trick for attention? Who would care? Not Velma, if she knew. She'd rather chew nails.

Dorothy miscarried that night. My aunt says her father wasn't there and came the next day. But blending this miscarriage with my grandmother's death, I imagined an entirely different scenario:

When everyone reached the hospital, the doctors hurriedly prepped Dorothy for surgery. They made a dismaying discovery.

"Mr. Stafford," one of the blue coats muffled his words through the mask. "We need you in the room."

When he entered, smelling of stale beer and cigarettes, likely covered in another woman's lipstick and perfume, he was pulled around to the bottom of the operating table.

"We couldn't save the fetus."

"What the hell you say?" Cliff said, ready to fight. The doctor pointed.

Stunned, Cliff opened his sterilized hands to catch the sixth girl child, which had a tumor wrapped around her neck. Stillborn. This part is true.

Grandpa Stafford took the dead child from between Dorothy's tired, fleshy legs; she was too doped up on medication to know what was happening. He cried. The damp smell of old whiskey seeped through his pores and farmer green hunting jacket. He cried and couldn't stop. The still limbs of the child in his hands. He cried some more, for everything, for Frieda, for himself, maybe for Dorothy, but most certainly for what the silence and flesh in his arms represented. Death happening to them again. Another ending without a beginning. Africans stolen from Africa sorrow. American Indians massacred and forced off tribal lands sorrow. Mixed bloods without ceremony and a fire sorrow. Ceremonies with no cedar, sandalwood, or sage. No libations poured.

That winter night at the hospital, he wrapped this quiet infant in a blanket and rounded up his daughters, now women with their own children.

"Your mother had another child," he said matter-of-factly. "But she was born dead. And your mother is dying. She was fulla cancer when they opened her up."

Stunned, the daughters didn't know if they should or could cry. The way their father was looking at them was unnerving. He talked as if he had to take out the trash and wanted to know who could hold open the goddamn door. Their mother was dying because the medication had caused the cancer or blood clots, but also because of Cliff: his betrayal had killed their mother.

"Lily," he said, turning to her, "since you the youngest you get to name her."

From somewhere, a fresh breeze moved and stirred under their tongues. Marlene.

"Marlene," Lily said without thinking.

That part is true, except Cliff only supposedly told Lily about the baby. No one else, at least not in that moment. Clifford took the dead child away, wrapped like a meat package in a hospital blanket and left the hospital.

Years later Lily remembered the sister no one spoke about.

"He wouldn't even let us see her," Aunt Lily later said. "He took her right out to Frieda's grave and buried the baby girl on top." Cheaper that way too.

Frieda, dead of brain cancer, and the baby girl. In the same grave. No funeral. Years apart but together. Did they die because it was their time, on accident or on purpose? From heartbreak or lack of love? I'm positive that a lack of love can kill you as much as the wrong kind of love.

If he cried that cold, dank day he was digging the second grave, I don't know. His heart, was it grieving or grateful? Possibly he got a splinter from the shovel handle or sank to one knee to pray for Marlene's floating soul. He probably asked the baby girl not to come back and haunt him. Not to make him miss her.

There had been five girls. Then Frieda closed her eyes for the land, for her father.

Marlene never opened hers.

Ever so briefly, five again when no was looking, when the still-born Marlene came and went, leaving four. Mildred was an adult with her own babies spilling down her thighs, leaving the sisters to themselves. Velma, Phyllis, Lily. Three. Then Phyllis ran away. And there were two. Until Velma married at sixteen and moved out. There was one until Lily married Bull, then there were none. That born-silent baby girl must have known. She wasn't going back.

There was no childhood to be had in that family. On that farm. There was no ceremony. That last girl child was stillborn yet all-knowing. *Damned* if she'd stay and let her father drive her to drink and fight. *Damned* if she'd marry a man with the promise of heather in his pocket, but instead showered them with rock fists. *Damned* if she'd pray all night long on bruised knees. *Damned* if her children would follow in her footsteps, down the same path. In all the indigenous stories I know, there's always a sacrifice, a suffering for the vision quest, and for the people. Yet in the sacrifice, strength comes. I recognized that strength, that rebellion, the act of that child's death, that anger, the acceptance at having been born into a lesson instead of a miracle.

28

The Dreamers

A STORM TOOK my grandfather.

But he didn't die in it; he died, I'm sure, because of it, with his white knuckles around the storm's neck, hollering, cussing, and spitting snuff. Like any cowboy failing to tame a beast he'd tried to tame all his life. It was the kind of storm that addled the minds of every decent Kalamazooan, making common sense difficult, dreams more intense, rivers flood up on the banks and push out ancient debris and pollution; the roads were oil-slicked and deceptively dangerous, less discernible in the haze. Besides the weather puffing up and filling its lungs—holding our manners, equilibrium, and tenderness hostage—all the signs had come.

Rochelle woke up on her sixteenth birthday with her eyes red and puffy. Her brown skin was finally starting to fill out and develop meat over the bones that had earned her the nicknames Frog Legs and Roach. I forget what question I asked her that morning in the kitchen, but she turned and stared at me as if balloons were coming out of my mouth. Her eyes held that pensive, see-through look in her face all day. She walked around dazed, and eventually dragged her feet to the mall to get her ears pierced, but when she returned, she cornered me while I was using the upstairs bathroom.

"I dreamed Grandpa Stafford was in a car accident and he and White Betty died."

Betty was his third or fourth wife.

I flushed the toilet and stared at her, apprehension filling my stomach. "That's crazy." I had to pee again. I hated when Rochelle confided things like this to me, when I was supposed to be the baby girl. She needed someone to talk to, but I was never allowed to make any decisions. I just caught all the ear crap.

This time, though, she followed my advice.

"Don't tell Mama," I said.

"Okay, good," she replied. That was too easy.

"It was a dream, Rochelle." I peed and flushed again. "Just nothing probably."

We looked at each other; we knew better.

The Iroquois have dream societies. They practice interpreting dreams like others practice a golf swing. We should have told someone. Several weeks later, robins and blackbirds started flying into the house and crashing into windows.

"Shit, Tyrone, get the broom," Mama screamed the first time it happened. "Just open the Goddamn door."

"We trying, Mama," Tyrone said.

The boys beat at one bird until it escaped out the front door. Huffing with the exertion, my mother shook her head.

"Well, someone's 'bout to die."

Rochelle and I eagle-eyed each other. She shook her head *no*.

To this day, whenever I've seen or heard of a bird or bat getting into someone's house, I shiver, and then inevitably, someone crosses over. Call it an old wives' tale, or African lore passed down from our enslaved side, but when the birds lost their way, we held our breath.

Over the next few days, three robins flew straight into our front window, making the sharp cracking sound of instant death each time they hit.

My mother grimaced. "Well, there goes another one."

But those birds seemed to come from someplace else, from Mattawan, from that farm, guided or misdirected as they were. Years earlier, when a blackbird got into the house, Grandma Manuel, Mama's grandmother, died. A year after that, Jessie's mother died within weeks of another bird's frantic flight in our living room. We'd had a bird's nest in the light fixture on our front porch since we'd moved in, but they'd rarely strayed inside our house.

A few weeks later, one fall day while watching TV with my best friend Jayda, I heard my mother's maroon Monte Carlo skip, *Dukes of Hazzard*-style, and slam into the slight hump in the driveway, scraping the fender before skidding to a halt. My heart leaped into my chest because Jayda wasn't supposed to be there. Jayda was my road dog from fourth grade onward, throughout middle and high school. We stayed friends despite the fact that her brother Darrell and my sister Rochelle had broken up within six months of their courting. But Mama bolted through the front door, past our opened mouths, and snatched up the telephone receiver. She dialed frantically.

"Y'all heard from Daddy?" she asked someone. She waited for the reply. "You sure? Well, I been calling and he ain't answering. He answered for you?"

We all knew the grayness of the day warranted rain, but she'd heard that there'd been a freak tornado in Mattawan and people had died. On the ninth ring, Grandpa Stafford picked up. He'd been out in the garden picking beefsteak tomatoes and couldn't hear the phone until he passed by the house.

The second time Mama sped home from work, Jayda was there again. We were playing jacks on the porch. And again I was terrified because Jayda wasn't supposed to be over, but my mother's car ripped up the driveway and she ran into the house without a second glance at Jayda and dialed a number on the phone, as if the first time had only been a dress rehearsal. Another tornado had been spotted out by the farm, and I think it was the one Rochelle saw my grandpa riding in her dream. This time, after many rings, Mama got no answer. She called Aunt Mildred.

A car crash.

"No, shit. Oh, God no." Her yellow face turned three kinds of red. She leaned against the dark-paneled wall, crying hard. From the heaving of her body, it seemed as if somehow she'd been expecting it. How did Mama know? Maybe she'd dreamed it too.

The car crash that killed my grandfather had been gruesome. A drunk driver ran a stop sign and plowed into Grandpa Stafford's black El Dorado from behind while it was in the turning lane. The drunk driver pulverized the bumper and shoved my grandfather's car into oncoming traffic. He and his ex-wife, White Betty, were killed instantly, along with several other people in other cars. It was one of the worst pileups that small town had seen.

At my grandfather's funeral, the mourners looked pasty and damp. My mother, stepfather, and I were seated to the left of the door in the third row of the family section. My brothers and sisters and cousins were behind us in hard chairs. I watched the people walk in, "curiosity seekers," poet Margaret Walker would have called them. I don't think that anyone believed my grandfather was dead because evil never dies.

Clad in polyester and cotton, they filed into the funeral home at the edge of downtown Kalamazoo, in singles, pairs, threes. I can't remember faces; I only remember the different hues of skin that had floated out of the marshland our clan had settled on: sallow amber, cornbread yellow, blotchy pink, reddish brown. Underwoods, Patterns, Staffords, Robertses. I remember polyester and corduroy pants. Several white people sat stiffly in chairs. Betty's son and daughter clung to each other. There was very little difference in her white folks' complexions, though; they could have been Grandpa Stafford's blood relatives just as well. My Great-Aunt Katheryn was probably at the back of the room, happy that Clifford was dead but also disdainfully ticking off those who she knew were related to the Manuels and Staffords and had married Black men, diluting what she thought was her full-blood American Indian and white line even more. Or maybe she hadn't shown up at all.

Suddenly my velvet dress was choking me. I fidgeted something awful. Though the dress, skeleton white bobby socks, and black shoes covered my body in the usual places, the rest of me looked like it'd been rinsed head to toe in Vaseline. I tried to rub some of the oil into my legs, first with my hands, then by rubbing my legs together like a cricket. My dress hem itched my knees. I scratched. My head itched, stinging from the nest of hair pulled up into a tight bun. I scratched. In the muggy little room, heated further by eighty-degree weather hugging the building, an oily puddle gathered in my underwear.

Sitting between Jessie and Mama made me nervous. They had given each other evil looks in the parking lot and walked into the room in stony silence. They made me itch too. My mother kept bringing my hands to rest back in my lap, giving me her crinkled evil eye, but I couldn't help moving, as if I was trying to avoid something that was coming right at me in that hard-backed chair. No one cried out loudly; they were more like country flowers wilting into each other, attempting sorrow but not really reaching the emotion.

Then it came, landing on my chest.

Something entered me.

I started to cry quietly. Faces blurred. The feeling—a hand, an arm—was choking me. I whimpered.

"Shush, Shonda," my mother said. "It will be okay."

Tears made my chest heave. I let out a howl.

Jessie pinched me on my arm, but that only made me wail louder. People turned to look. Mama and Jessie were embarrassed but shifted their glances to say, "Poor girl misses her grandfather."

In reality, I had somehow inhaled all the grief and anger that surrounded me. There was too much heartache and pure unhappiness in that room for my waif body to bear.

"I'll take her out." Jessie finally rose and hustled me out to the parking lot to calm me down. Even hysterical, I shrugged off Jessie's concerned, heavy-handed parenting. I disliked him so much I refused to say his name, just like I refused to say my father's new wife's name or call her mama like everyone else. I always called her by the name Daddy did, which was appropriate for a witch, Creola. I yanked away from Jessie, refusing to let him touch me because he too was an outsider, not my blood. But also, I seemed to feel the insides of anyone who touched me, and I would vomit if I could feel Jessie's emotions.

"I'll be alright," I blubbered, my hands and face vibrating like hot crystals.

Grandpa Stafford had made most of the people in that room irritated enough to put his eyes out at one point or another, either by whupping them, arguing with them, or sleeping with their wives. Underneath the sorrow, there was a deep layer of anger in that room. The daughters glowered with it; possibly it was guilty relief, but I know they, like my mother, had bit down on the resentment and frustration Grandpa had caused them, still seething at their father for things he'd never apologized for doing. Things he never knew he'd done to them in a drunken rage. Things he'd said that had cut them to the marrow. They remembered the love, but also the time he'd abandoned them to men like himself. I have always wondered what my mother felt driving home to call her father that second time, before she knew for certain he was dead. Was she secretly relieved or saddened?

The day after he died, things fell apart in a weird way. My mother and her sisters had gone out to the house to sort out his and their mother's things. My mother, at this time entrenched in gambling debts, scoured the old house.

"What the hell are you doing, Velma?" Lily asked her.

"You know Daddy left some money around here."

Lily looked over at Phyllis and wound her finger at her temple.

My mother ignored their laughter and continued banging on the ceilings and walls for a secret hiding spot. She looked in the shed and even the outhouse for money her father supposedly had hidden.

Then Aunt Mildred did the wackiest thing and created an estate sale out of dust balls and a double-barreled shotgun and a bait house. She priced everything on that farm, down to the pails of nails Grandpa Stafford had collected in the bait house.

"Mildred," Lily confronted her. "Are you out of your mothafucking mind? Ain't none of Daddy's shit worth nothing. His shit is too raggedy to warrant an estate."

"Well, people will want to buy stuff. If you want something, you can buy it out too."

"I ain't buying shit out of there," Lily told her. "Everything up in there is mine."

"Well, I'll buy it for you," Mildred said.

"You go do whatever you got to do."

Aunt Mildred bought several things out of the house for Aunt Lily, but she really wanted the youngest sister to live there and take over the land, five acres, now that it was vacant again. She didn't want strangers living in the house, but for some unspoken reason, Aunt Mildred didn't want my mother to move in, though Mama was the only one who volunteered. Between the banging on the walls and the bogus estate and old resentments resurfacing, Aunt Lily knew she'd made the right decision to leave Kalamazoo for Lansing, about an hour and a half away.

"Me and Phyllis would be looking at each other, laughing," Aunt Lily later told me, giggling at the memory. "We'd be in back of the car hitting each other, like, these muthafuckas is nuts. They was two greedy people. Just greedy."

But before my mother got to that place, when her debts carried her away on a treasure hunt, what was she thinking when she realized she'd never talk with her father again?

I can see her traveling the distance from Galesburg to Kalamazoo, down Gull Road or East Main Street, turning familiar corners she knew but didn't register. All the memories pushing up her throat numbed her, and maybe she practiced saying words she wished she'd said to her father but never could, for fear or anger. She'd never get the chance.

The first tornado was a warning; the second tornado, though it had never touched him, came and went and took Grandpa Stafford with it.

I can almost see him riding that beast like a bronco into the darkened sky, riling and cursing it out for moving too swiftly or cutting a sharp turn he didn't expect. "Hold still, you Goddamn sonofabitch," I hear him say. And before he disappeared, maybe he made a fist to punch the twister in the jaw, maybe he made love to it, but he definitely made a scene.

THE WEEK AFTER Grandpa Stafford died, he appeared to my mother at the edge of her bed in the middle of the night. He told her, she said, that he was well and that no one should worry. She relayed this on to us with satisfaction. She called her sisters and delivered the message just as if she were talking about how hot the summer day would get.

Grandma Manuel had visited my mother one winter night weeks after she'd died. The front door blew open, my mother said, and our grandmother walked in and sat in her old rocking chair by the wall. She rocked and creaked for a short while, then the chair stopped and she was gone. Rochelle and I were sleeping in bed close by, Mama said, and I swear up and down I remember the distilled scent of November cold, then turning my head to see the falling snow blown in by the wind, swirling around a small space. I remember seeing my mother get up to close the door and return to her crossword puzzle by the fireplace, as if she was accustomed to fully closed doors blowing open in winter. I remember the chair rocking, but maybe that scene is merely lodged in my memory from the telling and retelling.

I know I'm not a miracle baby. It's just the way we are, the women in my family. We dream and things happen. Or we dream the thing that's happening or about to happen. I know this comes from our African bloodlines (to where, exactly? West Africa? Ethiopia?). I've always felt at home in Cornwall, England, and since my DNA test pointed me there too, maybe my Celtic fairy ancestors would one day lead me back to Morgaine le Fey. But there's no proof of any of this, no records, no land deeds. Besides, those are not my stories.

My stories are my mom calling me to say, "Your dad came to me last night." Her confidence in the matter is always assured and unquestionable. "Said he's fine. Everything is alright."

I've never doubted my mother's words. I did wonder if she told him to go fuck off.

For the longest time, I thought it was normal for people to communicate with their dead. I thought dreaming of the future or the past was something everyone had access to, but as I grew older and told the stories I'd grown up with, the incredulous looks stopped me and made me choke back my words. Whether from the land, the black earth that we shook off our feet while we ran, or the weeping willow branches that shaded our secrets and shielded the blood of slaves and indentured servants coursing through us, I realized my family had a collective, inherited gift of sight. We had that thing you hear about in movies and read about in books. I called it a subconscious that protected and warned us, forever open and ready to receive messages from beyond.

If my mother remembers barely anything about her childhood, my Aunt Lily, the baby girl, remembers everything for her. Lily was the watcher. The family recorder. In fact, she remembered before she knew what memory was. My Aunt Lily remembers seeing herself born. It was May. The spring sun flecked hints through the windows of how the coming summer would steam the ground, boil the streams to thin trickles of water, and dry up Wolf Lake. My Aunt Lily's first view of the world as an infant, not even owning a name or a stitch of clothing, was twofold: a wet kitchen floor drenched by amniotic fluid and her mother's head.

"Seem like I was sitting up in the ceiling of the kitchen and everybody was scurrying," Aunt Lily once related to me.

The floor splashed with water and her sister Mildred was below her with a rag, frantically wiping the floor clean. Her father entered just then.

"Goddamnit," Grandpa Stafford yelled when he saw the mess and let out a wail of curse words, angry that the floor was doused, and probably secretly a little scared that his sixth daughter had been born at home, utterly unexpected in the month of May. The scene faded for Aunt Lily when she heard her father's voice, broke her concentration like a curse. She then remembered her mother climbing into a truck and "riding high and sitting up, but looking down [at me] too."

As she grew up, every time Lily told Mildred or anyone what she remembered about her birth, the elder sister would argue with her that she couldn't have remembered that. Mildred wanted nothing to do with dreams and ghosts; she didn't want nothing to be said about her family that wasn't already being said: "uppity Mulatto niggers," "Black Indian country trash." "Lying drunks." "Woman beaters."

"Now, I never ever say anything," Aunt Lily told me. "Because every time I'd say certain things, Mildred would get upset. So I quit telling people anything I knew or saw."

If we would have had teachers, mothers from the clan, maybe our lives would have been different. If we would have had someone, anyone, a grandmother or a West African elder or tribal healer, show us how to use our second sight to change things, maybe we wouldn't be so messed up. Maybe we'd have been back home in the village in North Carolina, having dream contests like the Iroquois do every fall, and shaking rattles for healing, pulling out an ailment. Singing someone's illness away. If we would have listened to our dreams, to our ghosts, to that baby girl who was never born in Mattawan, maybe we'd have been okay.

Instead of staying sick, we'd help ourselves get well.

PART III

Four Directions and Cowrie Shells

The house Clifford Stafford built on Route M-43, Mattawan,
Michigan, where my mother and her sisters grew up.

29

Getting Well

NOT ALL AMERICAN Indians dance at powwow or go to sweat lodges or have horses. Not all of them live on reservations, or stay on the reservations to which they were born, but reservation life is no fucking joke. Not all indigenous Indians look "Indian." Not all Black Indians are alcoholics, or poor, or say "cousin" in every other sentence, or beat their wives and children. Not all Mixed Indians want to remember that they are Indians. Many of my relatives don't want to claim the Black family members that their fathers, grandfathers, or great-grandfathers married; or the children their mothers birthed; or aunts and uncles who were ceremonially adopted. And this makes us ashamed, muted, and not want to claim Indian blood at all. They call us Mixed blood. Biracial. Mulatto. Half-blood. Heathens. But not Indian. They call us African American, Black, Negro, Colored (because of the stigma, land allotment policies, the one-drop rule, the U.S. Census, the massacres and trauma, our own ignorance), but not white. We are African transplants, African in the blood—but for so long, historically, subconsciously, anything associated with racial Blackness, with my beloved continent that colonization carved up like a Thanksgiving turkey, was subverted, ostracized, punished. All the roads back to Africa were under the Atlantic Ocean.

And others, grandmothers and grandfathers—Black, Indian, white—one way or another would force us to forget. Would kick, punch, scratch any memory out of you as to how you got there in the first place. It hurt too much to remember. Slavery. Removal. Migration.

When I visited Senegal for the first time in 2004, it was both a culture shock and a warm glove over my heart. I was home, but I was a foreigner too. The clothes were beautiful, the children coveted my locks, Wolof flowed from the mouths of Africans, and once my Senegalese friend turned to me, laughing: "When my friends talk in our language, they sound like they are fighting. I don't sound like that, right?"

"Not really," I lied. My daughter snickered but averted her eyes.

It was gratifying to see Black flesh everywhere I turned, but I didn't know where to look for *my* ancestors. I knew, however, where my direct descendants had lived their last moments in Africa: Gorée Island, the slave port. It took me three days to go there because I honestly didn't know if I could handle the ghosts. On the ferry ride over, I could see slips of them rising from the water in the silver mist. With every footfall on the graying dirt, I seemed to kick a resting spirit. From the prison rooms that once held hot, tortured African bodies—rooms labeled Les Hommes, Les Femmes, Les Enfants above the doorways, separating families—I heard echoes of wails, sorrowful hunger, and confusion. Then I retraced the steps of millions of mourning Africans, reportedly over one hundred and twenty million, who were transported in the slave ships during the Middle Passage. I walked slowly down a dirt-packed narrow corridor to that spot, that hated wooden frame: La Porte de Non-retour.

The Door of No Return.

This was the last place, last dirt, last smell, last air of Africa that the newly enslaved experienced. Never to return until we African Americans, we Mixed bloods, we Black Indians returned to honor and thank them. I stood in the threshold, looking out to the sea, trying to find the faces of my blood relatives who had stayed alive on those slave ships, had endured the unendurable. Those ancestors I prayed to in sweat lodges that had become my church. I leaked from every pore. "Are you okay?" my daughter asked as we walked away from the Door, because I could not stop crying. Salt slid into my mouth as I bent down, grabbing a handful of dirt that I stuffed in my pocket.

"No, but I will be." I hugged her. I took out my pen and wrote in the palm of my hand in blue ink (because I had no paper), "I have never seen with eyes like these." I took a picture of my open palm, pink flesh under the smearing blue lines.

My lifeline was the rock that would not break under the hammer of time.

I *had* returned. I was still here.

But I thought back to the overly aggressive street vendor who had hounded me the day before. He was just one of many who pushed their wares in my face, demanding exorbitant prices as soon as I opened my mouth to say, "Naka Emberi?" How are you? Everyone knew I was a foreigner. I got so frustrated because I thought they *saw* me, recognized the Black African Indian blood flowing in my veins no matter how pearl brown my skin was in the sweltering sun. Finally, I turned and shouted a phrase in Wolof I'd asked my friend to teach me:

"Manla African neo!" *I am an African like you.* His eyes grew round with surprise and he covered his mouth in laughter. "Okay, sister. You African. Wow. Good for you." Then he cut his price in half.

Manla African neo. But I wasn't. Not fully. I was a cartography lesson. I was the geography of the intersection of enslaved Africans, Eastern Shore American Indians, indentured white servants; their journey was on my face. I was the seed of a memory that my grandparents wanted to forget.

Sometimes, all you could do, wanted to do, or were able to do was forget. Many of us practiced forgetting. It had become a coveted magic trick. We survived like that. We loved like that. We hated like that.

In Michigan, in my family, forgetting was our art. No matter what the blood said.

ALL THOSE YEARS ago, when Rochelle had an abortion at sixteen, it devastated her. She could never forget. She couldn't get well. When she got pregnant the second time, only months later, she ran away all of five miles down the street to live with the father of the baby and his parents. She did have that baby. Jason. She did start her own lopsided family. That turned out to be the shithouse mistake of Rochelle's life. Dropping out of high school, becoming Philip's punching bag.

But I owe my life to Rochelle. I never realized until recently that I had rarely been in the room with her when she was doing her hard drinking. Somehow, I had never been in the same room with her when she shot up or snorted, or whatever it was that she did, and for that, God forgive me, I'm grateful. She always shielded me, protected me from the ugliness, from her junky, itching friends; people she owed money to; her Northside pushers and pimps who looked at me with gutted, questioning eyes; from the devil in the street that ran white-hot in her thin veins. From herself. I saw her after, and I heard stories of the walls she hit, or the brother she tried to stab when she blacked out. I heard many stories.

In life, there is a door you wish you could step back through, defying time and space, and change everything else that happened from that moment forward.

Her first pregnancy was our first door I wanted to step back through.

Back from her telling me about the abortion, and the brutal men she would love; back from quiet-as-kept molestations; back from the drugs and dim corners and back alleys and packs of cigarettes she'd smoke while gulping down black coffee on an empty stomach just to get a high; back from Jason and Rodrique seeing it all and wilting, shrinking into themselves. Back from that Detroit night in Cass Corridors at that homeless shelter, where we slept with Janice and our cousin Debbie, both skinny as moonbeams. All three of them gurgling with crack-addict secrets, laughter spilled from their mouths like swamp stars.

"Girl, I remember that time I took my baby girl in her stroller through the knee-deep snow to use. Left her ass outside and came out dazed as a mothafucker, but I got my baby home."

I was twenty-three and Rochelle was twenty-five or twenty-six.

"Um-hum, I remember when my son had to help me to the toilet to throw up. So many times he helped me. I blacked the fuck out all the time. Don't know what I would have done without Jason. That was some crazy shit."

And y'all laughed and agreed, that was some crazy shit. But you're clean now, you're all clean.

That night she first told me she was pregnant was Door Number One.

The Before. It was her chance. And we all have that chance to take the other door. Don't we? I never ever asked her if she wished she could have made a different choice and not aborted the first child. But we got us Jason, and then years later, Rodrique. Beautiful boys.

Door Number Two: her dreams. Rochelle was open like a country window that all the spirits could come through. She was a soothsayer who dreamed the future but those dreams scared the hell out of her. Death, betrayal. Long, dark hallways and hospitals. If we'd had had a tribal elder, some African griot or other knowledge source, who said yes, those visions come to you for a reason, maybe we could have learned about our magic. But when she dreamed Grandpa Stafford's death and it happened just like she dreamed, she felt guilty, as if she'd caused the terrible car accident that opened up his chest, simply because she saw it first.

"I wish I would have had someone to help me through those dreams," she told me years later. "I knew it had to do with us having Indian blood, but no one helped me. No one could tell me what to do. I didn't know what it was."

THE DREAMS AND our memories were unwanted gifts as permanent and tenacious as our fingerprints, as real as our long, spongy, wavy hair from the Native American and African in us, a trait we shared along with a black mole in the middle of our chests, above our women's hearts. These memories were as real as our ghosts. It was that which I'd run away from, and that which left me wondering how I'd gotten out and they hadn't. My mother and her sisters didn't tell the weeping willows everything.

They left just enough for us to tell.

I used to think I'd almost made it. I'd left Kalamazoo and Mattawan behind. Then, I realized that I was only an escape artist. In the middle of folding clothes or having dinner with a friend or cooking for my daughter in our small Inglewood kitchen, the memories would come faster, so much so that they'd spill into whatever I was eating or drinking. The taste of Kalamazoo's black earth filled my mouth. A freezing, weeping winter Mattawan night engulfed me, stole my breath; the sound of the natural spring water plunging into the pond that Grandpa Stafford gouged out of the earth rung in my ears, and I would hold my head, thinking, *man, I didn't run far enough.* I hadn't really gotten out; I might have lived in the City of Angels, but it was only temporary.

Family reunion or a funeral, you always returned home.

Rochelle and my other sisters, and my mother and my aunts and their daughters, all showed me with their actions the things I promised I would never let happen to me. To my daughter. There was always a strained stillness in the air, as if we were waiting for one collective blow, and if there wasn't silence, there were screams, echoing out across the sinking, seedless land. The deer-haunted forests, through the willows. The sounds were an infant-like inability to say what exactly was hurting; we just knew something was wrong. I realized I would not walk forever tied to our heredity, to a legacy seemingly intractable from the landscape—from the years of not knowing who we were. I wanted off the Trail of Tears in Mattawan.

Over the years, I told people I learned to trust about how crazy and hyper, beautiful and magical, ugly and insane and funny, they—we—all are, and of my devotion to their—our—country essence, my shameful embarrassment of their—my—faults. My straw-filled conversation, the salt licks, and country breeze showing through.

I told people that Michigan wasn't big enough for my mother and me, and I had to put a country between us to love her better, but really, I loved my entire family so much I had to leave. I didn't want to fight my family. I left because I refused to participate in the vicious cycle I saw growing up. I refused to be shaped by the visceral pounding, the gladiator love they held in their fists, the type of love we learned from the end of an extension cord, a broom handle, a horse whip. From enslavement and eradication.

Now, I was no longer a runaway in an adult's body and life. An escape artist. I had been running from that swampland from the moment I could read and write because the violence, the fraught identities, *pained me*. It was time I turned around and said, "Thank you for my life and for teaching me with actions instead of words." Even though I would want to add, "I don't want to hurt you or have you hurt me. Please stop hurting each other." But I couldn't tell them anything; they wouldn't listen to me. Not a one. I was the last girl, the only child of the second marriage, not even full-blood to the first five siblings or the last one. I was still the baby girl.

Anyway, they would run off and tell Mama, and she'd tell Rochelle, Rochelle would turn to Bobbie Ann, Bobbie would pull Tina aside, Tina would catch Tyrone, he'd inform Loren, and then Loren would call Popeye and tell him. By the time it got back to me, I would have forgotten who I told, as that's the way with stories and big families. Besides, wasn't it the story that counted and not who was telling it? Because somehow it would get around to everyone who counted, the living and the dead, especially those who visited my mother at the edge of her bed shortly after they'd deserted this realm. We would show our dead that we'd survived. How do I know? My Black, Indian, and yes, white bones. They had grown with the weeping willows in the front yard of the farm in Mattawan, roots drinking swamp water. It seemed like we, our entire family, had grown so far apart and had so many wedges between us, they were almost impossible to mend. We were bare-fisted honest and we lied; we were immoral and gorgeous, crass and sensitive, all at once. My family would love you and crush you with that love and then crack a joke. "Look, she can't even breathe. Shit for brains. She dead."

You would be expected to laugh because all you could do was laugh.

Even if it were your last breath.

Like Marlene and Frieda, I was one of the keepers of secrets unspoken, watching over our family, never breaking, only bending in the wind.

30

Mothers and Daughters

MY DAUGHTER IS in the back seat of the rental car. My mom, wrapped in her winter coat, hums next to me in the passenger seat.

The roads look as if they're melting, the snow turned to dirty white slush from the plows. Kids are outside throwing sloppy snowballs at each other. We used to do that. I drive my sturdy black rental car from one end of Mattawan to the other, past the family graveyard in Almena County and an old house I never knew she'd lived in. She curls her lip in a half smile as if to say, "See, you can ask all the questions you want. You don't know me at all."

"Turn down there," she says. I flick on my blinker and turn. We're in Gobles, and Mama points out the church she and her sisters went to every Sunday when her daddy and mother were together so long ago.

"Mama always had us looking nice." My mom's eyes water a little. "Did our hair up. Oiled our legs."

In the pictures, they looked like spit-shined Indian pennies. I look over at my mother, one side of her head still partially swollen from her recent operation.

"Y'all look so pretty in your pictures," I say, trying to ignore her pulpy face.

For over a year, she'd noticed that the skin on the inside of her mouth was peeling, and the suspected diagnosis was bone cancer in her cheek. My Aunt Lily told me later that the place the doctors diagnosed had been the exact same spot where Junior Bynum used to hit Mama when they were married: "He used to smack her right there and send her ass flying." Turned out it wasn't cancer but a gristle of skin and bone meshed together: proof of survival. Having had to crack my mother's skull open down to the jawline to get at it, the doctor told her it would be months before she looked fully like herself again.

"Mama, when did you and Daddy meet?"

She folds her arms. "Shonda, I don't want to go there, back to the past."

I remain silent, not wanting to spook her by my immediate desire to stop and shove her out of the car. I want to ask her the real question, about something Aunt Lily said last night when I'd interviewed her, but I can't yet. Over the years, I learned so much about their lives, but I still can't ask my mother some things. Things I think will make her cry.

"He's my father. Those are my memories, too."

She looks out the cold window.

"Not even if they make me happy, to talk about Daddy?"

"Nope. They're mine," she says. "You can't have them."

I already have them. Reverend John Al Buchanan was a soldier, a janitor, a preacher, a womanizer, and a drunk. Why did he make these choices? *He's my father*, I want to yell, but melodramatics like that only make our family laugh. *That's some white people shit*, Mama would later tell everybody, *Shonda done lost her damn mind.*

I change the subject and let her talk about lesser things as we drive through the backroads and down M-43. She points out places that hold good memories for her while my tape recorder runs inside my sweat jacket pocket. She knows the tape is running because she'd seen me press the button and is trying her best to ignore the small whirring sound. Though sometimes she snaps at me, irritated that I'm not playing the game more smoothly. I've never been a good partner in this charade that our family has no secrets. My hands grip the rental car's steering wheel. My daughter is quiet in the back seat. I bite my tongue while Mama stares out the window with a small smile, commenting only when she wants to.

"What's that?" From the back seat, Afiya points ahead to the side of the road.

"What is that?" I repeat. Molty dark spots and then a long line of brownish-red stain atop the snow appear on the road and curb. They get wider as we drive on.

"Looks like blood," Mama says, averting her head. We both hate to see roadkill. "Yucky."

"It's an accident?" Afiya, the horror movie queen, asks. "Let's stop and see."

"Let's just go," Mama says. "Damn. Y'all both crazy."

Afiya's mouth drops, taken aback that her grandmother has lumped her in with me as "crazy," but she keeps quiet.

Soon, there is a ridiculous amount of blood on the roadside, as if something had been hit, then dragged. The crayon-red trail leads up and down a white mound of broken snowbank to a small clearing. We're on Red Arrow Highway, the fastest thoroughfare that everyone takes to cut across from Paw Paw or Alameda to M-43.

"It's a deer," I say.

"Naw," Mama says.

"Maybe it's dead." My time in the California mountain American Indian sweat lodge kicks in, and I realize that we could say prayers over it and maybe use pieces of this sad death for some good.

I slow down. "We could get the antlers."

Mama cuts me a hard look that says, *You natural-born dumb ass.*

"What, Indians used all parts of a deer," I try to joke.

"Shonda," Mama says in a tight voice. "Don't stop here."

"It's just a dead deer." I crane my neck to see.

"Aw, someone hit a deer." Afiya's voice is low and sad.

"Let's keep driving." My mother stretches her neck. She barely has any feeling in the right side of her face, she's been telling us. She is scheduled for another doctor's visit.

"It might be alive." I put the car in reverse.

"It's not. *Goddamnit*, Shonda Theresa Buchanan." Her ears burn baby doll pink and my face is turning purple. With the evocation of all three of my names, I know I'm about to get popped. "You got to be out your damn fool mind."

I look behind me. There are no other cars. "We just wanna see the deer. It was an accident. Maybe a sign."

"Don't nobody wanna see that goddamn dead deer." She is practically yelling at me, and I sense that her anger has nothing to do with the moment. All at once, I remember the night before, a part of Aunt Lily's interview that I was afraid to ask my mother about.

"Was my mother ever raped?" I had asked my aunt. All my life, my mother acted like someone who'd been tampered with. It was in her actions, her lack of affection, something in her eyes that carried an ancient anger, and yet, she was afraid to tell. Rochelle acted like that too.

"I don't know who it would have been," Aunt Lily paused during the recording. *"Oh yes!"* She snapped her fingers as if uncovering a long-lost memory. *"She did tell me that."* Lily paused again. *"Oh God. This is when she was staying with Mildred and this is why she left Mildred's house."* Aunt Lily took a deep breath.

"John A. and a friend of his—he actually brought a friend in there with him to help him do this. And I think that's why he got so upset about her leaving, cause he thought she would tell somebody. And she never told. That's what it was. And that's when she really turned. That was the turning point. That's when she became really mean and angry. She had every right to be that way. It's a shame, though, that we never had the right to tell it. Because if you told, they would have said, 'You did something.' So she kept it to herself. That's why I think she hates Mildred

so much, because Mildred didn't protect her. She just hates her. I don't care how much I try to bring them together on something. Mildred will do something and Velma will get so turned off and just shut down all over again."

Did Mildred know? They say every woman knows when a girl child is being violated in her home and simply denies it. Who knows how long the raping continued? No one knows but my mother, who can't look at the murdered deer I want to look at like a silly fool. No one knows but the murderer, John A. Cloud, who is now dead.

God forgive me, but thank God.

I edge to a stop in reverse, see the deer's body almost cut in two, and know that my mother, who averts her eyes, is that deer, as innocent and warm and leaking blood. I haven't known any of this. I, the voyeur, the writer, faithfully sick to my stomach when I saw any roadkill, but sometimes, for reasons I've never attempted to decipher, I'd force myself to see the animal and name it.

Always on the outside looking in, I know I ask too many questions, that I haven't understood my mother's need for privacy. To forget. Have refused, in fact, to respect the silence. I've apologized for my persistence but not for my need to know, already positive that she would never be proud of me because I couldn't corroborate with quietude. I read too much. I think too much. In her eyes, I think I'm smarter and better than everyone because I went to college and work at a magazine. I've ignored my family's resentment and continued to search. I always thought I had to find some key into my mother's head to help us understand each other better, but all she wants is quiet. No remembering. No memory. Then her heart won't hurt so much. I've been a shithead daughter. The past lay there, nice and dead, and I should have let it lay. But here I come, just when she thought the Stafford-Manuel legacy was all buried and calcified, the memories silent, here's a daughter starting to dig.

A daughter who wants to see the accident, the dead or dying deer by the side of the road. In so many ways, I've suspected that I failed as a daughter because of my inability to keep silent, but I've never known why. I thought that meant I was brave, but now, looking at my mother, I'm only ashamed of myself. Shame on you, Shonda.

I didn't know there were secrets that could kill you twice. Kill you three times; kill you every day of your life. "Okay, Mama," I say, revving the engine. "Let's go home."

My mother, she'd be okay if she never sees another dead, bloody thing in her life.

She has seen enough blood.

31

The Making of an Indian

As WE ASCEND the last dirt hill into a clearing, I look around at what my boyfriend, Charles, calls a Native American preserve, not a reservation, where several old trailers dot the outskirts of the encampment in Los Padres National Forest. A few in the center look like lean-tos. We're in a hip pocket of the California mountains.

It has taken us—my boyfriend, his mother, and three other women friends—three hours to drive from Los Angeles up the winding mountain roads and get coughed out into a dry, shale-laden, rabbit sage–riddled valley. The pungent scent of the sage is so strong it's intoxicating. We've driven on unnamed roads, over bumps that nearly popped our tires, and now, with the windows open, the evening air is clean and clear, smelling like crystals would smell if they had a scent. I feel like I'm inhaling water as I drive and I didn't know I was thirsty. It's like I'm asleep and waking up at the same time. Elated to be out of the city, in Real Nature, I think, *I have to bring my daughter here*, and it's almost as if I can see the words floating before me in the air.

"This isn't the only preserve in these mountains," he says, gauging my delight from my intense "wow" every few minutes. He rolls up his window against the mountain chill. "There are others."

In the clearing, dogs, five or six mixed breeds, circle our van barking ferociously, until Charles lowers his window again and calls to them: they recognize his soft voice and trot away, waving their tails abashedly. Our rental van skids to a halt before a low, oblong structure, covered in blankets and what looks like a light green parachute. We're a short distance from a pile of freshly chopped wood, and I smell smoke and ash. The sun has just set, the day's heat seeping out of the air as soon as the last rays of light disappear.

"Oh no." Charles cranes his neck. "You might be too late. It's either about to start or already started."

"Late for what?" We tumble out of the car, pulling out backpacks and towels.

Charles starts over to a fire pit dug deep into the ground. The pit has a circle etched in the sides that you can walk all the way around. He grabs a handful of tobacco, holds it high toward the sun, and tosses it in.

"Hey, Charles," two women call, "good to see you brother. Is this your mom? And your girlfriend?"

"Yes, and I need a bathroom," his mom says. One of the women takes her to the outhouse toward the back. Always loving and publicly affectionate with me, Charles folds my arm in his.

"This is my companion, Nyesha, and she's here for the women's sweat."

Eh, no Nyesha isn't. Despite having opened myself to taking a community name—Nyesha, which means "rain" in Kiswahili—to help me get cleared of old habits, my first instinct about the traditional women's sweat is a hard-edged Stafford-style "no." I don't want to go in there. I don't know what to expect. Charles hasn't told me anything as we've been driving up the mountain drinking air. Controlling, self-protecting, I need a little more warning to get nekkid in front of strange women and crawl around in the dirt. Nope. I'm not doing that. Not me.

Not Velma's daughter.

It isn't a Christian upbringing protest; I've long since abandoned my father's Baptist ways and what feels to me like the hypocrisy and prison-like nature of churches. My father had let me go my way as long as I believed in some kind of higher power.

Even though I never lived with my father and his second boring family, out of all his children I was the one who *read and discerned* the ideas and philosophies in the Bible on both a spiritual and an intellectual level. He seemed to cherish when I came to visit him on my trips home at eighteen, nineteen, and twenty. I'd knock and push open the door to his little office behind the choir pew in his little white church on Douglass Avenue. He'd be underlining passages for his next sermon, always in red.

"Hey, fella!" he'd say, hugging me, smelling like peppermints and hot toothpicks. Every visit, curious how he saw things, I had a different question:

"Daddy, what's the role of women in the Bible, really?"

"Daddy, how come Constantine got to decide what the Bible looked like when he kicked all those other religious leaders out of that conference?"

"Daddy, aren't there several more books of Moses that aren't in this version of the King James Bible?"

"Daddy," I began one day, and he cut me off.

"Shonda, believe what you want. As long as you are a good person and believe in God, you're gonna do fine."

A janitor at local middle schools for years, when he came to the church he was a different person, seen in a different light on Sundays, and while I had no curiosity about how he felt cleaning toilets, he'd always welcomed my questions about all the discrepancies in the Bible. As long as I believed in something, I was a good daughter. Over the years, I prayed to God as I had constructed this entity. I woke up with prayer on my lips, held God in my hands when I drank water, and meditated at the beach. I walked in prayer. I went to bed with prayer for my daughter's well-being and for my family. I knew some thought it was odd, but I had not seen the inside of a church in years.

Still, this little round structure in front of me? No, I don't think so. Whatever this is, it is Not for me.

But it starts to rain and if I don't go in, I'll be alone with the dogs. Charles had disappeared with some of the men. Somehow, something gets me to the women's changing area. Somehow I am shoeless, in a long skirt and a T-shirt, and have a towel wrapped around my shoulders. I'm asked to turn around in a circle as a cloud of sweet hot smoke burns my throat. I crawl on the ground and follow what the thin white woman at the entrance of the sweat lodge says: "as you crawl around to your seat, bring your people and your ancestors with you by saying, 'all my relations.'"

It is dark in the lodge, the ground dirty and hard. As much as I edge and edge away from them, my butt seems to find all the rocks. Finally, I give up and cross my legs as the hot mist rises from the water poured over rocks, and the sweet woman, Bonny, a veteran to this ceremony who adopted the culture through her husband, part indigenous Indian from Mexico, tells us what to do. When our turn comes, we are to offer a prayer.

When my turn comes, I don't know what to say. I say something like, "Thank you for letting me be a part of your ceremony." And when asked if I know any songs, I sing a harvest song from my West African dance class and then my favorite American Indian song off of a CD, something from the Montana Chief Cliff Singers. I'm pretty sure I've embarrassed myself.

After the first round, the pouring of water on rocks that have just come out of the fire pit, it's so hot that I fall to the earth. The darkness is so dark. The darkest dark. Africa dark. Sweat wrings from my singed skin, but it feels good. The earth is cool where I lay my face. I can't see anything, but I don't need to *see* anything. I feel everything. This is my church. My roots.

Just like I'd felt in my first West African dance class, the ritual, the reconnecting to these old ways, moves something in my body.

My organs feel rearranged and my head relocated. Then the hot dark is a mother's breath in my ear and everything settles.

Again, I am home.

When we crawl out of the sweat lodge on our hands and knees, it is still raining. The warm summer drops seem to brush me in soft welcoming strokes. I lie on my back on the ground next to another woman and just breathe and breathe; I didn't know sitting in one place for two hours could be so hard. *I will never do this shit again*, I think. But it's a lie. One of those lies we tell ourselves for comfort, out of fear. Something begins that day; it lodges itself in my rib cage and cracks it open. It looms next to my heart, pumping my blood through my veins. My ancestors are not just watching over me; they are with me. All my relations are with me—Black, Indian, white—as I pray in that one hard spot, on that ground, leaving my prayers in the dirt.

For the first two years of attending sweat lodges on that sacred land and elsewhere, I never know what to say. We weren't raised in ceremonial ways. I just keep quiet and listen. When it dawns on me why I've spent the next few years soaked in tears, blubbering, sitting in the West direction or Western door, I start to find my own direction, not just as a daughter of the Staffords but as a person, a woman, a mother. Why, I never ask Creator until much later, but it comes to me that the West is the door of transformation and winter when things are quiet and sad and powerful; the West is the direction of Bear medicine, of Africa and Africans, from how I've understood it and have been taught; every reason for my sitting there points me back to Kalamazoo: I represented the West. The Midwest. Africans. The sad ones. The resilient ones. I had to learn to stop crying and feeling sorry for myself, for how and where I was raised. I had to grow up.

I needed to heal. I needed to get well.

Having spent years clean and sober, Rochelle sinks back into drugs, her brown eyes wild and tormented, disappearing from our family as if she were a ghost. We talk about her in soft funeral whispers, sharing our rare sightings of her; we know she is doped up in some drug house on the Northside of Kalamazoo.

Another knock on our door—someone is dead. Another knock, we think my mother has cancer in her jaw and the hospital where my mother has the surgery is the same hospital where her little sister Frieda died all those years ago. I can see the fear in her eyes as they wheel her into the sterile room. But sitting in the West, in the sweat lodge, I listen. I mend. I think about my connection to these ways, to nature, and how I have always listened to the wind, even if my grandfather didn't teach us that. As a child, I scrutinized any mammal, bird, or bug that crossed my path as if they had a message for me. I still do.

"Shonda, you were weird," my brother Tyrone laughs, reminding me how I used to tell my brothers and sisters I'd *seen* things: aberrations, shapes in the sky, shadows that looked like people, dead family members in my dreams. "We thought you were making some of it up."

Like my Aunt Lily, it never occurred to me to make any of it up. I remember at age ten when I took it into my head that I was Jana of the Jungle, a character from one of my favorite cartoons. We had lived on my grandfather's farm for two and a half years after his death, and I decided I was going to commune with the animals, like Jana. I don't know where my mother was, probably working, but I had a lot of time to myself to listen to things. Barefoot, in a slip of a nightie, I went out behind the house, about thirty yards away, and found the greenest mound of grass I had ever seen in my life. It looked like Arthurian knight fairy grass. I lay down in that patch, trying to hear what the forest wanted to tell me.

Maybe I did read too much, but I was determined to connect with Nature. Apparently, nature was determined to connect with me too, because I started to feel swift pangs on my legs and arms, and when I jumped up, a happy swarm of mosquitoes lifted like a giddy wave over me, feasting on my flesh.

I was like free breakfast to them. I ran out of the woods and into the house, laughing, pride hurt, welts covering my body. I never told a soul.

It wasn't until I sat there in the sweat lodge that first day, and the years after, that I knew my childhood instincts had been correct—go into the forest, find a quiet place, and listen. God is there. Without a guide or teacher, elder-less, I just did it ass backward. With the people who came to the American Indian preserve where Charles brought me, and sitting and listening and asking questions of the head of the camp, I found peace, and what felt like a direct connection to my American Indian ancestors, even though in North Carolina, Virginia, Mississippi, Delaware, and Oklahoma they probably did it differently. No nation, or every sweat leader, does a sweat lodge in the same way. But the main ingredients are the same across the country: come humble, come without alcohol or drugs in your system, come with respect in your heart and actions.

Over the next eleven years, though I am already a grown woman, I grow up in that sweat lodge. I blubber, spit, and pray for my family, for Rochelle, and my mother, and all the women I love, for Aunt Lily, and the other two aunts and their daughters—all of us, at one point or another, abused in some way. It takes a long time for me to say prayers for myself. Despite the hardship of being a single mom, somehow I've felt as if my family needed them more. Even though I am over a thousand miles away, I'm not whole if they aren't whole.

More importantly, I am lucky to raise my daughter on that land, whisking her away from the City of Lost Angels every chance I get. Already we have immersed ourselves in the African heritage: we dance West African dance and practice the values and philosophy of what feels like traditional African culture. It isn't hard; almost every Black person in Los Angeles in the 1990s wanted to Go Back to Africa. But having found the sweat lodge, or the sweat lodge having found me through Charles, and the community of people who pray like me, I feel as if I'm starting over on a new path, on what I know now to be the Red Road, a path of ceremony.

The same year I attend my first sweat, I attend my first powwow in Los Angeles. A powwow is intended to be a gathering where you get to see relatives and friends you haven't seen all year, while scouting out the best Indian tacos and watching the competition dances. Sometimes, there's even competition between drums and women singers, as well as a hand drum contest.

Hay litters the fairgrounds; vendors line the long walk to the dancers' arena. As the drummers and singers play, and the day grows hotter, Native Americans swirl in their bright outfits. At least eleven women come into the dirt circle, some dancing gravely while others twirl, spin, and raise their fans high; everyone seems to know what to do but me. My mother had never taken me to a powwow.

"It's an intertribal," Charles says. "Do you want to try it? You just need a scarf to drape around your shoulders."

At this time, I'm not a dancer. I don't know a Women's Traditional dance from a Men's Fancy dance from a Jingle Dress dance. Until I start going to the sweat lodge, I don't know that the Four Directions—north, south, east, west—honored many aspects of the culture, the land, the 500 Indian nations, the animals as well as the seasons.

But in my jeans and T-shirt, I walk slowly around the circle with another woman who'd come with us taking steps back toward what we lost on that trek from North Carolina. I have so much to learn, but it's a learning journey I'm willing to go on and complete for those of my people who could not dance their dances or speak their languages or pray in their sweat lodges when the government outlawed anything Indian in the 1900s. It isn't until eight years later, in 2006, that I dance around the circle in my own ribbon dress at the Monacan Powwow in Virginia, tears sliding down my face. And a year after that, I dance in a buckskin I helped make. I am stunned and immensely proud when Afiya, a sewing queen, makes her own beautiful chocolate and turquoise shawl and Jingle Dress. It takes her two years to get up the courage to dance in it, and before that, to ask an experienced Jingle Dress woman for help by offering her a pouch of tobacco. Tobacco is sacred to many American Indians, and the offering is a respectful way to ask for the elder dancer's counsel as my daughter learned to dance in that medicine dress.

To the best of our abilities, and in a good way, my daughter and I are walking in the footsteps of my great-greats: those who first came on the boat from Africa in the 1500s and escaped to an Indian village, married into the community, and made beautiful Mixed babies. Those 1600s Indian slaves and indentured servant women who slipped back away into the night with their new Black African husbands, purchased to marry after their men folk had been killed or imprisoned in the French Indian wars, and they made beautiful Mixed babies. Those Maroons, those Mulattoes, those slaves, those shoe shiners, those coopers and livery men and blacksmiths; those survivors. Yet no consistent records of their lives exist.

My life is their unrecorded testament, the proof everyone is searching for.

I didn't just live my ancestors' journey to and in America; like James Baldwin says of history, their journey, their struggle, their Mixed blood stories live in me.

32

Afro-Native Daughter

Dropping off a book at the Hampton Public Library, I glance at the counter and see a licorice-red flyer that says, "Come Join the Weyanoke Association: African Americans Honoring Our Native American Heritage." I look around. Is someone playing a joke on me?

Charles and I broke up three years earlier, and in August 2004, my daughter and I moved to Hampton, Virginia, for my job at a Historically Black College. Our first year was hard and lonely, and we desperately missed our poet friends and other communities in Los Angeles and in the Los Padres National Forest.

"I hate it here," Afiya said at least once a week as she tried to make friends in the ninth grade. I tried to placate her with the proverbial "give it time" talks, but I had moved her away from her friends at fourteen, just as she was about to start high school. We had many "I hate it here" fights until she joined a leadership group at the YMCA and a choir, and, without telling me, found a boyfriend. I found a few good Virginia poetry groups, but there were no folks like me. No sweat lodges. No African dance classes. I was just as bereft as Afiya.

The Saturday I walk into the community room to see *Black-looking* people in *Native American* regalia blows my mind. Black folks with their old black-and-white family photos with placards of who is what tribe. *They know their tribes.* They have handmade drums, dancing sticks, dream catchers: things *they've* made *themselves.* One man wears beaver pelts on his head and around his shoulders, and a *loincloth.* In *the library.*

"Hi, I'm Little Beaver," he shakes my hand in welcome, and I try not to look down. Another woman, one of the lead singers, wears a beautiful multicolored African outfit. Others don Western clothing, jeans and jackets, with leather and beaded vests, earrings, and cowboy hats. One man, Ogunjimi, who is a Babalawo, and his Togolese wife, Alida, are beautiful in full West African outfits. Another African American man *with locks like me* wears a ribbon shirt, which I later find out is a traditional men's shirt to wear at powwows or when they're singing with drums. There are full-bloods and white people there too, our lighter-skinned cousins.

Unable to keep my mouth closed, I know people are laughing at me. They can clearly see I'm floored by the open display of Mixed heritage. No one is hiding it. No one is apologizing.

"Welcome," a woman in an African outfit with Native embroidery approaches me. "I'm Anita Harrell. What's your name, sister?"

Reeling, I try to close my mouth like my mother has taught me, but it's hard.

"This is amazing," I say. We find seats near the front.

When Anita, who turns out to be one of the two lead organizers, co-founders of the organization, stands up to speak and leads the group in a song it is as if they have popped out of a dream I had long ago; I can't quite believe it. They know and sing Native American songs. They *know* things about the culture that I know. After being in Hampton without community for a year, it is like finding one person out of a hundred people on a deserted island who speaks your language.

The organization was formed to educate people about the intersections between African Americans and American Indians. The association is for everyone: those just curious, those just learning, and RedBlacks whose narratives aren't hidden but out in the open. There are elder Black Indians there who, unlike my family, sought out others and *talked about* their past and their history. Each speaker and panelist tells a different version of the same story. Either they have great-great-grandparents whose Indian blood they are trying to trace, or they already have the documentation and are trying to get a tribal enrollment card, or they are just here to memorialize and honor their Native American (American Indian, Indian) ancestors. But whether they're descendants of Creek, Seminole, or Cherokee Black slaves who were adopted, or possess a full-blood great-grandmother like me, doesn't matter. We are of one accord; we know the blood of two peoples runs in us.

Recently appointed Chief of the Nottoway Tribe, Lynette Alston, a historian who looks like my aunts, presents the history of her tribe and discusses both Black and European intersections. Everyone applauds. Dressed in blue and red regalia, with a woman's powwow fan and a beautiful shawl draped over her arm, the regal Anita Harrell stands up again.

"We'd like to thank everyone who came today, and thank you to our wonderful panelists. We'll now have the question and answer session, but please feel free to get food and come back to your chairs."

Someone made fry bread. I almost cry. I haven't had fry bread since California. At the end of the Q and A, Anita closes the program.

"We encourage every Black person, and anyone who has Native American blood, to find, celebrate, and talk about their shared heritage. Since the first African village in Charles City, to the first Indigenous American and African union in the Americas, we want everyone to know that we are still here."

I gasp. *We are still here. We. Are. Still. Here. All our relations.*

How could she have known? I want to cry, or jump up and give witness, or tell this woman my whole story. There is a volcano in my mouth, but I don't want to scare her with my eagerness, and my sheer relief, that there are people participating in the culture and who pray like I do. For years, I thought our family was the only family who didn't like to talk about the past, about what we had lost, who couldn't trace their roots in records but rather depended on family lore to connect us to a past that we knew existed, a past that so many others in this country have fought so hard to keep hidden.

Anita and Alida become dear friends. I join the Weyanoke Association as a member, and later a board member, and discover that apparently I've had my head in the Michigan sand. Numerous RedBlack communities exist all over the country, and in fact, because of the slave trade, all over the world.

The most Black Indians I've ever seen powwowing are in Virginia and on the East Coast, and all along up to the Hamptons, where the Shinnecock Indian Nation, one of the oldest and continuously self-governing nations, holds a huge powwow on their tribal grounds. Not only are Black Indians head dancers at powwow, but some are council members on their tribal associations and have stories about their RedBlack struggle. Others have *proof.* Proof. I am giddy with the knowledge that the Virginia Nottoway Nation, Chief Alston's tribe, honors that RedBlack connection through sharing their history, even if they aren't yet recognized by the state as a legitimate American Indian tribe. Some whisper that not all Virginia Indians want tribes that are visibly Black to be recognized. Others believe that racism against Black Indian tribes prevents this recognition. I have seen many Black Indians get unfairly "carded" at powwows such as the Chickahominy, who have a reputation for harassing their darker cousins, while the "white-looking" Indian dancers go unmolested.

Today the number of Black Indians in America is unknown, as we do not have a box on the census. Yet when the powerful "Indi-Visible" exhibit comes to the Smithsonian in 2009, detailing both the recent past and contemporary Black Indians' lives, and showing the evolution of the influential Mashantucket Pequot Tribal Nation, it is a validation for us. For the North Carolina Manuels, Robertses, and Staffords; for my father's Mississippi Choctaw Buchanan line.

So many of our popular Black figureheads have always claimed their Native American heritage—Langston Hughes, Jimi Hendrix,

Alice Walker, James Earl Jones, Jesse Jackson—but as a nation, we seem to discount the connection as legitimate.

Black Indians are living alongside everyone else, going to work, shopping at grocery stores, but come powwow season, or if there is a special event, we wear our regalia proudly. From the first Maroon communities with names like "God Knows Me" and "None Else, Disturb Me If You Dare," to the secret Black Indian communities that William Katz explores in his compelling book, *Black Indians: A Hidden Heritage*, we are still here.

We are not going anywhere.

Still, it's hard when I claim my Indian heritage and some African Americans see it as a betrayal. As if to say that I am also American Indian or Native American allows me to escape participation in the derogatory stereotype of being Black. As if by not claiming full Black I am somehow trading in my Black card for a red one, my Sunday black-eyed peas and cornbread for fry bread and maize, or for the stereotypical image of a bow and arrow, a horse and a longhouse. Instead, I live with the burden of two stereotypes in my blood. I live with comments from others, my darker-skinned girlfriends, who stab me with words like, "You're not pure Black, not really Black. I mean, look at your nose. Your hair."

What the fuck is wrong with my nose? Straight and narrow, not wide enough. Like my relatives'. The Indian and, yes, the white side. My hair. Coarse, not straight shiny, like my mom and aunts, but like my dad's and mom's hair combined: soft, long, black. My cheekbones high and defined. Like my mother's and father's. African and Indian. My eyes, slew like a wolf. The Indian in me? Still not Black enough. What's wrong with my skin? Not brown, really. Too light, too many freckles. I have freckles on my tongue.

"I'm both," I say. "Two sides of a coin. Different picture but the same thing."

It's never good enough for people who want me to expand the definition of Blackness by maintaining a mostly Black persona. They want me to disregard how I am also expanding the definition of Indigenous American Indian, mixed with that Sub-Saharan blood, mixed with Jewish, mixed with Irish and British, people I have never met. We Mixed bloods are our own tribe.

Why can't I be Black Native American or Afro-Black American? Who makes the decision? Not Black academicians. Not researchers. Over the centuries the U.S. Census, established and run primarily by white male politicians, has made those calls. Can a government office, first designed to segregate for the purposes of land-grabbing, tell me or anyone that we can't be both ethnicities? Claim all our blood? Instead, I and other Mixed bloods are given labels like Mulatto. Mixed. Half-breed. High yellow. Octoroon. Red bone. White chocolate.

Milk in the coffee Black girl. Not Black enough. Not really Black. *What are you mixed with?*

"Who yo' people?" someone would ask.

"Staffords."

We'd wait for the cringe. The shrink back. I can't tell you how many times I've heard, "Don't fuck with them crazy ass muthafuckers." Even though it wasn't true for all of us, in Mattawan and Kalamazoo, the Stafford name was synonymous with every backward, high yellow, no-count, stomp-a-mud-hole-in-yo'-ass man or woman that plowed a narrow row in that black earth. Maybe it was my grandfather's doing. Could one man single-handedly destroy the name of people who once owned hundreds of acres of land throughout Michigan and Indiana? It couldn't be all him, but I know we didn't get invited to anyone else's family reunions. People would come up to me in the seventh and eighth grade and tell me we were cousins, but I had never heard hide nor tail of them.

After years of resenting blood quantum discrimination, the DNA blood count police, I finally spit in the tube: from my matrilineal line, my DNA says I have a fourth-, fifth-, sixth-, or seventh-generation full-blood American Indian ancestry from 1700 to 1790, so less than four percent. The kit also says I have over fifty percent African and over thirty percent British and Irish, with a full-blood Ashkenazi Jewish ancestor on the tree. But no one called us Jewish, Irish, or British, although my great-great-grandmother was a Mahoney. Growing up, while my mother told me we were "French, German, white, Indian, and a little bit of Black," it turned out the order was mixed up for me, especially being my father's daughter. But no record I ever came across said we were Jewish. And I never saw or met a full-blood white-blood relative. My family records for "Race" include Colored, Mulatto, Multiracial, White, Delaware Pequot Indian, Cherokee Indian born in Oklahoma, Freeman, Black. I lived as *and identified* with who I saw at family reunions, in pictures, from the darkest on my father's side (Black and Mississippi Choctaw by family lore) to the crisp light-bright on my mother's side, but we were still all labeled Black. How was that possible? One reason: this country punished, fined, or jailed interracial couples like the Lovings. It would not be legal to marry interracially in Virginia until 1967. In the 1800s, magistrates confiscated and bonded out Mixed race children as work horses. Historically, Mixed peoples were not allowed to claim or acknowledge white or Indian blood publicly, even though it was a quiet-as-kept secret. These are the struggles that many of my friends who celebrate their African American and American Indian heritage find themselves in time and time again, no matter where they are in the world.

They'll call us Black because of the one-drop rule; they will never call us white.

No one wants to call us Black Indian until we make them.

33

A Good Sweat

I CRAWL AROUND the sweat lodge in a circle on the hard, cold
ground, cutting my hands and knees on both the loose stones and
protruding rocks embedded in the earth; I have known some of
these rocks for over nine years. When I settle on my haunches, I
recognize them like cousins, the hard rise of their shoulders lodged
in my softness. I pull my knees to my chest, circle my arms around
my legs, and wait as the warmth of the first stone in the pit ema-
nates heat.

Usually I sit in the western door, or section, of the lodge, but
this time when I come to the mountains, both Friday and Saturday,
I notice with trepidation that I keep getting closer and closer to
the sweat leader. I am closer to the north door, and in the next
day in the women's sweat, I'm right next to the leader, a Hispanic
woman, an elder with beautiful, fiery, but cautious cat eyes. I can tell
from the care with which she talks to us in the darkness that she's
been sweating for years; this is her way. Before I came here this
weekend, I had said I wanted to learn the ways of this ceremony
more thoroughly, participating as a disciple, one day leading my
own sweat, not just someone who prayed. I had said I wanted to
learn to keep fire and eventually, when I was ready, possibly older,
pour water in each direction to honor our ancestors. But it is a
lifetime commitment, working with the fire, the water, and rock
people. I don't know if I'm ready or if I will ever be ready. It will
be hard, something like writing, to always have to ask myself, *Am
I doing it right?*

In the lodge, when the flap closes and the darkness engulfs us, my throat tightens. I have been sweating for nine years but I want to leave immediately. There are too many new people. I'm not focused like usual. My stomach begins to hurt, a small hard knot forming there as the sweat leader begins to pour the sacred water over the rocks. The hot mist rises like fine powder above our heads and descends, lodging in every crack and crevasse. It is a ninety-eight-degree summer day outside; I'm sure it has to be about 115–120 in the lodge. I want to ask permission to leave, but not because of the heat. Something just doesn't feel right inside me. Maybe I'm not praying right. If I ask to leave, it will be a first for me as long as I have been on this Red Road. I have never asked permission to leave because I thought it would end the prayer I began with when I first entered and kissed the black earth with my forehead. No one told me this. It's something I've felt over the years. And most always, because they were prayers for my mother, my sisters, the women who grew me, who raised me up from a scraggly weed, my women, whose hard lives of abuse and addiction have been my best reminder, I stayed. It was my choice.

The day before, the sweat leader, a frail elder from Mexico, and his wife, a husky-voiced Canadian, sat nearest the door. As we sang and prayed, I could hear how hard it was for the people who have been sweating for years. It wasn't just me. Their labored breathing sounded above the water spitting from the hot stones, the stone or rock people, we called them. Several people asked permission to leave. The sweat leader let them go, and paused after he poured water: "Some people think it's easy for the people who've been doing it for years. It's not. We suffer too in this ceremony for the Creator."

But we suffer in a good way. How is that? My daughter, and many of my friends' children, grew up in the lodge and around these ways, honoring our ancestors: Indigenous Native American,

African, African American, French, German, and Japanese. I am eleventh-generation Coharie from North Carolina and Black African from some Sub-Saharan tribe I never knew. We'd had Catholics, Christians, and Baptists enter the lodge and humble themselves. People come from all walks of life to pray in this way, giving thanks to the people who started this ceremony and thanks that we're able to use it and continue to heal ourselves. My pastor father's Baptist church never healed me in the way that the sweat lodge does, no matter if the sweat is a gentle one, where the water sputters on the rocks and gives off cool air, or if it's as hot as it is this day. Every lodge, or sweat leader, is not the same.

The knot in my stomach calcifies into a wedge of cold lava. I try to breathe it away, inhale the cedar and copal into my lungs and force them to thaw the pain. But it doesn't work. Then I can see how hard it is for Sarah-girl, a woman I have known for years. She popped a disk in her back the week before. Last year, she had completed her Sun Dance—four days and nights without food and little water—with an ear infection that turned into a staph infection. No one forced her to continue her dance; it was her choice. Half lying, half prostrated on my legs, she shifts uncomfortably in her small space. Her drenched dress clings to her body. She doesn't complain. If she can stay, I can't complain. And here, on this land, I have learned that when the flap closes, in the sweat lodge there is no color. No Asian. No white. No Black Indian. There are only your honest prayers.

Some full-bloods hate that there are sweat lodges that let half-bloods and non-Indians in. Occasionally, like in the terrible and sad episode in Arizona where three people died, if the lodge is led by untrained, non-Indian people, it hasn't been done right. Charlatans or non-traditionalists give the sweat lodge a bad reputation. You don't have to grow up on a reservation to know these ways, but you do need to follow the traditions taught by someone who also learned them from an elder. In those instances where an inexperienced person "borrows" or uses the ways of an ancient ceremony for profit or gain, that person is unable to take care of the medicine, the people, and the prayer. They are not sweat *leaders*. They are capitalists.

But here, in the lodges I've attended over the years, there is nothing New Age-y about it; it only matters that you're respectful, that you listen, learn, and pray. And that's how it should be. We have all been through too much not to be allowed to lay our words in a line and promise to do better. Because that's all any of us can do anyway.

I remember when I first started on this road, trying to stamp out the crazy weirdness, the engulfing violence, of my Kalamazoo, Michigan, childhood. Before tracking down the family lineage, before I knew what it meant to pray with my face to the earth, I instinctively drove up to Joshua Tree National Park with my friend Kim, about three hours outside of L.A. I needed to hear Mother Earth and I couldn't hear her in the city. Not where I lived in South Central.

While Kim stayed with the car on the side of the road, I climbed under giant crops of boulders, down into a quiet, lush green canyon. With the smell of sagebrush and desert flowers on the cool morning air, I sat on a table-shaped rock, extremely proud of myself for having gotten away from the city and to this very rock. Above, two large ravens circled, gawking, miffed at my presence but curious. They watched over me. Then my country upbringing kicked in: there might be snakes, spiders, and rodents. The ravens above my head might not be watching that closely, might not be fast enough. I had grown up around cottonmouths and rattlers springing from underneath rocks and stairways, crossing my path in the cornfield. But I wasn't quite ready to leave. In the middle of the canyon sat a large craggy boulder about the width of an SUV. As the sun slipped behind the clouds, I crawled on top of the boulder, sat lotus-style, and closed my eyes. I inhaled, mouth forming quiet O's, letting the wildflower scent seep in.

From far away, I heard a sound, my name on the wind, and for a moment thought, *Yes, I hear you. I hear you, Mother Nature.* I had connected. *Shonda.* Shonda! I opened my eyes.

"Shonda." It was Kim yelling urgently at me. "Look behind you." She pointed. I turned and saw them. Four fifty-pound coyotes were jogging confidently toward me. I froze. *Don't run* shot through my brain like a lightning rod, instinct from childhood when packs of dogs roamed dirt roads and city streets I used to walk by my dumb self, always trying to connect with nature. But I had survived so far.

The canyon's echo carried Kim's frantic screeching above and beyond me, trying to let the coyotes know I wasn't alone. I couldn't move.

Wait, a voice whispered. *Just wait.*

I wasn't supposed to move. Was it my thirteen-year-old Aunt Frieda's voice from the grave, the one who I thought watched over my family? The fear started as an itch on my left ankle and slowly crept up my leg, shoulder, neck, to my scalp, becoming a quiet panic. The coyotes, heads turned away from me, split in twos right at the edge of my boulder, two sets on either side, never once directly looking at me it seemed, but I could see their sideways glances sizing me up. They were five feet away from me. Maybe four. Food, they must have thought. *Stupid food.* I was Red Riding Hood, ridiculously far from home. But instead of pouncing, they disappeared into the far edge of the brush toward the open desert as silently as they appeared. Were they even really there? My accelerated heart rate said, "hell yes," so I waited ten minutes just to make sure they'd gone, and then scurried off the boulder and up out of the canyon.

We all have a moment like this: that split-second moment where you have to decide something because you asked for it. The test moment, when a stupid mistake, someone choosing to sit on a boulder in coyote country, a horrible incident, can destroy you. It's your decision to run and hide, or stay, face it, and fight. Or run and come back to fight another day. After having run all the way from Kalamazoo, this time I stayed. Those ravens and coyotes were my medicine. Lessons for me to learn from; lessons for me to learn. "This is life or death sister," Turtlehawk, one of my elders, told me years later the first day of my Vision Quest.

Life or death.

That day something small and at once important erupted.

That day, for me, my ceremony began.

In the lodge, sweat pours from my skin and the salt stings my eyes. My legs are covered in dirt. My calves and arms are as slippery as eel skin. I shift to the other haunch and try to get comfortable, breathing that new hardness into submission. I sit. And I sit.

Part of this ceremony is about the prayer but it is also about endurance. Not physical endurance of a sport but the endurance of facing yourself. It is at once a reflection of your relationship with the Creator, God, Yahweh, and the relationship you have with yourself. What you are made of. What you must overcome. You are not a person sitting there sweating out all the excess liquid in your body until the blood begins to wonder if it should follow. You are a rock in the fire. A part of the community breathing with one lung. *I am a rock in the fire*, I think, and slowly my knot begins to dissipate and I am only the prayer coming from my lips in the darkness. This is where, and how, I really grew up.

And here is the perfect metaphor for life. For marriage, relationships, and friendships. For family. For our world. Learning to endure. But also learning when not to. Letting go. Whether it is blood kin, or the family you'd woven around you on your walk through this life, or a job that's depleted you, you listen to yourself and let the unhealthy leave your life. Even if, like me, you grew up in two tribes, black and red, and each of your siblings felt like they had two tongues and two skins. No one identity. No clear direction. A childhood that haunted you for years. Still, you learned to let go while enduring.

The difference is, in the lodge, the good sweat leader will take care of you; he or she will let you leave because even the rock breaks in the fire. In life, you have to decide when to let leave before you break.

It is not easy, sitting there with yourself, so close to the earth, and sweating from every orifice, crevice, and pore. The hush and stillness of movement, the crush of thighs, and the rustle of clothes and limbs scraping the ground. The discomfort and cooling dark.

The next day, in the women's sweat, I immediately sink to the dirt after a cloud of mist rises and envelops me, so hot it chills me to the bone. *Wait. Just wait,* a voice whispers. My aunt? Myself? I stay there. I pray, lips to ground. Trying to get comfortable in my new position, I shift, cutting both big toes on two sharp rocks on either side of me, rocks I've known for years. It is hard. It is supposed to be hard. It is life. I am a rock in the fire.

It's a good sweat. Mitakuye Oyasin.

All my relations.

PART IV

Mixed Blood Ceremony

My sister Rochelle Bynum.

Journal Entry, date unknown

Trying to finish what's been started. When you break away from the ground you were grown in, finally uproot yourself and begin to walk-crawl away from the wolverine pack, you think you've made it. When you look back, you think you beat them. You think you've grown up and away and out of the shade. Think that those savagely gnarled branches can't reach you. That you've escaped and the swamp won't wrap her legs around your trunk and force you to fuck her with a bag over your head. But you return home and you realize that you got your savagely gnarled hands honest. And you had never gotten away really. You'd only shaken the dirt off and cleaned your fingernails.

Like a good little girl.

34

Willow Women

A MONTH AFTER I arrive home from my Aunt Phyllis's funeral
in 2000, I leave the U.S. for Belize. Alone. My daughter is so
happy to stay with her dad's mom in South Central L.A. instead
of being sent to her crazy Michigan relatives. I don't really have
the money, but my rent is paid, and so I call it a "writing trip"
to finish my novel and write it off on my taxes, but really, I am
running away. I'm escaping again, this time to a place where no
one who lives in the state shaped like a mitten can call me and tell
me their dreams.

In Placencia, Belize, I spend numerous hours rocking lazily in
the white-knit hammock on my second-story veranda; I stare at my
pink toenails in the sand as my feet darken from Indian-summer
brown to eggplant; I swim with barracudas, and snorkel, and write.
I actually finish a three-hundred-page draft of my novel.

But nothing helps me forget Michigan more than gliding in
the ocean over the second-largest great barrier reef in the Western
hemisphere and swimming above luminescent brain coral, striped
fish with lopsided heads, and scary stingrays.

The sky is a crisp-shirt blue, no clouds. The water warm and a
soothing mermaid green.

"You like my country?" Rob, my snorkel guide, says, when I
clamor into our little speedboat.

"Are you kidding?" I slide my mask off. "I want to live here
one day."

"Serious?" He quirks his eyebrows. His skin is a tough, tanned,
reddish yellow. When he smiles, a missing front tooth sucks in light

and distracts from his otherwise handsome face. He tugs down a white cap over sunburned ears.

"If I could get a little slip of land here," I pause, surprised that he's surprised. "I'd build a small house here in a minute."

I look down into the ocean, trying to see everything at once and wondering aloud how far down it goes.

"Watch me." He dives off the boat, and I watch him push down and down until he disappears in the silver depths. Two minutes pass, then five. I look around. No one's in sight for miles. What if a whale swallows him up and I'm adrift? Well, I'd figure out how to turn on the motor, but which direction would I go in? I yelp when I see movement under the boat and realize he's coming back. He has two conch shells in his hand when he clamors into the boat.

"Shit, I was scared," I laugh it off.

He smiles and holds up the conch: "You want some?" He beats a white form out of the shell and takes a bite. "Sushi." He grins at my vegetarian face.

"I'd be lucky to live here," I say. "Even if it was part-time, I'd be so grateful."

For the next few days, I ride a wobbly bike down dirt roads, drink rum, and eat rice and beans that melt in your mouth.

I retreat and recover. The other side of recovery is sweet.

My last weekend there, while Bill Clinton is making the head-lines for some presidential faux pas that Belizeans kept asking me about as if Bill and I are best buds, a hurricane runs over the country like a giant, possessive hand, leaving us without running water or power for three days. Trees that I'd passed on my beachcombing ex-cursions are washed out to sea. The two-story, four-room building I'm staying in shakes and moans, and then there is midnight quiet. By myself, I've survived one of the worst hurricanes in the history of the Caribbean; when it gets to Guatemala, it kills over five hundred people. But I am from Michigan. *And shit, if I can survive Michigan,* I think, looking at the destroyed cove, *I can survive anything.*

I ALWAYS THOUGHT I had my mother's hands—long, elegant if knobby-knuckled, foal-soft inside the crevices—but not as strong. It isn't until I see my sister Rochelle's hands at the second funeral that I realize she is the one with our mother's hands, and our mother's suffering too. She, like my mother, is the real survivor.

While we were planning and laughing and making our beds, life unfolded something in the sheets when we lay down to rest, something we had no inkling of. Call it a dream, a nightmare, maybe a gift from the Weird Sisters, the virgin, the mother, the crone, spinning our lives in one hand each, into Rochelle's hands.

One morning in the middle of September, only a few months after Aunt Phyllis's funeral, a few weeks after I returned from Belize, I have a dream: Jason is lying down on a bed, or the ground, in his shirt and jeans; he is cocooned in something, arms tight against his sides, unable to move. He smiles, trying to tell me something, to talk to me, but suddenly he becomes my youngest brother, Popeye. They are almost the same size, hefty young men, and I know with the dream awareness that whoever it is, my brother or nephew, he is dead. "Don't worry, Auntie, I'm okay," I finally hear him say.

When I wake, my heart is a hot anvil in my chest. I once had a vision in a dream of a line of my ancestors in the sky, leading me back to the place we called home. But I refuse to see this one. Shake it off like a wet dog shaking off water. I shake the fractured prophecy out of my body and go to work.

You're a dreamer. From a family of dreamers.

No, no, no, I whisper to myself as I go through the motions of compiling stories for our next magazine issue at my desk. *No, no, no, no.* I had been crying in the dream, heaving dry tears. I should call·

home, I think, but *no, no, no*. It can't be true. I'd also had a dream earlier that month that my sister Bobbie Ann had died from her bad knee operation, but in the dream my sister became my Great-Aunt Gladys, my father's aunt, and I wasn't sure whether the huge dream funeral was for her or my sister. As soon as my eyes flew open I said, "Shit."

All day, I was afraid to tell Bobbie Ann, so I called Rochelle and Tina, asking them both if they could tell Bobbie Ann to go see a doctor. They refused.

"Uh-uh," Rochelle said. "You got to tell her that mess yourself."

"What you think, I'm a messenger?" Tina said.

When I mustered up the nerve to dial Bobbie Ann's number, she beat me to the punch. "I heard you got something to tell me." She'd already been to the doctor, she said. The tension left my body and I clutched the phone less tight.

"That wasn't me, Shonda," Bobbie Ann said reassuringly. But the feeling nagged.

So, with that misfire, I try to think of this second disturbing dream, about my nephew becoming my brother, as another false alarm too. Because I am still angry at Jason, I figure I'm even dreaming mean. The Stafford in me.

I become embroiled in my day. I immerse myself in magazine production. One of the ads has a virus in the file, and I hound the company to get a new one. I don't call home. I pretend everything is fine, that nothing will find me in sunny Los Angeles, that the past will not seep into my skin, through my blood, into my veins.

Later that night, as I'm talking on the phone, my second line beeps.

"Shonda." My mother sounds as if she's choking.

"What?" *Oh no,* I think. *Just please, no God. Not again.*

"Jason is dead. He shot himself in the head today."

Wait. Stop. Rewind.

"Mama, nooo. No. You lying. Wait." *No, no, no, no, no.* I don't believe her—even though I know she's been an evil woman all her life, I never thought that even she could say such an evil thing.

A hot sour rush of hate floods my head for everything that she is and has done and has never done for me, for us, her children, and even as this anger floods me, I know I am avoiding blaming myself. *It's your fault,* a small voice says. *You could have called home. You could have stopped this. You could have warned someone.*

Numbed, I click over to the other line, performing the perfunctory courtesy of letting the other caller know I need to go. When I click back to my mother, she has hung up. I knew she was lying. I dial everyone in Kalamazoo. All the lines are busy. Finally I reach Bobbie Ann. She is crying hard.

"Bobbie Ann." I start to cry, too.

"He gone, Shonda." Her voice is wooden. "Your Aunt Gladys also died of cancer today." She seems to add in Aunt Gladys's passing as if that might make it better somehow.

I'm the keeper of secrets now. The gift of prophecy is mine now. My dreams had already told me everything and I'd ignored them.

"Jason had been playing Russian roulette with some friends," Bobbie Ann sniffs between her tears. "And according to their story, when he put the barrel in his mouth and pulled the trigger, the bullet came out and splattered his brain against the wall. His friends, they just ran."

35

Rochelle's Opus

IT COULD HAVE been anyone's son.

That circle of men-boys with a gun. In that neighborhood Jason wasn't supposed to be in. On the couch of one of the boys he wasn't supposed to hang with. It could have been anyone's son. Who were the others who survived? Who'd watched him put the gun to his mouth? Who'd watched him smile and pull the trigger? Where did they get the gun? Which one of them had held the cold metal last and was grateful they'd given it away? Which one of them knew my nephew was about to swallow a bullet?

This time when I land at O'Hare and drive to Kalamazoo, I'm not looking for understanding, reconciliation, or love, like at my aunt's funeral. *How could Jason do this to my sister?* I fume through my tears. When I walk through my mother's front door, though, my resolution to be angry at everyone dissolves.

"Hey, Cisco," my mother greets me, hitching up her pants. She's equally as angry. She isn't playing cards. She doesn't hug me. Her eyes are rock hard, red but dry, like a bull's. I remember the girl from her pictures: the innocent girl, with the big, serious, adult face and charming smile. Before me now stands a mother who will not hug me for fear I'll make her cry; she will not cry, because if she does, the whole family, the entire day, the light and the earth will break.

No one ever sees the willows weeping.

As if we've rehearsed this, Mama points me toward the guest bedroom. I find Rochelle there, sitting on the edge of the bed, rocking herself, a fistful of tissue mangled. I drop beside her and squeeze her until the tears flow like thick milk.

One by one, like a tribe coming home for the harvest, my brothers and sisters arrive. They file in, all of us crowding Rochelle, leaving her no space, touching her legs and arms, folding around her like rose petals, and she's the pistil, with pollen leaking from her pores, her hands limping with uncollectable sap. We, the petals, hope to catch something, to save her.

"I don't believe it." She muffles a sob in my shoulder, then turns to Loren, the eldest, who flew in from Las Vegas. "I don't believe it." Loren holds her tight. At intervals, she looks full from our love and attention, puffed up, and then the memory of her son's death returns and she is as hollow as any chicken bone, her marrow dry.

"I think," Loren says, "all y'all's fat asses gone break Mama's bed. Then she gone beat y'all, not me."

Self-consciously, we rumble laughter low in our throats. Loren's presence, his stinging mirth, Farmer Brown–strong, pushes back the sorrow for a time so that we can loosen up. It's good that he is here. Like peacock feathers, we spread out to give Rochelle room to breathe. We circle her room, coming in and out, studying the floor patterns and measuring our steps around each room in my mother's house.

We wait.

Throughout the day, she and I talk. Eyes rubbed pink, she blames herself for not having been a better mother. Although she won't say it, she blames the entire family for not taking care of her baby boy. *If someone had taken him in*, her eyes say, *he would never have had that gun in his mouth.* Rochelle can barely meet my eyes because she blames me too, for the argument Jason and I had had four months earlier.

Popeye blames himself. He and Jason had been road dogs for a time. Popeye thinks he should have been watching out for Jason better, steering him away from that crowd. Popeye even feels somehow responsible for the scene of the shooting.

My mother, without looking up from the spread of solitaire on the kitchen table, says, "When Popeye heard what happened, he picked up the end of a car that held two of the boys who'd been in the room with Jason. He was gonna kill them."

It was like a scene from *The Incredible Hulk*. Popeye had snatched them out of the car and tossed them like rag dolls in the air. When my mother and Bobbie showed up, they wrestled him away from the boys and the wary police; they put him in their car so he wouldn't get arrested. Apparently, he'd done those boys damage, and they'd be looking over their shoulders for the rest of their lives.

I don't need Rochelle's incriminating eyes. I blame myself too. I should have called home when I woke up the morning after I had the dream. Why didn't I call?

As the funeral arrangements come together and Rochelle busies her mind with who should and should not be there, I confide in Aunt Lily.

"You couldn't have saved him," Aunt Lily tells me when I share the dream with her. "Whatever was supposed to happen would have happened anyway."

My Aunt Lily is wise like that. But I still feel blame sitting like an elephant on my throat.

In an unspoken agreement, between packs of cigarettes outside on the front porch since my mother doesn't allow smoking in her house, we take turns watching over Rochelle. It could have been anyone's son. But it wasn't.

"Shonda." Tyrone pulls me by my arm into the star room. "I want you to stay close to her because she needs you. You're good for her."

Good for her. I wonder if this is true, but nod anyway.

His shuts his eyes tightly and rubs them for the tenth time in the few minutes I've been standing there. He blames himself too.

He has always protected Rochelle first, above all the rest of us, no matter how much they've fought over the years.

Rochelle is everyone's favorite sibling. She has always given us her best of everything, despite her addiction, and we let Jason die and betrayed her love. We all know this, wear it like an insignia.

The phone at Mama's house rings off the hook. People from the past have picked up the scent, the news in the air that one of ours has died so horribly. Rodrique, Rochelle's youngest son, sulks in every corner of the house, unable to quell his mother's agony. We hug him too, but of course, we can't do so without thinking of Jason. Rodrique doted on his brother; to him Jason was Superman.

Jaws locked, Tyrone keeps clenching his hands into fists, then releasing them. When he hears Mama talking to Jason's father, Tyrone stops and says loud enough for the person on the other end of the phone to hear, "Philip is not welcome at the funeral." Tyrone spoke in a hard, flat, murderous tone. "I promise I will break Jason's father's back if he approaches her."

I think that this is fair.

Philip had gotten her hooked on drugs. He was two years older than Rochelle, eighteen when Jason was born, and he crushed Rochelle at every turn. Rochelle was unaware of what "cycles of abuse" meant; she was just trying to survive one round.

I flit from room to room like a discontent Jane Austen character, useless, ancillary, barely talking to my mother because I don't want her to say something bad about Jason that I will yell at her for and regret later. When Aunt Lily enters, her energy perceptively lightens the house, her karat-gold laughter ringing like chimes. Having escaped to Ohio, my aunt seems to have fairy balm in her hands, rubbing Rochelle's back and shoulders.

When Rochelle finally takes an afternoon nap, I pull on my coat and get into my mother's car. I stop at Bobbie Ann's house, our old house on Southworth. Tyrone bought the house to keep it in the family, and Bobbie Ann is currently renting it.

"Hey," I tell Bobbie Ann's son, my nephew David, "come with me."

Tall and country as an Alabama tree, and gay before he knew it himself, David looks at my face and follows me without question. His self-involved nervous chatter is exactly what I need on the ride over to the funeral home for the viewing. The wake.

David, a willowy, hazel-eyed twenty-five, is a plain-spoken man, and cuts down family members' stupid comments within five minutes. His words are as vivid and slicing as his mother's, though he'd hate for me to make that comparison. I hadn't wanted to do this, the viewing, to see Jason in a casket, but it's the only way I'll be able to walk the next day at the funeral. He makes me laugh for a little while, but when I enter the room and see the prone body of the man-boy supposed to be my nephew—his sallow face, dead skin the color of eggplant—I'm unable to take one step closer.

That is not my nephew. That body in the casket is not Jason.

"Take your time, Auntie." My nineteen-year-old nephew Jeremiah, Tina's oldest boy, rubs my shoulder. In the cool room, I am leaking from every pore, every gland that holds water. I'm afraid to approach the dark thing resting in the silver casket, surrounded by white satin. But if I'm going to be any good for Rochelle the next day, I have to.

I gather myself to walk to the front, and maybe to make sure that it's true, I touch his cold hand, an act I couldn't do for my Aunt Phyllis. His skin is much too dark from the makeup. He lies there, finally at peace. No mother or grandmother telling him what to do, yelling at him, no auntie like me calling from two thousand miles away, begging him to do right by us, by his mother. I remember when he was a baby and used to bite himself on the arm when his father pummeled Rochelle. How do you have a childhood against that reality? From our legacy? From poverty? From the loss of a heritage you didn't even know you had?

"Jason, I'm sorry."

He's joined the other ghosts that roam Grandpa Stafford's farm; he'll find Frieda, and the baby girl, and Aunt Phyllis in the family cemetery. He'll find all those RedBlack ancestors sleeping in that lush Michigan, Indian, North Carolina dirt and tell them about us. They'll watch over us.

I step outside into the cold September air. Jeremiah follows me. Having joined the army right after high school, Jeremiah's forearms, boot-camp hard, ripple under his T-shirt. I hug him hard, grateful he's reached manhood. Jeremiah's face holds a confused but accepting look. He and Jason had been close, but when Jeremiah realized being young and Black in Kalamazoo meant selling drugs or having a gas station attendant job, he quickly joined the army. When he left for his first assignment, he put the deeds he and Jason used to inflict upon us behind him. Two years younger, Jason hadn't been able to do the same.

Protectively, as if he were older than me, Jeremiah folds his arm into mine and escorts me through the parking lot where other distant cousins I don't recognize stand around. They are catching up politely, talking in hushed, strained tones. Others I recognize and hug, but say little to. We haven't seen each other in at least fifteen years; maybe they just hadn't seen me because I hadn't wanted to be seen.

It's true. I don't want to belong to them, to Kalamazoo. To Death and more Death. As I back the car out of the parking lot, the mournful crowd seem to be extras in a movie, mouthing lines no one will hear.

After I drop David off, I find myself on my ex-boyfriend's rundown porch, my butt pinched between the sagging, peeling stairs. Leon, my very first real high school boyfriend who had taken me to my prom, had carried his "rock harder" attitude from high school into adulthood, and every now and then sported an afro-like Mohawk. He now lives in a condemned house on the cusp between the Eastside and the Northside, but it is definitely Northside living, just behind the train tracks and downwind of Kalamazoo River's stench.

He isn't home, but I wouldn't have entered his house anyway. There are holes in the ceiling, rodents, and no heat. A deathtrap, just the way he likes it. Leon was the boyfriend that my mother tried to send me away from, my very first love that everyone expected me to marry, but I knew better. It would never happen. Our love was best left to the young people we had been in high school, listening to Lionel Richie and Rick James songs in his mother's car all night long. Cars slow by on the main street to get a good look at me, a creature on the neighborhood weirdo's porch. I don't care; I had loved Leon once. I ignore their bold stares, opening my journal, knowing I am a weirdo too.

The cool autumn breeze shifts the oak leaves across the street. I write a poem about a boy who was born to an elephant tribe, one that laughed loud and hard and long, and he never ever forgot who he loved.

THAT NIGHT BEFORE the funeral, Rochelle can't sleep.

"I keep seeing Jason's face whenever I close my eyes," she says. I hover close by, her handmaid, awaiting her thirst, hunger, and sudden onslaught of tears. Tina had stopped by earlier, and when she saw Rochelle's agitation, she decided to stay the night. Aunt Lily was already camped on my mother's living room floor, so we pulled out more blankets and laid them out in front of the fireplace. If Rochelle can't sleep, none of us will. Instead, we push our words into my sister's ears like cotton, attempting to soak up her internal wounds. The sounds of our voices, our harsh laughter against the crackling flames, keep everyone in the house awake. I know Mama hears us from her bedroom, but she doesn't yell this time, or come out twitching her trademark evil eye. It's an old-fashioned slumber party, the likes of which none of us has been to in years. At about one a.m., we raid the kitchen for leftovers. Rochelle microwaves popcorn.

We spread out on top of the blankets and eat in front of the fire as it cracks and smokes. We bubble over, holding our stomachs with laughter, then grow quiet, whispering and wiping tears from our eyes as Aunt Lily tells us family secrets, answers questions I didn't know I had. We share sex stories and more family secrets, talk about our children and misunderstandings between ourselves. For years, after a falling out, Rochelle had resented Aunt Lily. She'd told Rochelle to get help and stop using drugs, to stop using Mama. Rochelle felt Aunt Lily was always in her business, judging her: "acted like she herself hadn't had a drink a day in her life," my sister told me.

But Aunt Lily was trying to guide Rochelle, her niece, away from her own miserable experiences. *Clean up. Get well. Get a fucking job, Nigga, and a better life for yourself and your children.*

Aunt Lily didn't stutter. She said that shit clear and plain and loud enough for everyone to hear.

Fuck secrets, my aunt's eyes said. *Niggas is dying over here.* We are *dying.*

But That Night Rochelle Can't Sleep, they reconcile. We move on, hang old boyfriends out to dry, and talk about Rochelle's job, and finally, of course, her sons. Rodrique is staying the night with his father instead of with us. He can't comfort her; he's a child. The women will do it.

"Jason told Rochelle," Aunt Lily confides to me in the kitchen, "when he visited last month, that he was hearing voices."

Shit. Schizophrenia.

Apparently, Jason had started talking to himself a few years ago, sometimes as if he were having a conversation with someone.

Rochelle didn't think anything of it, or ignored it, but my Aunt Lily, a health care worker with the Red Cross for over twenty years, quirked up her eyebrows at the mention of voices in her great-nephew's head. Mental health issues. That was the beginning of schizophrenia, she'd immediately thought. Another of the Black community's silent diseases. But she stayed silent. Because no one would believe Aunt Lily anyway, except me. The women in my family don't listen to anyone but ourselves.

"Are y'all fat butts gonna sleep or what?" a groggy Loren scratches as he walks through the living room to use the bathroom.

"Aw, go back to bed Nigga," Aunt Lily says. We hush and shoo him back downstairs to the basement. I know Mama must be hearing us and smiling in the dark at our laughing and crying.

"I keep thinking he's going to appear," Rochelle finally says, wiping her tears. I know she is a dreamer, too, but Rochelle has never told me if she'd inherited Mama's seer gift, the one where the dead come back to tell her that they are alright.

"I do too," I say. "But just like I told my daddy, I'm not ready for that. I don't want to see no dead people. I'll just dream."

I don't tell Rochelle my dream, the one I had the morning Jason died. It lies like a hot poker between us. I'm afraid she'll blame me: *Why didn't you call me and tell me? We could have warned him.* We. I keep it to myself. "Yup, I don't want to see no dead people. Just dream them."

As I say this, I remember two distinct dreams. One I had when I was twenty. There was a ceremony of women in a forest, near water. Some of the trees were bent and spindly, others had fleshy trunks beside the river that tossed its sounds across the bank and in the hollow spaces between our bodies. We were aware of and at once a part of every living thing in that forest. High overhead, the moon lit the night and the women under weeping willow trees. I felt a sense of peace and comfort there, with all of my women, young and old, alive and dead.

Years later, at thirty-two, I dreamed that I was walking across my grandfather's farm as a big truck was being pulled by two huge thoroughbreds. The horses were being guided by someone trying to cage me in from taking water to a bunch of thirsty kids, young girls who were actually dying of thirst. I finally slipped out of the truck's path and ended up walking across a small marshy river, but every time I put my feet down in the water and lifted them up again, the soles were embedded with baby tree roots. Finally, I heard my grandmother's voice: "pull the roots out so you can walk upright and take the water to the children."

The night before Jason's funeral, with my aunt and sisters, I feel as though we are taking each other to the water, walking upright and straight. Gazing into the fire and listening to them talk, I want my daughter to walk like this—with women, even my mother, whom I've begrudged for not being the woman I need her to be for me. This is where I've had to come to—to let go of the night she and Robert Gene tussled in the snow that Christmas Eve years ago. It's taken me a long time to get here, to come to this place where my desire to know the secrets of the past is not so strong. I still want to know, to blame someone or something—my grandfather the loudest of the ghosts—but not as much anymore. I'm able to look at the family photo albums now without shuffling resentfully past my grandfather's photos. I've looked closer to see that he sometimes seems to be gloating, and other times to be in honest pain.

His ghost is almost quiet.

When I was a child, I heard another story about a mother losing her eldest son. Rochelle had dragged me along when our mother said if she wanted to go to cousin Val's house on the next block over, she had to take me with her. We'd just gotten to Val's house when Aunt Louise, his mother, got a phone call. The other grown-ups slapped cards down on the table in a friendly game of bid whist in the small, grease-scented kitchen.

"Shush," someone, probably Pete, Val's uncle, said, trying to listen to the phone conversation.

I looked over suspiciously, but Rochelle dragged me down the stairs like a Raggedy Ann doll, clunk, clunk, clunk.

My cousin Michael and I began a manic game of seeing who could bounce their back the fastest against the couch. I admired his ingenuity at developing games out of thin air. He was the cousin who could stretch his entire mouth around the biggest chip or cookie like Stretch Man.

By way of the bigger kids, the story filtered downstairs.

A woman had taken her two sons fishing in Spring Valley. The woman was one of our cousins by marriage. I had seen her once or twice but never remembered her name. Her younger boy, Mark, a dark, gingerbread brown, had gone to my elementary and middle school. I can't remember the name of the older brother, but his face is a vague, fleshy, taffeta-skinned ghost in my memory. Some-how the boat had tipped over and the family went overboard. The mother was able to find one son, Mark, and shove him up high over her body, away from the rushing current, but the other boy, the older boy, had gone under. He was nowhere in sight. She must have felt as though she had failed her son. She must have called his name. She must have cried, yelled, screamed to God the unfairness of this unforgivable act. One boy in her hands, the other in the mouth of the river. There seemed to be no lesson.

Later, the story I heard included a gruesome detail that made it bigger than a river, bigger than our neighborhood, bigger than Lake Michigan, Lake Huron, and Lake Erie put together. Ap-parently, after the boat tipped over and they all fell in, the older boy had gotten caught in an undercurrent, tangled in the reeds, and somehow he'd ended up directly beneath his mother. She was standing on him. Standing on her eldest son. Her feet on his back.

She had no idea that she was standing on top of her son's lifeless body. What must that have felt like? Standing on one son and holding the other. One child under her feet and the other clutched high above her head in Spring Valley. The tears and water plastering her forever undone face. There was no way God could justify himself for taking her child's life like that. For allowing her to use his body to support herself and the other son. It wasn't her fault—the boat tipping, the plan to fish—but God's; she wasn't to blame.

Neither is Rochelle, but she doesn't know it. She is still standing in the river, Jason beneath her feet, ready to be let go. She is holding onto the wrong son and standing on top of the other, her feet planted in his chest.

Rodrique still needs her. I overhear him mumbling to himself, "It should have been me. Mama don't love me like she loved Jason."

"That's not true!" I catch him and hug him to me. "She loved you both equally. Never say that."

I hug him harder.

Rochelle needs to see her youngest son now, but she can't, she hasn't for a long time. Yet it is time to switch them, to believe that it's okay for her to be alive with one son left. There is nothing else she could have done and nothing she can do now except live. And that's the sorriest lesson for the ones left to bury the dead.

Although everyone says that Rochelle needs me to be there for her, in my mother's house and at the funeral, that I am a great source of comfort, in my opinion Aunt Lily, who has gained an impressive source of spiritual strength and wisdom from her Buddhist meditations, is the strong one. She has always been the one to know what goes on, the real keeper of our bones. I am only the scribe, laying them down in the land, these words like seeds from the willow trees, for myself, and my women, for my daughter and her own, so that one day we can grow tall, nourished from the natural spring water from that farm that, despite my grandfather, lives in our memories. We could grow into stronger willow trees, weeping in name only. It's a desperate hope I've had, a hope I've had yet to dream.

Finally, at about three or four in the morning, while the fire ebbs to embers, the elephants in us quiet and we sleep.

The next day, the funeral home is packed with our family and friends, Jason's friends, people who genuinely love us and are not simply curious to see how we mourn. The Staffords, the Manuels, the Bynums, the Buchanans, all kinds of Mixed bloods from North Carolina, South Carolina, Alabama, Georgia, Mississippi; even Popeye's cheating father is there. They hover around and in the parking lot like bees around a hive; their bodies and cars line the block. Kalamazoo and Mattawan people know this is a tragedy beyond tragedies. A Black Indian boy dead at seventeen. By his own hand. A gun in his mouth. Our blood. Our harvest. Our son. This funeral is the family reunion that we should have had in June. That Aunt Phyllis should have been invited to, that we should all have shown up at with food and laughter and smiles instead of tears.

Despite addiction, despite her short fuse, Rochelle has at one point fed, loaned money to, or used with every person in this room. Kalamazoo knows her. She is the heart of our town, cracked and still beating. She is at once our sister, our daughter, our niece, and she is in pain. The funeral home owner turns people away.

Rochelle is our Kikalamazoo. Our reflection in the mirror; our bubbling hot water on the river that surrounds our town, our lives, and she is a mirage. For a brief second in time, she was more beautiful than all of us put together. But her young adulthood came and went, slipped by her and us so fast, it's as if it had never happened. The Door closed.

If you blinked you would have missed it.

36

Stories We Sing

THE SEPTEMBER DAY is a cold oyster gray.

Barely able to walk, Rochelle peals out a scream when she sees the casket. I wish it were just a movie; I wish she were just playing a part in a sad, sad tale.

She throws herself on the casket, rocking the silver box, almost knocking it into the freshly dug grave. Her hands, knuckles soft, are desperate and grabbing for another chance on the casket's hull.

"Shonda, take her away," Tyrone orders through clenched lips. Eyes furious black dots in his face, his lips are so tight they're white. Having notified Jason's entire family that he will bury Jason's dad in this cemetery next to his son if Philip so much as looks at Rochelle, Tyrone is on the lookout. His face is a block of granite, but his helplessness is etched in the corners. He is as distraught with grief as Rochelle, but he wants to help his sister. He doesn't understand that she needs to do this. To break down. Although she has one son left, Jason had been her baby boy. He'd grown up with her. He saw her through her worst and kept her going when she probably could have just lain in some corner and died. He was the man in the family. Her husband, brother, uncle, grandfather, father, and son.

"Shonda," Tyrone repeats. "Take her."

I ignore Tyrone. Rochelle's scalp, braided tightly in intricate cornrows, seeps with sweat and sorrow. I refuse to ply my sister away from the casket, from her son. Instead, I rub her back and whisper meaningless words as she weeps deep, wracking sobs. I hold her, and feel North Carolina swamp water seeping from her back, sticking to her polyester shirt. Finally, one of the Bynum uncles, Pat, comes and shakes her shoulders gently.

"It's okay, nobody is going to take him from you, Rochelle," Pat says. At his words, she releases the casket and lets it be lowered into the waiting, bitter ground. She lets herself be led to my mother's Cadillac and climbs inside. She dabs at her face with a cloth and blows her nose.

But it will take her years to let Jason go.

Rochelle holds birthday parties at Jason's gravesite for him, and at first lots of people show, and then finally it's just her. "You know what Rodrique told me this year?" Rochelle says to me on the phone one year, sometime in between these parties. "He said, 'Mama, we forgive you.' And I finally realized why I'm still so fucked up about this shit is that I can't forgive *myself*. My sons knew I was sick the whole time when I was using. But I just can't forgive myself."

It has been years since she's been able to look at her own face in the mirror.

"You've got to Rochelle. It's time," I say. "That's why Rodrique told you that, so you'd know that they both love you and forgive you for everything. That's the first step. You've got to forgive yourself."

"Jason was doing so good, going back to school and just doing good for himself without me even knowing it. He was just like me and that's why he used to piss me off. But he made me laugh even more."

When Rochelle comes to my wedding in Virginia in 2009, she whistles like a farm hand and lights up a joint somewhere behind the bathroom; I can smell the sweet smoke wafting over to me. Then she invites some hungry strangers to the reception. That is her heart. She's less antsy, snaps less at us, and talks only half a mile a minute. She's lost weight and looks good in her black spandex dress, tattoos across her chest and an orange leopard one on her leg. Still no real boobs to speak of, but she is here. She is smiling.

Like our mother, Rochelle has settled some of the voices in her head.

Finally, she's started forgiving herself for everything. Her life, her failures. She grew up, became a vegetarian, tried to let the past go. She is not dead; drugs, the addict life, have not killed her. The death of her eldest son has not killed her. She can find a small measure of joy in life and not just fake it; she can love us without hating us.

She is the rock that did not break in the fire.

There is, and always will be, a gaping shadow called the past; some might call it hell's pit in our living room, others the end of the world. My sister almost died there, in the feces and piss of junkies and whores, and the blood-dipped needles littered there like an ocean of bad dreams. It was where she had lived and no longer lives. She has endured. My mother and aunts have endured. I keep my daughter away from Kalamazoo because I never want her to learn to endure a man's hands pummeling her.

Whenever I think I might have had it hard—a single parent in Inglewood, a struggling writer, living next door to crack addicts, ignoring the drug dealers' friendly rape-glare—then I think, *I never had it that hard.* I could never have survived what my sister survived.

I would never have made it out of myself alive. Not like that.

WHERE I LIVE in Playa del Rey, the croak of bullfrogs on a humid summer night reminds me of Mattawan; the scent of moist earth is the same, sharp and haunting.

There is even a giant eucalyptus tree with sea-spent leaves that reach the ground on a corner where I turn on my last stretch home, the largest one I've seen in Los Angeles. The tree mimics the weeping willows that stood watch in my grandfather's front yard, the weeping willows that I think my mother and her three sisters told their secrets, pangs, and longings to.

We didn't have tobacco or sage to clean us, to take our prayers to our ancestors; we didn't have any African traditions to fall back on when we lost our way. We didn't have anything except our dreams. Still, I knew the ghosts *saw* and watched us through the veil. I was convinced (or nuts, my family said) that our ancestors, Black, Indian, *and* white (wherever the latter came from, Ireland or France), watched me and my daughter learning West African dance in an Inglewood park center. Watched me take my first steps into the powwow circle in Virginia. They watched us praying to our African deities as well as in the sweat lodge. Watched my mother and sister in church. Hovered over my daughter as she stitched together her first Jingle Dress, and me, my first buckskin dress. Maybe they came in my dreams and said, *not that way, but this way.* I tried to listen. They told me I had history in this country as well as Africa.

Told me I was, we were, not who they thought I, we, would be.

A Mixed blood child of theirs. Not pure to either but still whole.

In their graves, my Aunt Frieda and the baby sister, Marlene, shift. They are ready for it to end. It was only a matter of writing it out and naming the things, of dreaming. We are at our most powerful when we are dreaming.

So forget I am spinning a yarn of Kalamazoo and Mattawan, but don't forget how the moon is sometimes so crisp in the swamp-black sky, her reflection used to press my daddy's shirts. Forget I am the drum under their deafening laughter but never forget my tribe. Don't forget their ways, and their breaking love and masterful tongues. Their golden scarab faces. Their ability to survive. And don't forget, no matter how much I speak or write or run, don't ever forget that I belong to them.

I will tell, Mama. I will tell.

"Shonda," my mother waves me over to the car. She wants me near my sister. I slide next to Rochelle and hold her wet hands, hands like my mother's. My mother, unable to cry for fear she won't stop, keeps looking at Rochelle in the back seat. John drives us away quickly over the bumpy frozen dirt road that leads out of the cemetery. He glances back twice, then glues his eyes to the road. I hold Rochelle's hands tightly.

After it all, I know now that history can tell us where we've been, but it cannot tell us who we are: *this* we tell ourselves. In our stories, in our songs, through the eyes, the hands, the breath—we tell ourselves. Anyone looking for bruises will find none: they are all under the skin.

I watch the landscape as we climb out of the cemetery, the one next to Borgess Hospital, rather than the family cemetery where we buried Aunt Phyllis six months earlier, and everyone else for hundreds of years, our bones and blood feeding the earth. Fertilizing the ground. Or singing. Or dreaming.

I hold my sister's hands so tight.

Outside my window, patches of weeds, grasshopper green despite the coming winter, shine between smudges of dirty snow on the sides of the little road that will one day lead us all home.

Acknowledgments

THERE ARE SO many people and institutions to thank for helping this book come to life, and I cannot possibly name them all. First thank you goes to my daughter, Afiya Lewis, who watched me and encouraged me and supported me every step of the way in the writing and researching of this book. Next, I must thank my editor, Annie Martin, for believing in this story. Annie and the Wayne State University Press team had the courage and vision to acquire this book and see it through. Without you, Annie, your tireless gaze, this book would not have been possible. Thank you so much to my steadfast copyeditor, Polly Rosenwaike. I also thank Chris Jackson, publisher and editor of *One World*, for your very first encouragement that this was a good story that needed to be told. Thanks so much to Christy Fletcher, who was also an early champion of this book. Thank you, thank you to the venerable Marie Brown for loving this story and providing incredibly helpful notes. I must extend a profound thanks to the Kalamazoo Public Library Research room and the librarians there for keeping the records of all Kalamazooans, which show the establishment and continuing presence of Mixed race communities, and their extensive contributions.

Thank you to my dear friend Charles, who first introduced me to Muhu Tasen; thank you to Bonnie and Rudy Gonzalez and all your beautiful children for being keepers of the land; thank you to my entire Muhu family, to the medicine, the Bears, and these ways.

Thanks to Ancestry.com, the North Carolina Genealogy Room, the Paw Paw County Registrar's Office, the Hertford County Registrar's Office, and FamilySearch.org. A million thank-yous to

Anita Harrell, former librarian, and her initiation of the free services at the Hampton, Virginia, Public Library Genealogy Room. Thank you to Hugh Harrell, possibly the smartest man I know, for all your insight as you tirelessly organized the Weyanoke Association events with Anita by your side.

Researching the lives of people who lived hundreds of years ago is no small feat, and without the help and support of my daughter, Afiya, and nephew Christopher, who were my first research assistants, I might have missed a few vital elements.

Thank you to my cousin Angelica Roberts for allowing me the chance to compare notes and hold our Great-Grandma Felicia Roberts's Freedom quilt, and thanks to the kind librarian at the Kalamazoo Public Library who put Angela and me in contact for that memorable day. Thank you to the Jentel Foundation for providing me with a summer fellowship that helped me revise the last drafts of this book, and to my fellow residency artists who talked me through my many contract questions. Thanks so much to Chris Blaker, editor at *Michigan History* magazine, who published the first excerpt of my family history, as well as to New York University's *Black Renaissance/Renaissance Noire* for publishing the first excerpts of my book. And of course that could not have happened without the introduction of Jeff Allen, one of the most supportive writers I have met. Thanks to my good friend, and writing partner, E. Ethelbert Miller for answering any question I had about writing over the years. Thanks must also be extended to William Loren Katz, the historian who wrote *Black Indians: A Hidden Heritage* (published in 1986), the first extensive collection of research in this area. Without this book, many would never know of some of the great contributions of Black Indians. Thank you to all the tribes who don't card, who allow their darker-skinned cousins the right to dance and honor all our relations. Thank you to my drum families, Four Rivers, Eastern Sky, Many Nations, and Colorblind. Thank you Vincent, Charlene, Marvin, Tracy, Michael Butler, Sylvia Nery Strickland, Jane Price, Michael Manard, and so many others on this red road for always being courageous, kind, and good-hearted people. Please know that if I danced with you, sang with you, or did ceremony with you, you have contributed to my life.

I owe a great debt to my dearest friends and writing community, especially my tribe of women—Rhonda Mitchell, Ruth Forman, Kim Benjamin, and Amy Osburn—for reading and rereading drafts over the years, or simply believing in me: you never gave up on me or this story.

Yet my deepest thanks go to my family, especially my mom, my Aunt Lily, and my sister Rochelle, for sharing your stories with me, and also for your bravery in allowing me to dig deep. I hope I have done us justice to help us heal. Ultimately, I hope our story allows others to heal from personal, family, historical, and generational trauma. Aho.

Selected Bibliography

Forbes, Jack. *Africans and Native Americas: The Language of Race and the Evolution of Red-Black Peoples*. Urbana: University of Illinois Press, 1993.

Green, Rayna. *Women in American Indian Society*. New York: Chelsea House Publishers, 1992.

Katz, William Loren. *Black Indians: A Hidden Heritage*. New York: Atheneum, 1986.

Minges, Patrick. *Black Indian Slave Narratives*. Durham, N.C.: John F. Blair, 2004.

Straus, Terry. *Race, Roots & Relations: Native and African Americans*. Chicago: Albatross Press. 2005.

Tayac, Gabrielle. *IndiVisible: African-Native American Lives in the Americas*. Washington, D.C.: Smithsonian: National Museum of the American Indian, 2009.

Taylor, Quintard. *In Search of the Racial Frontier: African Americans in the West, 1528–1990*. New York: Norton, 1999.

About the Author

AWARD-WINNING POET AND educator Shonda Buchanan was born in Kalamazoo, Michigan, a daughter of mixed bloods, tri-racial, and tri-ethnic African American, American Indian, and European-descendant families who migrated from North Carolina and Virginia in the mid-1700 to 1800s to southwestern Michigan.

For the last eighteen years, Buchanan has taught creative writing, composition, and critical theory at Loyola Marymount University, Hampton University, and William & Mary College. An Eloise Klein-Healy Scholarship recipient, a Sundance Institute Writing Arts fellow, a Jentel Artist Residency fellow, and a PEN Center Emerging Voices fellow, Buchanan has received a grant from the Arts Midwest/National Endowment for the Arts Big Read Program, the California Community Foundation, and several grants from the Virginia Foundation for the Humanities.

Her first book of poetry, *Who's Afraid of Black Indians?*, was nominated for the Black Caucus of the American Library Association and the Library of Virginia Book Awards. Buchanan is the literary editor of Harriet Tubman Press, as well as a freelance writer for the *LA Weekly*, *Indian Country Today*, the *Los Angeles Times*, and the *Writer's Chronicle*. Buchanan is completing a collection of poetry about the iconic singer, concert pianist, and Civil Rights activist Nina Simone.